Democracy and Indian Christianity

Public Theological Explorations

Democracy and Indian Christianity

Public Theological Explorations

Gnana Patrick

Christian World Imprints

First Published in 2025 by

Christian World Imprints
Christian Publishing & Books from India
A-71 Group, Wazirpur Industrial Area
Delhi-110052
cwidelhi2017@gmail.com
www.ChristianWorldImprints.com
Phone: +91 11 41526079

ISBN: 978-93-6065-992-9 (HB)
ISBN: 978-93-6065-482-5 (PB)

Printed in India.

Dedicated to

Prof. Felix Wilfred (1948-2025)
A singular inspiration for lifelong learning…

Contents

In Gratitude…

I wish to thank all those who, directly or indirectly, contributed to the making of this volume. The different chapters of the volume were written on various occasions during the past seven years. It includes a period when I was actively involved in the running of the Department of Christian Studies at the University of Madras. The potent questions I encountered from co-learners like students, staff and other scholars in classrooms, seminar halls, and study circles helped my learning and I heartly thank all of them. I gratefully acknowledge the creative inspiration received from Prof. Felix Wilfred in whose unexpected demise we lost a uniquely stimulating scholar.

I take this opportunity to thank the members of the Global Network of Public Theology who are co-learners in the field of public theology. Their explorations in various parts of the globe are a source of encouragement to my continued learning. I express my gratitude to my Catholic Diocese of Kottar, its bishops, clergy, religious and people, who respect and support my study and research. It's my joy to acknowledge the care and concern I received at the pastoral centre of the Archdiocese of Madras-Mylapore, Chennai, during my long stay over there. I am happy now to find a home at the office of the Catholic Priests Conference of India, Bengaluru, and I am grateful to the organisation. Finally, my appreciation and thanks to Mr. Sudhanshu Kanda and his team at the Christian World Imprints, New Delhi, for the elegant publication of this volume.

Gnana Patrick
20 April 2025

Introduction

Religion and politics are being related to one another in unprecedently complex and crucial ways all over the globe today. While the times of monarchical rules, which by and large took religions to be part of their royal powers, are generally gone by, the era of democratic politics opened contextually nuanced ways of relating religion and politics or even separating them. One of the salient ways of imagining the relationship between the two had been named as the liberal democratic framework which had come to be adopted by majority of the modern states of the world. But today the scenario is changing.

Liberal democracy is facing a crisis all over the world. Democratic political systems, built upon inalienable universal rights of human individuals, are changing their characteristics under the weight of the communally divisive forces, which have come to sail on the wings of populism, corporate capitalism, religio-cultural nationalism, regionalism, ethnic nationalism, racism and other retrogressive elements. Signs of emergence of dictatorial rulers, using the democratic framework paradoxically though, is clearly visible on the global political horizon of the present day.

Not merely at the manifest political level, but also at the level of civil society one finds the preponderance of voluntary agencies or initiatives founded by or oriented towards the ideologies of the Right. Forces of domination, constituting and legitimating themselves with resources from "traditions" which have been, beside being identity markers, also serving as sources of hierarchies, discrimination, and regressive power, seem to gain salience in the civil sphere.

At a personal level, an individual seems to experience one's individuality not so much for one's own worth, dignity and freedom, but in terms of one's affiliation to an identity that dominates the world of art, culture, and politics. The inalienable human rights seem to reorient themselves towards a regime of rights associated with various identities. The ethical self of an individual seems to be anchored on the so-called pride and honour of one's outward identity. The depth dimension of the self and the ethical anchoring of personhood seem to dissipate into opportunism and crass individualism.

How can the vision and practice of democracy be salvaged from the onslaught of such deviant authoritarian political formations is a question that comes to the mind of any concerned individual. It is a concern not so much to reinstate the liberal democracies as to reclaim the virtues of politics, known under the broad nomenclature of democracy, that began to integrate the role of grassroots people for envisioning and implementing measures for common good. It is a concern to reclaim and nurture the democratic process with ethical ideals of economic equity, social dignity and equality, cultural and human rights, solidarity and collaboration for common good.

In this context, a pertinent question is: 'How can Indian Christianity, as a religious tradition, be meaningfully related to the democratic process today?' Though a politically quiescent minority religious community, Indian Christianity has been deeply associated with the roots of democracy in India at different levels. Right from the moment of the birthing of Indian modernity and the subsequent empowerment of the grassroots population in terms of education, skills of communication, and social uplift, Christianity's role has been no less significant in the formation of politically participating subjects. During its continual growth and development, the Christian agency nurtured the quality of democracy with its contribution to poverty alleviation, disaster management, developmental goals, higher education, human rights advocacy and social movements for subaltern empowerment. Indian Christianity stands at a crossroads today as regards its political engagements. It seeks to reflect over the challenges as well as prospects thrown open by the present circumstances.

This volume seeks to make its modest contribution in this regard. It reflects over the present-day challenges to democracy even while proposing the continued political engagement of Indian Christianity by way of doing public theology. The articles of the volume are laid out into three parts. The first part explores questions related to Indian Christianity, democracy, civil society, human rights, etc; the second part brings up, as an example, the potentials of Catholic Christianity for public theological conversations; and the third presents case studies on religious traditions whose potentials for public theological conversations are paramount.

The first chapter observes that Indian modernity, despite contributing to certain emancipatory transformations, is meeting with its dialectics today. The most perceptible field where the dialectics manifests tangibly is that of democratic politics, wherein anti-democratic elements like majoritarianism, religious communalism, hegemonic caste identities, and those of neo-liberal market have come to instrumentalise the democratic system for their own ends. This happens in an ambience of a global retreat of liberal democracy which had been centring almost solely round the rights of individuals. It is time democracy, as a form of political behaviour and system, took note of the role of communities and traditions, and lent itself for participatory practice of democracy. Participation in democracy can well be nurtured by conversations in public spheres. In such a context, religious communities, in this context, Indian Christianity, which has hitherto been an active contributor to the emergence of public spheres, would do well to pursue public theology, in the three arenas of the Church, academia and the wider society for the wellbeing of democracy in India.

The second chapter reflects over a typical challenge Indian Christians face today in their existence. Historically speaking, right from the beginning of Christianity as a religious tradition in the then Roman empire, Christians have been living out a "theo-political" existential in the sense that even while paying respect to the political authority, they always lived by a faith in a transcendent God. Down through their history, they developed their patriotic or nationalist spirit towards their nation-states so long as the latter served transcendental goals. Now they are in a predicament when religio-cultural nationalism seeks to substitute, in a manner of idolatry, itself with the faith in a transcendental God. This is a typical challenge posed to their theo-political existential in India today.

Chapter three explores the role of Indian Christianity to the strengthening of civil society and thereby to the maturing of democracy. It surmises that religions in our post-liberal world have come to exert a sway in the public domain, apparently more to serve the elites than the ordinary citizens. Can religion be freed from such elitist abuse and be channelized for the wellbeing of the democratic polity to serve the poor and the oppressed is a question that needs be kept vibrant today. In this context, this chapter attempts to reflect the way Indian Christianity, as a minority but a significant religious tradition, may contribute to the wellbeing of Indian democracy.

Chapter four reflects upon the status of Indian Christianity as a minority other. It observes that in the recent past, Christians in India have been made to become self-conscious of their identity as the majority's 'other' through a process of 'minority framing'. From being an ancient religious community which went about its life and activities in an ambience of relative freedom, the Indian Christian community is now made to become a 'communally conscious minority', concerned about its communal identity – vulnerable, ambiguous, shifting and so on. This chapter goes into the contours of the dynamics of 'othering' in the case of Indian Christians, and surmises that being a vulnerable minority other, even while inducing a sense of being a surrogate victim, stimulates pro-active involvement in the public.

Chapter five takes up a discussion on the question of human rights in our context of the salience of communitarian rights. The human rights discourse, much vibrant during the middle of the 20th century, had its remote origin in the many European revolutions, the Magna Carta, and the Enlightenment movement, which gradually took a turn to the human subject, its individuality, autonomy, freedom and dignity. As a result, the UN Declarations of human rights (1948) came to defend the inviolable liberal rights of individual persons, based on the vision of a universal humanism. However, contemporary political philosophies, especially those emerging from the west, dispute such a universal humanism, argue for communitarian origins of individual selves, and speak up for communitarian rights. Unfortunately, the present-day ethnic communitarian political ideologies of India seem to draw strength from this communitarian turn. To what extent this turn could be meaningful to India and how can it resonate well with Indian realities are the questions probed in this chapter.

Chapter six in the second part of the volume begins to highlight the resources available with the Catholic Church which could be of critical value for public theological initiatives today. Drawing upon the encyclical of *Fides et Ratio*, brought out by Pope John Paul II, the chapter argues for the contemporary relevance of approaching religious traditions within the dialectical relationship between faith and reason. Such an approach is particularly necessary for India where the initiative of religious studies, which initiates us into a certain dialogue of faith and reason, is in a very initial stage. While going into the historical factors which inhibited the emergence of religious studies in the Indian context, the chapter looks at the need of promoting religious studies to train the Indian mind to learn to treat different religious others in the best civic manner possible in a democratic polity.

In the seventh chapter, an overview of Catholic theology which developed in India after the second Vatican Council is presented. A relatively longer chapter though, it informs an interested reader to get to know the creative flowering of Catholic theologies in India. This rich theological flourishing is highlighted as a representative case of the general theological creativity Indian Christians in general have manifested in the recent past. It is pertinent to take note of the thick ethical orientations of these theological endeavours which, almost always, privilege the option for the poor and the marginalised in theological thinking. Such an orientation found in the Catholic theological oeuvre serves as a fountainhead for doing public theologies in India.

Chapter eight dwells upon the resources of the Catholic Social Teaching to create a civic structure of care in India. While thinking of a "civic structure of care" in India, one finds the Catholic social teaching (CST) resourceful to create a "civilization of love", wherein human freedom and dignity, premised on the transcendental orientation of humanity, is integrated with virtues of solidarity, fraternity and common good, resourced from the Christian faith-tradition. The CST contributes to a meaningful synthesis between the contemporary liberal and communitarian visions of freedom, common good and civil society. The Catholic Church in India would do well, especially in the present-day context of the "majoritarian communitarianism", to dialogically mediate the wisdom of the CST by involving in public conversations in the forums of Indian civil society.

Chapter nine analyses the public theological dimensions of Pope Francis who is able to communicate today values of common good across borders of religion, regions, and sociopolitical systems. Catholic social teaching on the common good, particularly as articulated and promoted by him as part of a culture of encounter, conveys a relevant message for our times. Approaching the pope's initiative from a South Asian context, the chapter argues that an engagement with *dharma*, a religio-ethical doctrine, can be part of this culture of encounter, especially in public theological conversations about the common good. Specifically, the themes of common good can converse with *dharma* for mutual enrichment, even while the basic teachings on human dignity, freedom, and inalienable rights can usefully enrich the latter.

Chapter ten explores the political engagement of Pope Francis. It argues that Pope Francis's model of engaging in politics could be taken as a public theological model. This model does not establish itself as a power at the state level, and therefore, it respects the autonomy of the political sphere. But at the same time, it does not abdicate its responsibility towards the "noble cause" of politics. Pope Francis's papacy does not argue for political establishments of religion, but yet stands for a robust political involvement in civil society for the common good, especially the good of the poor - a sublime value deeply embedded in the Catholic Social Teaching.

The eleventh chapter deals with a vibrant theme occupying the Catholic mind all over the world today. It attempts to relate Pope Francis' initiative of promoting a synodal church with the cause of strengthening civil society today. Going into recent social teachings of the Catholic Church, the chapter delineates how the relationship of the Catholic Church with civil society unfolded in a contextually sensitive manner. From an antagonistic stance, the Catholic Church has come a long way today to highly value the role of civil society and of its role in it today.

Chapter twelve, opening the third part of the volume, explores the need to situate our practice of inter-religious dialogue in a new light of public conversations today. It means that we need to go beyond the traditional framework of interreligious dialogue, which more often than not, showed an impulse to convince the other of one's religious truth. Public conversations, on the other hand, are aimed at mutual enrichment towards commitment for the common good. Religious teachings of different traditions need to come together to guide humanity towards their common goal. In this effort, we need to learn the virtues of public conversations to be meaningfully involved in them.

The thirteenth chapter explores how the teachings of different religious traditions can come together to shape up relevant theologies of cities or urbanity in the Indian context. Indian subcontinent was home to some ancient civilisations wherein cities were built with meticulous planning, where city-life flourished with considerable comfort and civic facilities, etc. However, it can well be ascertained that it was during the colonial era that cities with mass settlements emerged and grew with liberal civic ethos, to provide habitat for everyone in a non-discriminatory manner. While acknowledging this openness of Indian cities, we need also to reckon with the fact that Indian cities keep experiencing dynamics of exclusion, some of which do not augur well for the universality, equality, civic virtues, and urban creativity. A typical dynamic operative in the Indian cities is discrimination and segregation on the basis of purity and pollution. This chapter explores whether religions in India can come together on public theological forums to address the question of discrimination in Indian cities.

Fifteenth and sixteenth chapters are brief case studies on Ayya Vazhi and Tamil Buddhism, two subaltern religious phenomena, which arose among sections of the subaltern people of India in a context of ostentatious social oppression. They were, so to say, instances of public theological narratives which embodied and manifested great potentials for the birthing of democracy in the Indian context. They awakened the subaltern consciousness through a religious idiom and in a spiritual mode to empower the people with experiences of dignity and social justice. They are presented here as examples of the existence of hundreds of such religious traditions in India which can contribute to cultivating the spiritual roots of democratic virtues like human dignity and social equality so as to strengthen the democratic process today. They are also relevant for a volume on 'democracy and Indian Christianity' because they are meaningful samples of public theological conversational partners for Indian Christianity.

This volume on *Democracy and Indian Christianity* is ultimately a pointer to the resourcefulness of Indian Christianity to a continued commitment to nurture democracy in India. Its value lies in the realisation that an abiding contribution can made to political imagination and praxis at the grassroots civil society. Starting with redeeming the civil sphere itself from the clutches of the exploitative dominating elites, a robust civil society vibrating with political virtues of citizenship, participation, solidarity, conversations for social justice and common good can make significant contributions to the democratic process.

Part-I

Democracy, Civil Society and Indian Christianity

1

Modernity, Democracy and Indian Christianity

Making of the Modern India

It is general knowledge today that the Indian subcontinent came in for a multidimensional radical change along with its encounters and confrontations, accommodations and resistances, and, adaptations and vilifications of the western colonial modernity. 'Metanarratives' of social reform, progress and development, pursued through kindred projects of science, technology, industrialisation, mass education, rule of law, rationalised bureaucracy, and relentlessly advancing modes of communication and transportation, have indeed changed the social, economic, political and cultural terrains of the subcontinent in an *unprecedented* manner when compared with the multi-millennial 'pre-modern' era. However nostalgic one may be of the past glory of monarchical rules, however romantic may one be of the oriental philosophical heritage, however proud one may be of the nature's bounty in the subcontinent (rivers, mountains, underground minerals, etc), and however vituperative one may be against the colonial plundering, an informed Indian mind would never be able to discredit some of the thorough-going changes brought about by western modernity in this land.

Much before the winds of nationalism began to blow, this subcontinent had taken in some of the vital infrastructural components of modernity and been irreversibly impacted by them. Transportation facilities, factories, mechanised manufacturing units, trade and commerce, modern banking, postal communication, widespread schools for primary education, colleges for modern higher education, universities, civil administrative structures, judiciary, rationalised system of policing and arbitration, vaccinations, modern medicine, and other structures of statecraft were of no less significant when it came to the lifeworld of the people. Economically speaking the industrial mode of production, along with its market-oriented distribution and consumption patterns, was introduced to initiate the capitalist system in this country. Though colonial entrepreneurs dominated the system initially to exploit the Indian labour and resources, gradually Indian capitalists came to participate in the system. Politically, empires and kingdoms were replaced with presidencies and resident-controlled royal principalities to eventually unify a political unit under the brand name of British India. These interventions not merely *changed* the face but *churned* the socio-cultural terrains of this sub-continent.

Sociologically speaking, it was indeed a complex process. The reigning order of caste, embodying the 'homo hierarchicus' religio-cultural genetic code, came in for a jolt. The modern education, though supposedly purported to produce a class of people 'Indian in colour and English in thinking', opened up, in principle, the conduit of 'progress and development' to people of all strata of the caste society. Every segment of this society, mutatis mutandis, could participate in colonial education, administrative and military dispensations, to 'empower' themselves and reposition themselves in the caste hierarchy. A semblance of equality emerged in public discourses and relationships. As Charles Taylor points out, the introduction even of such prefixes as 'Mr.', 'Mrs.', or the word 'Sir' as part of the modern ethos of dignity, or the recasting of the experience of space and time through the introduction of modern transport system, went a long way in infusing a modern spirit of equality and universality in the subcontinent's sociality.

The cultural terrain got impacted radically. In addition to changes in dress codes, food habits, and life-styles attendant upon what is known as the process of westernisation, a new cultural ambience informed by science and technology, including modern medicine, came to construct new individual subjects, however small in number though, with a more affirmative self-agency. Availability of modern literatures, in new genres of prose, essays, memoirs, ethnographies, surveys, dictionaries, lexicons and translations, and that too available in print-forms, contributed to the emergence of modern consciousness, poised to think logically and involve in public debates and arguments. The genius or intellectual excellence of India, in such fields as mathematics, astronomy, physics, and so on, yearned to express itself in the western modern idiom, the case of Srinivasa Ramanujam being the best example.

A stream of Indian minds, perhaps the cream of Indian population, participated in the western modernity in the hope of transforming India. Starting with Rajaram Mohan Roy (known as the father of modern India), the founders of Brahmo Samaj and Prarthana Samaj, the young Bengal movement, and those who supported Lord Macaulay in implementing English education imbibed and mediated the western modernity, along with its Enlightenment ideals. Later on, it was Jewaharlal Nehru who came to embody the aspirations of Indians to make of it a modern nation, progressing in industrialisation, science, technology, and establishment of individual liberty and social equality. This nation for him, as he envisages in his *Discovery of India* was not pure and simple a western national variety, but one that integrated the diverse philosophies, cultures, traditions, and religions of India to emerge as a modern nation.

There was yet another stream of consciousness, emerging from the subaltern Indian landscape, which, having imbibed the spirit of modernity, sought to construct an alternate Indian nation wherein the oppressive caste system would stand annihilated, and equality established. Jyothirao Phule (1827-1890) founded the Sathyashodhak Samaj to work for the uplift of the lowly and presented his criticism of the oppressive society. It was of special interest to get to know that Phule wrote *akhandas*, religious verses, to speak of a creator God, who had created everyone equal. C. Iyothee Doss Panditar (1845-1914), a versatile personality, undertook to found what was known as *Tamil Buddhism* as part of his emancipatory struggles for the freedom of the Dalit-subalterns. There were hundreds of such individual initiatives or socio-religious movements which arose across the sub-continent to shape up a new consciousness and construct an emancipatory identity for subaltern people.[1] To cap them all, Ambedkar emerged as a singular personality, embodying the aspirations for a new India, wherein the democratic constitution would bring about revolutionary changes to achieve an egalitarian society. And it is in place to note that he embraced Buddhism as a socio-religious alternative to undergird the egalitarian practice of a democratic nation.

Dialectics of Indian Modernity

As we know, postcolonial studies have now opened a vantage point to critically look at the claims of modernity, western modernity in particular. They have underlined the contradictions implied in the universal claims of colonial modernity, the will to power embedded in them, establishment of empires of knowledge among the colonised minds, continuance of hegemonic dominance over different others, etc. They have exposed the Eurocentrism inherent in the western modern rationality, and therefore of its contradiction. Theories have been proposed to look at modernity in a context-sensitive manner, instead of throwing away the entire modernity lock, stock and barrel. The proposal of S. N. Eisenstadt for imagining multiple modernities is a case in point. He argues that "the best way to understand ... the history of modernity is to see it as a story of continual constitution and reconstitution of a multiplicity

[1] J. N. Farquhar, Stephen Fuchs, Kenneth W. Jones, Gail Omvedt, Anne Feldhaus, Manu Bhagwan, Chad Bauman, Christian Lee Novetzke and others have published collections of such initiatives and movements which emerged among the subaltern people as attempts at visualising an alternate modern egalitarian society.

of cultural programs."[2] Going by this insight, one might consider an Indian modernity, which unlike the western variant, created its own modern 'cultural program' by retaining a thicker content of beliefs and traditions, while taking in scientific and technological rationalities. Even while granting a place for Ashis Nandy's highly radical critique of modernity as the very form of violence, it is not possible to deny the positive and emancipatory effects of modernity in the Indian context. Leave alone the manipulative instrumental reasoning implied in the consciousness of the 'educated' class of Indians, that the western modernity brought about an opportunity for equality for the subalterns cannot be overlooked. That a 'silent revolution', as in the words of Christophe Jaffrelot, was witnessed to in the Indian society is no less a convincing reality. Indian modernity has had its empowering and emancipatory moments!

That we are witnessing to some of the worst forms of modernist negativities in India today is a sad reality to be reckoned with. The emergence and sway of ethnocentric cultural nationalism, religious nationalism to be specific, sailing on the wings of democracy, nay upon its travesty, is the case in point. Indian experience of nationalism has indeed a chequered history. As some prominent theorists on nationalism like Ernest Gellner and Benedict Anderson opined, nationalism, as part of the modern project of constituting nation-states, had its legitimacy in the imperial colonial context.[3] As a manner of achieveing one's freedom, the erstwhile colonised countries drew much strength from the spirit of nationalism. That the pioneers of Indian freedom struggle did draw upon Indian nationalism is part of the process of birthing of India as an independent nation-state. However, even at that context, some of the free minds like that of Rabindranath Tagore doubted the very legitimacy of nationalism and called it a 'menace' that corrupted the freedom of consciousness of a citizen. That Gandhi himself wished for closing the Indian national congress once freedom was achieved cannot be forgotten. What has, unfortunately happened in the post-colonial Indian context, is the caricature and manipulation of nationalism to distort it into an ethnocentric cultural nationalism to serve the need of managing the election-centric democracy in this vast nation. As Eric Hobsbawm has observed it has become an atavistic non-progressive ideology, and even as Edward Said, a postcolonial critique himself has observed,[4] it has turned into a sectarian divisive force in India. The mindless manipulation has generated much hatred between different others, especially between the majority and minority others, besides endeavouring to reiterate the dominance of the hitherto elites by a hegemonic dynamics of manufacturing consent. That India as a young developing nation, emerging out into the global arena, has a certain predicament or a need for constructing its own identity cannot be less

[2] S. N. Eisenstadt, "Multiple Modernities", *Daedalus*, Vol. 129, No. 1, (Winter, 2000), 2.

[3] Cf. Leela Gandhi, *Postcolonial Theory* (NSW, Australia: Allen & Unwin, 1998).

[4] Cf. Edward W. Said, *Culture and Imperialism* (New York: Vintage Books, 1993).

appreciated. However, the identity construction with the cultural resources of a perceived majority, at the cost of the very character of democracy and its pillars of equal citizenship, participation, respect for plurality and differences, etc., can never be legitimised. That such a malaise is not merely an Indian experience, and that the Indian case is relatively better when compared to some South Asian regional powers, cannot go a further legitimising step, especially when reminded of the fact that the number of victims would count much more than the neighbouring countries. Indian modernity has come to contradict its own wellbeing today.

The modern state, the cynosure of modern political power, the stage of high evolution of the Spirit in the Hegelian system, the paragon of public morality in a liberal political project, has given in to manipulative techniques of market-driven corporate magnates and houses, abysmal corrupt practices, high nepotism, and sectarian arbitrary powers. The Indian "democratic" state, despite a projected progress, has not improved its ranking in the scale of world democracies,[5] and continues to be weakened at vital points. The 'socialist' mixed economy envisaged in the Indian constitution has been given the go-by with the structural adjustment programme of the 1990s, and the corporate firms, local and global, have come to dominate the state's economic power. Poverty alleviation programme, remedying of social exclusions, and other welfare schemes have become tenuous, parodied by tentative populist schemes. Political leadership, barring some notable exceptions, is vested in the hands of the traditional feudal forces or the upstart corporate magnates.

The Achilles Heel

The Achilles heel of modern India remains to be the discriminated and skewed sequestration of resources in almost all walks of life. Political power, knowledge-domain, technology, economic process, educational facility, social capital and influence, and even religio-cultural resources sequestrate around a miniscule 'powerful' who, like the proverbial python, keep resurging against all odds. Several factors continue to cordon off spaces of power. Firstly, there is the factor of *externality* which sequestrates power from widening out. Then, there are the *exclusionary* dynamics, which keep repelling the base or the periphery from centres of power. And then, there are the *exploitative* forces operative in different fields, in tune with the neo-liberal cut-throat competitive phase of the advanced capitalist world.

---

[5] There are multiple agencies doing the ranking of democracies. The Global State of Democracy ranks the countries based on multiple indices like 'representation', 'rights', 'rule of law' 'participation' and the like. Accordingly India is ranked 71st under representation, 116th under rights, 80th under rule of law, and 104th under participation. Country Rankings – The Global State of Democracy 2024.

Externality of power is not a small cause in the skewed functioning of democracy in India. The modern Indian statecraft had its remote origin in the East India Company, then with the British Raj, then with the higher echelons of India (royalties, feudal lords, etc) and then with caste leaders, middle class and 'cultural warriors / saviours' (heroes of the silver screen, cultural nationalism). When Ranajit Guha founded the *Subaltern Studies Project* of historiography, his ardent desire was to 'bring Indian history to itself'. He found the then existing Nationalist and Marxist historiographies not highlighting the agency of the grassroots people of India. Power - social, political, economic and cultural, *had not come home* in India. In other words, the base of Indian nation has not yet *participated* in the power relations of this country; or, to put it otherwise, the people of our country have not turned *political* in a substantive and healthy manner. The top-down operation of power, or the ad-hoc recourse to grassroots humanity in such occasions like election or even populist schemes, have only de-politicised the people, and they still remain incapable of exercising their political agency. Occurrence of communal clashes would only support the argument that people who are brought to bear the brunt are not participating in the operationalisation of power. As Kanchana Mahadeven would surmise, it is the continuing depoliticisation of people, and replacement of political identity with sectarian identities that trigger and sustain communal violence in this country.

Secondly, it is no exaggeration to say that the *exclusionary* dynamics at work in the Indian society keep dissuading people from the practice of power, thus effectively sequestrating power for a privileged few. The exclusionary dynamics are deeply entrenched in the caste hierarchy and the ubiquitously present patriarchy. These negativities work upon a typical manner of *exclusionary inclusion*. It is not a pure and simple exclusion, but one that keeps excluding people within an overarching 'inclusive' pavilion. As Louis Dumont has pointed out, everyone or every community is fixated at a particular point or status from which it is impossible to exit. As Javeed Alam points out in an insightful article, Indian community organisation does not provide the right to exit. The deeply embedded religio-cultural belief-based practice of purity and pollution keeps the exclusionary device greased and well functioning. It is therefore no wonder that the Indian modernity, called aptly as 'retro-modern', repositions the caste hierarchy, rather than annihilating the system. It is a pity that even the alternate religious system like Christianity could not overcome in its own body these dynamics of repositioning of status. Gandhi, even Tagore and several other stalwarts, have gone in approval of the system, taking it to serve as the bulwark of toleration of diversity in this country. But as Ambedkar points out, it is this caste system which kills the public spirit of Indians. Similarly, the typically Indian patriarchy, a combination of caste and gender exclusion / inclusion dynamics, keeps including the female power into the systemically male oriented society. An equal section of Indian humanity, if not more in some regions, fails to partake of power, even while participating in large numbers in the 'festivals' of Indian democracy. Such exclusionary dynamics of the Indian society, sad to say, keep paralysing the inner sanctorum of the Indian polity.

Thirdly, the proliferation of *exploitative* urges with the onset of the market-driven liberalisation has contributed its share to the accumulation of the economic power in few hands. Late capitalism has succeeded in doing this job. *Freefall: America, Free Markets and the Sinking of the World Economy* (2010), a volume by Joseph Stiglitz,[6] the former WB vice-chairperson, argued that North America, the epitome of capitalist liberalisation, had become an economy 'of the one percent, by the one percent, and for the one percent.' Shrinking of the beneficiaries of advanced capitalism, even in its celebrated home, has gone with the emergence of several owes, including the experience of 'ontological insecurity', as found in the 'victory' of supremacist far-right political discourses. While that being the case in North America, the market-driven capitalism has gone about the globe with its exploitative prowess, especially in plundering natural resources, thereby causing devastating climate damages. There was a time when commentators spoke about apocalyptic fears caused by nuclear war heads hanging over our heads ever ready to destroy the human race; now, one speaks of apocalyptic fears incumbent upon biological warfare, global spread of viruses, alarming levels of climate wreckages, etc. That being the case in the global scenario, 'make in India' discourse in India has wide opened the doors to global investors, as a reciprocal gesture to others opening their doors to Indian capitalists, going mindlessly exploiting natural as well as human resources. Despite the shine supposed to have been seen in India, as per the official account, 25% of our people live under poverty line. Majority of our people do not participate in the economic resources of our nation. There is a caste-class symbiosis which keeps excluding people from the lower strata. The apparent promise of the neo-liberal market, the 'invisible hand' of Adam Smith, colludes with the caste system to keep excluding the oppressed people. Interestingly, as Arvind Rajagopal observes, "[T]he rhetoric of market reform and that of an insurgent cultural politics went public together and interacted to express a new historical conjuncture... Liberalisation and Hindu nationalism shared their technologies of transmission for expanding markets and audiences respectively."[7]

India's predicament now can no less be pitied, and far from being envied. A very populous giant, emerging out into the global arena, to compete with

---

[6] Cf. Joseph Stiglitz, *Freefall: America, Free Markets, and the Sinking of the World Economy* (USA: W.W. Norton & Company, 2010).

[7] Arvind Rajagopal, *Politics after Television – Religious Nationalism and the Reshaping of the Indian Public* (UK: Cambridge University Press, 2001), 2-3.

global others in terms of economy and political power is suffering from internal contradictions. Added to the challenge is the one to construct an identity of its own to negotiate itself with others in the culturally poised global order. Presenting a cultural identity has become a necessity for India to vie with others on political and economic fronts. Looking at India from this global need, the discourse of cultural unity, rooted in a hoary past, embodied with great wisdom, become a pertinent Indian need today. It is so, especially against a western prejudice which viewed Indians as people of passivity, given to superstitions and obscurantism, unable to 'develop' themselves or progress towards the heights of modern civilisation, to which the western civilization was thought to be destined for. However, this unity cannot be built upon pretentious and skewed pillars in a monolithic imperial fashion.

Possibilities for a Civic Republican Participatory Democracy

An experience of liberal democracy remains external to majority of people in India. It has adapted itself to the systemic structures of "exclusionary inclusion" and has become a tool in the hands of corporate capitalism. Liberal democracy has indeed come into question in several parts of the globe today. In a book titled, *The End of History and the Last Man* (1992) Francis Fukuyama argued that with the fall of the Berlin wall (and of the end of the cold war), human political ideological evolution had come to an end and that there was no alternative anymore to liberal democracy in the world. The euphoria of this victorious 'proclamation' unfortunately did not last long. Liberal democracy all over the world had to face up to the challenges of terror in the name of religion, religious nationalism, racism, and other sectarian identities which manufactured hatred towards different others; it had to reckon with a burgeoning regime of corrupt practices catering to the greed of individuals and corporate houses, and with 'naked' public spheres devoid of values and solidarity. Questions were seriously raised and are being raised today as to whether a liberal democracy which hinges solely on the liberty of the individual subject would take us further.

Against this context, amidst attempts to revise and reinterpret the liberal political philosophy to come to terms with the contemporary challenges,[8] there is an attempt also to revisit and revive the republican democracy in a contextual manner. While republicanism has a strong historical tradition (Aristotle, Roman *res publica*, Machiavelli, Rousseau, etc) which is generally seen as a conservative and elitist political philosophy, its revision today as *neo republicanism* (Hannah Arendt, Charles Taylor, Michael Sandel, Philip Petit, Iseult Hanon, Cecile Laborde, and others), especially as *civic republicanism* offers several insights which seem to be very relevant for us today. Its basic philosophy is that human beings, as political animals, can realise their nature only in self-governing communities, and that the community they constitute is *essentially political.*

[8] John Rawls, for example, makes a sustained effort to reinterpret it for our times.

Unlike liberalism which begins with the natural rights of individuals, civic republicanism treats rights as basically derived from social living characterised by traditions, but continuously being propounded through a political culture. This derivative right hinges on or becomes effective in shaping up a substantive citizenship, which is built upon the pillars of rule of law, participation, non-domination, and freedom from arbitrary powers. *Participation* means not just involvement but joining in a political process by cultivating the civic virtue of solidarity with different others to work for common good. It would mean evolving a public political culture from below, recognising the validity of different others, and dialoguing with different others as the very manner of existence. *Non-domination* stands for 'a condition or a possibility' wherein a citizen is not coerced or made to act in a particular way. It differentiates itself from 'freedom of self-mastery' and 'freedom from interference', which are considered to constitute the liberal citizenship. The important difference is that neo-republicanism treats the presence of non-domination in the social ambience as indispensable for the ability of an individual to be free. It is not enough to say that no one is visibly interfering in your freedom, but also vital to consider whether the condition created is free. *Freedom from arbitrary powers* stands for freedom from factors which do not become public or do not participate in the public political process, but exert undue unconstitutional authority.

Civic republican democracy has features which have much relevance to the Indian context today. Its central vision characterised by participatory democracy, absence of dominance and non-interference from arbitrary powers has much to offer to a context of discriminatory sequestration of power, rigidly hierarchical and exclusionary social system, and undue dominance of market forces in conjunction with casteist arbitrary powers. A republican vision is not new to India, and it has already been intoned by our constitution. The preamble of Indian constitution presents India as a democratic republic. Bhikku Parekh, the Indian born British parliamentarian, points out that in the original draft the word 'republic' alone was used, and in the next, it was replaced with democracy, and in the final version it became 'democratic republic.'

Indignation to liberal democracy also has not been new to India. Ambedkar, the architect of Indian liberal democratic constitution, himself had to come to terms with the inadequacy of the liberal side of Indian democracy, which ignored the other kindred values of equality and fraternity. He said, "[P]arliamentary democracy developed a passion for liberty. It never made a nodding acquaintance with equality. It failed to realize the significance of equality and did not even endeavour to strike a balance between liberty and equality, with the result that liberty swallowed up equality and has made democracy a name and a farce."[9] He continues: "Without equality, liberty would produce the supremacy of the few over the many. Equality without liberty would kill individual initiative. Without fraternity and liberty, equality could not become a natural course of things."[10]

Democracy, in Ambedkar's vision, is "a form and a method of government whereby revolutionary changes in the economic and social life of the people are brought about without bloodshed."[11] He said: "... political democracy cannot succeed where there is no social and economic democracy... social and economic democracy are the tissues and the fibre of a political democracy. The tougher the tissue and the fibre are, the greater the strength of the body."[12] Ambedkar cautioned also against the 'divine right' of the majorities. He said, "Unfortunately ... Indian nationalism has developed a new doctrine which may be called the Divine Right of the Majority to rule the minorities to the wishes of majority. Any claim for the sharing of power by the minority is called communalism while the monopolizing of the whole power by the majority is called nationalism."[13] Sukhdeo Thorat says: "In Dr Ambedkar's view, a democracy is not confined just to a form of government and state apparatus; rather it is more than a system of political governance – it embraces social governance... is primarily a mode of associated living with an attitude of respect and reverence towards fellowmen. Therefore, the roots of political democracy are located in social relationship among the people in a society."[14] Jean Dreze, the well-known economist, is of the opinion that Ambedkar had a visionary conception of democracy which needs be rediscovered today. In his words: "The future of Indian democracy depends a great deal on the revival of Ambedkar's visionary conception of democracy. This vision, I believe, also needs to be enlarged and updated in the light of recent experience."[15]

To reconstruct our democracy along the line of Ambedkar's more integrated emancipatory vision, I think we could draw upon the features of the contemporary civic republicanism to transform Indian democracy. This is not, however, to claim that Indian democracy has gone too far in liberal democracy. Even as per the yardstick of liberal democracy, India, as mentioned above occupies only lower positions in world ranking. It would mean that neither

---

[9] As quoted by Jean Dreze, "Dr. Ambedkar and the Future of Indian Democracy," in *The Radical in Ambedkar – Critical Reflections,* eds. Suraj Yengde and Anand Teltumbde (USA: Penguin Allen Lane, 2018), 172.

[10] Ibid., 171.

[11] Ibid., 170.

[12] Ibid., 171.

[13] Sukhadeo Thorat, "Forword", in *Dr. Ambedkar and Democracy*, ed. Christophe Jeffrelot and Narender Kumar (New Delhi: Indian Institute of Dalit Studies & OUP, 2018), xvii.

[14] Ibid., viii.

[15] Jean Dreze, "Dr Ambedkar and the Future of Indian Democracy", 170.

has liberal democracy matured in this country. Unfortunately, India presents a kind of political hotchpotch, drawing elements from different political philosophies, but not maturing in any; thus resulting in a vulnerable state wherein un-democratic forces – be they cultural nationalist, market, feudal, casteist, and other anti-people ideologies can run the riot. The 'tissue and fibre' of our nation are not strong enough to dispel these undemocratic elements. It is therefore incumbent upon us to create a people-based participatory democracy, non-dominating, networking and free.

Public Spheres, Public Ethics, and Public Religion

Public spheres, indeed, are the primary forums of participatory democracy. Jurgen Habermas, with whom theorising on modern public sphere is generally associated, understood public sphere to be spaces wherein debates take place to form public opinion which weighs upon decisions for public life. He thought of three types of public spheres: 1) public spheres in the political domain (a domain which is proximate and yet different from the state, preparing individuals for statecraft, 2) public spheres in the 'world of letters' (discussion and debates in the domain of literatures, academia, press, clubs, etc), and 3) public spheres in the 'town' in coffee houses, salons, etc. Jose Casanova, a more recent scholar of public religion, thought of different public spheres operative at various levels of civil society, political society and the state: civil society in its voluntary organisations / initiatives, political society in legislatures and political parties, and state in its bureaucracy. Thus, there are different categorisations and identifications of public spheres. The commonality among them is that they are discursive fora, contributing to the formation of public opinion and the general will of the people. Discussion (lexis), according to Habermas, embodies the *public reason*, whose characteristic elements are neutralisation of status, inclusiveness, and debates on matters of public concern. 'Neutralisation of status' meant a certain 'disregard' for status-positions of the discussants involved in discussion, and inclusiveness meant a seamless universality. These characteristics make the public debates effective carriers of public opinions, which participate in decision making on matters concerning public policies, common good and public life in general. Creating appropriate fora of such public discussions, learning the skills of public debates or discussions, and actively participating in public spheres need to get priority in constructing a republican democracy.

There has been much debate as to whether any normative argument of ethical or religious nature could be appropriate for public reasoning. The concern of liberal democracy has been whether such normative arguments could be universal enough to represent the voice of the general humanity, or those concerns of the general public. It used to be argued that normativity would base itself on particular traditions which would not be intelligible to outside others or on particular sources of authority which would come into conflict with the universality and the neutrality of public reason. However, there have also been questions as to whether public reason, devoid of normative ethical or faith-dimensions, could be historically factual and effective to inspire actions for common good. Liberal theorists like John Rawls tried answering the questions first by acknowledging the value of ethics and religion for public life and then by suggesting the method of 'translation', that is, translating the message of ethical or religious doctrines into 'secular' language so that it could be intelligible to all. The contemporary post-liberal world has cast serious doubts upon the effectiveness of Rawls' suggestions, and has come up with other methods like 'conversations' between different incommensurable ethical or religious comprehensive doctrines for common good.

It is to be noted that the contemporary post-liberal political philosophy, by and large, accepts the need of bringing in ethical or religious doctrines into the public sphere for the cultivation of virtues of solidarity, sacrifice, respect and reverence to different persons, etc. Similarly, it is positive towards the role of religion too in the public sphere. Such a positive openness is born upon multiple realisations: first of all, religion as an influential category is already present in the public sphere, controlling the political behaviour of individuals and collectives involved in the political process; secondly, the attempt to be neutral under the garb of being secular has not been a successful endeavour, because secularity is not a neutrality, but a position against religion or a bias against religion; thirdly, there is a growing realisation that the so-called secular liberal public spheres have not succeeded in achieving universally egalitarian politics, but, on the other hand, have impoverished the political process of morality, ethics, and experiences of transcendence. It would therefore be necessary to acknowledge the publicness of religion, treat it as any other language or perspective, and integrate it in public conversations. Religions, indeed, have been active components in public spheres or political decision making across space and time. The Indian experience would vouchsafe for it. Religion, religious sentiments, visions, doctrines, and beliefs are indeed present in the modern Indian political processes. However, there has been a hesitation to articulate its stances openly. What passes for in such situations of hesitation is a taken-for-grantedness of the legitimacy of the religious presence or influence of the dominant or the numerical majority, while those of different others, especially of minority others, get vilified or antagonised. It would therefore be a matter of fairness that religious presence in the Indian public sphere is acknowledged and articulated in public conversations or dialogues.

We need to be involved in an educational praxis, both formal and informal, for participation in public spheres. Similar to the informal education or literacy campaign in which different civil society organs, including the churches, involved in, we need now to be involved in 'education for public reasoning', which would focus on political participation, citizenship, dialogue of cultures, religions and ideologies, social justice, equality, solidarity for common good, decentralised power for statecraft, etc., along with fine skills of argumentation, disputation and conversation. Education, in its multiple variants, has been at the root of transformations, and education aimed at public reasoning would transform an individual to be a citizen, a particular will to be the general will, individual aspirations to be ideals of the state, and individual frustrations to public acts of resistance. It will bring the particularities of culture, religion, ethics, and aesthetic preferences into dialogue with one another, and synergise a vibrant public resource. In an important way, it will also help learn to live inter-subjectively with different religious others, without fear and hatred.

Indian Secularism

When religion becomes public in such a sense, what would happen to the 'secular' character of our constitution or polity could be the pertinent question. Indian secularism, as it is generally understood, is not like the French laicite or North American wall of separation, but equal treatment of all religions or equidistance from all religions. Rajeev Bhargava, an ardent supporter of Indian secularism as enshrined in the constitution, interprets the constitutional secularism to mean a contextual secularism, open to ethics and religion, working with a method of 'principled distance'. Bhargava clarifies that Indian secularism keeps religion away from the 'level of ends' (whether to establish or disestablish religion at the state level like the theocracies), and the 'level of institutions' (administrative structures), but be a part of the 'level of law and policies', the level of civil society wherein religion can contribute to healthy conversations on religions, eventually to bring about an ethically oriented and religiously inspired public policies and commitment.

A Public Church / Indian Christianity

'What would be the role of Indian Christianity in constructing the base of a participatory republican democracy?' could be a meaningful question to end this paper with. Since a substratum of thick public sphere, along with a vibrant civil society, would go a long way to give life to values of common good, solidarity between different others, public reason, social justice, virtues of public life, non-domination, citizenship, plurality of religions, and dialogical existence, Indian Christianity would do well to contribute to the strengthening of this substratum.

It would perhaps begin with creating public spheres within the churches themselves. It is in place to recognise the fact that a practice of democracy within the churches could simultaneously be an experience of democracy in the Indian nation, enhancing the quality of Indian democracy. Aparna Sunder's argument in this regard is a case in point. In order to understand her argument proposed within a scheme of 'New Subaltern Studies', we need to situate it within the stream of subaltern studies which arose during the 1980s. We are all familiar with it, and of the volumes which carry a good number of studies on the histories of subaltern agency. The New Subaltern Studies finds that the SSP works within a modernist approach to culture and religion and by and large eclipses the latter in relation to their subaltern agency. Against this criticism, Aparna studies the presence of the Catholic Church among the Mukuvars and makes an argument that participatory structures within catholic churches are themselves an experience in power, a manner of democratic experience by themselves. The very manner of being a Church is an experience in democracy. Similarly, being a church in India itself is a manner of living out a polity, which has come to wield an alternate or even a subversive presence in the predominant contemporary political landscape bending itself for dynamics of homogenisation. Being a Church or being a Sikh or a Muslim community for that matter, constituted by beliefs and practices, becomes a point of contestation and resistance, constituting a thick public sphere.

Further on, Indian Christianity can undertake to do a public theology as a manner of nurturing the elements of Indian public sphere. It may have two angles to it: one *ad intra*, and the other *ad extra*. Public theology *ad intra* is a way of learning, interpreting, assimilating Christian doctrines or the tenets of Christian faith with a conscious attempt to relate them with a public other than the Christian public. It would involve gaining certain level of knowledge of other publics around. It would be like the dialogical dialogue proposed by Raimon Panikkar, except that it would add the element of the political dimension of the publics. Public theology *ad extra* would be a manner of presenting the tenets of Christian faith to different others - religious, 'secular', non-religious, etc. by way of working towards the common good. It would involve that we learn the art of *conversing* with different others in a public space. In addition to the fine art of rhetoric, we need to be equipped with substantive knowledge of Indian history, constitution, religio-cultural traditions, life-histories of great leaders, socio-economic systems, etc., which constitute the gestalt of Indian nationhood.

Finally, Indian Christianity can inspire other religious or philosophical traditions too to evolve their own public theologies. In his article titled, "Religion in Politics and the Politics of Hinduism", written as an introduction to his edited volume on *Political Hinduism – The Religious Imagination in Public Spheres*, Vinay Lal ends the article with a query whether a political Hinduism – a Hinduism that is sensitive to the political goals of establishing justice, citizenship rights, human rights, community rights, development and peace is not possible. He calls it a political Hinduism, which is far away from the Hindutva variety of political ideologies, but one that represents the religious aspirations of most Hindus to construct a polity which is deeply democratic and egalitarian. Such Hinduism, according to him, can be shaped up, not so much from the Brahminical religious traditions, but from the religious traditions of the subaltern or marginal people of India. A public sphere, fecundated by such the dialogue or conversations of such religious traditions, will go a long way in constructing a participatory democratic republic in India.

Conclusion

This chapter has tried to show, directly or circumstantially, how making India a civic republic is the need of the hour. The paper has arrived at this point, by tracing the itinerary of Indian modernity, its positivity and negativities, its Achilles heel of sequestration of power and the need for creating a civic base, with features from republican democracy, to make the people citizens of a civic nation. Religions, particularly Indian Christianity can play a significant role with its public theology, inspiring others to do their public theology, and bring them to the public sphere to be synergised by one another and journey towards common goals of freedom.

2

Being Indian, Being Christian
A Theo-Political Existential

The Christian Theo-Political Existential

"My faith, my country" - the cryptic but "tell it all" phrase embodying the position of Samuel V. Azariah, an Anglican bishop at Dornakal, in the context of a conversation[1] with M. K. Gandhi, seems to very pertinently indicate a pattern of relationship between Christian faith and nationalism (or patriotism), especially in India. It is a manner of bringing them together, without collapsing one into the other; it is a way of preserving the distinctiveness of both, even while endeavouring to bring a close relationship between them; and it is a manner of living out and giving shape to a unique interface, creatively forged through a configuration of contextual factors.

This manner of interfacing is premised on a Christian theological vision and practice, which has come down to us from ancient times. The relationship that the early Christians tried to maintain, both in positive and negative terms, with the Roman Empire manifested the primacy of their Christian faith even while standing for their "obedience" to the political authorities. Augustine of Hippo articulated the Christian commitment to the Roman Empire, even while holding the empire in judgement with respect to the *City of God*. A dialectics between transcendence and immanence, i.e., faith in a transcendent God and commitment to a temporal polity, seems to work at the core of this Christian approach.

It could also be named in the Christian tradition as the "incarnational" Christian existential, which embodies a vision of "rooted transcendence",

[1] Susan B Harper, *In the Shadow of the Mahatma – Bishop V. S. Azariah and the Travails of Christianity in British India* (New York: Taylor & Francis, 2000).

wherein materiality and spirituality, history and mystery, present and future, heavenly and temporal dimensions closely cohere, in a manner of *perichoresis*, i.e., indwelling of one in the other. When looked at in a comparative perspective, this existential could be distinguished from, even while being complementarily related to, the Islamic surrender to the totally transcendent Godhead and the Upanishadic call for the interior realisation of the *atman* as the *Brahman*.

This Christian theo-political existential had its pedigree in the Biblical notion of political authority, especially in the First Testament (Hebrew Bible). Political authority of the time was exercised in a dialectical relationship with priesthood and prophecy. Though started apparently with a theocratic combination of the three, the political authority progressively differentiated itself from the latter two, beginning with the time of Samuel.[2] Down through their history, the Biblical Israelites, lived out a creatively tensive relationship with the political authorities – be they native or foreign, primarily on account of their faith in a transcendent God.

The medieval "Christian West" had its ups and downs in continuing with this dialectics down through its history. During the pre-modern era, though endeavouring to keep the dialectics working by postulating two sources of authority (temporal and spiritual) represented by the person of the king and the pope, it became a story of certain give and take, depending upon the circumstantial issues of power and authority. As Aristotle Papanikolaou and George E. Demacopoulos observe "the history of Christian political theology in both the East and the West has been one form or another of Justinian *symphonia* in which the Church feels it is justified to use the power of the state to advance Christian objectives, and where the state makes use of the institutional church and appropriates Christian discourse to advance the interests of the state."[3]

The modern era witnessed to more complex ways of the dialectical Christian engagement with the political. The Reformation, though primarily a religious event, resulted in the formation of independent political units ruled by the German princes, freed from the grip of the Holy Roman Empire. This independence was wrought, in no small measure, as a cumulative effect of the newfound freedom for individuals to read the Bible on their own as per the Reformation theological maxims of "sola scriptura, sola gratia, and sola fide" and the doctrine of the "priesthood of all believers." The concomitant formations of multiple denominations and their political leadership in various regions of Europe, leading even to decades of wars (known as the wars of religion) and the consequent peace accord arrived in Westphalia (1648) – all had in them a dialectics between faith and politics.

---

[2] 1 Samuel 8

[3] Aristotle Papanikolaou and George E. Demacopoulos, "Outrunning Constantine's Shadow" in *Christianity, Democracy, and the Shadow of Constantine*, eds. Aristotle Papanikolaou and George E. Demacopoulos, New York: Fordham Press, 2017, 5.

The birth of the scientific world and its initial struggle against the ecclesiastical authorities and the simultaneous development of the modern political theory of the separation of state and church and the institution of what came to be known as the "secular" states – all these political events too, even in their apparent denial, had subtexts of the Christian doctrines embedded in them. For example, the birth of the modern sciences in the west had to do with a teleology of progress and development, which were nothing but secularised versions of the Christian vision of eschatology (Interestingly, the birth of Artificial Intelligence in our present-day context, as some authors argue, has to do with the Christian apocalypse[4]). Even the secular Enlightenment values of "liberty, equality and fraternity" of the French Revolution, which vehemently opposed the supremacy of the clergy, were mirror images of values born out of the Christian anthropology of the *Imago Dei*.

The modern political philosophies of the West on civil government originating from John Locke, developed further by Jacque Rousseau's Social contract theory, coming down to the present-day liberal contractarians like John Rawls, have an embedded Christian theological vision, even while the philosophers openly critiqued and even distanced themselves from the Christian narrative. This embedded vision could be seen especially in the biblical vision of the covenant relationship inspiring the formation of civil governments, constitutional polities, a commonwealth of nations governed by the rule of law, the binding force of civic relationship, etc. We saw this covenantal relationship reflected in the founding text of the US constitution beginning with the phrase, "We the People...", and this Constitution is treated by many as the text of a civil religion for the US.

A criticism stands out that Christianity's affinity with the modern liberal democracy, though occurring differently with different denominational backgrounds (for example, the Catholic Church becoming antagonistic to liberal democracy in the post-Enlightenment era), has ultimately helped the exercise of power by oligarchy, aristocracy and capitalist magnates. Persons of these categories, as landlords, plantation owners, etc., stood out to be leading Christians of the time. Needless to mention that they were also known for slave holding, and exercise of oppressive power! But it is also true that slavery was overcome in the North American context with the reinterpretation of the Bible from the perspective of the Black people. Similarly, we have examples like Latin America where due to the blossoming of liberation theology, Christianity has helped resist or even overthrow dictatorial powers; or the case of apartheid in South Africa having been overthrown with the activism of Church leaders, even while the Dutch Reformed Church was backing the white hegemony. We,

---

[4] Cf. Robert M. Geraci, *Apocalyptic AI – Visions of Heaven in Robotics, Artificial Intelligence and Virtual Reality* (Oxford: Oxford University Press, 2010).

thus, have differential and dialectical accounts of the role of Christianity when it comes to taking on elitist political powers during the modern times.

The Indian Christian Experience

Christians and the Indian Political Sphere

Lalsankima Pachauau's book titled *Indian and Christian* speaks of the creative and dialectical interface in the Indian context. It may well be said that the political consciousness of Indian Christians is situated on a continuum between the poles of being Christian and being Indian, integrating them contextually in differential manners. As Pachuau himself observes, "there were church leaders who ... (were) as nationalist as anyone else but who maintained their Christian distinctiveness as their point of departure. For Christians, there is a doctrinal call to be prophetic and, thus, to maintain critical distance."[5] He points out that Christian leaders like K. T. Paul and V. S. Azariah "upheld a position that was different from mainstream political nationalism, although they rightly maintained that they were nationalistic."[6] We can see that this kind of dynamics of 'standing for faith even while becoming part of the culture of the land' was at work from the very early stages of Christianity in India.

The St. Thomas Christians of India, from a very ancient time, represent a thick integration of being Indian and being Christian. The anecdotal statement made by Pacid J. Podipara that Indian Christianity of the time was 'Hindu in culture, Christian in religion and Oriental in worship' conveys the dialectical character of the relationship. Being a trading community that had established commercial relations with others and had struck marital ties with the natives, Indian Christians of the time had been to a large extent socio-culturally integrated, but continued to be religiously distinct. As A. M. Mundadan would put it, "[T]he life St. Thomas Christians had been leading till the arrival of the Portuguese spanned two worlds: the geographical, political and social world of Malabar or Kerala (India), and the ecclesiastical world of East-Syrian or the Persian Church..."[7] Though spanning the two worlds, the Syrian Christians (St. Thomas Christians) lived their lives more as natives than outsiders, and as Susan Bayly would put it, were "honoured and rewarded" by native rulers on account of their being "warriors, traders and Church notables."[8] The native rulers seemed to have constructed Church buildings and donated lands, finance, etc., to the Syrians. Such a benefaction, as Bayly would narrate, points out to

[5] Lalsangkima Pachuau, *Indian and Christian – Historical Accounts of Christianity and Theological Reflections in India* (New Delhi: ISPCK, 2019), 56.

[6] Ibid., 57.

[7] A. M. Mundadan, *History of Christianity in India – Vol. 1: From the Beginning up to the Middle of the Sixteenth Century* (Bangalore: Church History Association of India, 2001), 145.

[8] Susan Bayly, *Saints, Goddesses and Kings – Muslims and Christians in South Indian Society 1700-1900* (New York: Cambridge University Press, 1989), 243-44.

a considerable level of integration of the Syrians with the native community. Moreover, they shared a rich content of religious beliefs and cultural practices with the natives, including their purity-pollution laws.[9] Thus a specific manner of native existence, though sharing in different socio-cultural and political worlds, characterised the lifeworld of Indian Christians from ancient times. It would imply also that they had established a relationality, including a discursive field of communication – cultural, religious, and even political with the native people.

During the early modern era, the dialectical relationship was tangibly manifest, especially in the political roles some of the Christian missionaries played. Francis Xavier played a political mediatory role between the Portuguese power and the native king; Joseph Constantius Beschi apparently served as the *diwan* of Chanda Sahib, a *nawab* at Arcot; Christian Fredrick Swartz played a mediatory role between the East India Company and Hyder Ali; Charles Mead served as a civil judge for a while in South Travancore; etc. There are many more similar examples.

While these being exceptional political roles played by some outstanding Christian leaders, the culture of "associations" in the modern sense was introduced in the civil sphere by some Indian Christian leaders as part of their effort to bear witness to their Christian faith in a context of emerging nationalism. Examples like Bengal Christian Association, Madras Native Christian Association, Western India Native Christian Alliance[10] attest to this fact. It is instructive to see how some members of the Bengal Christian Association like Kali Charan Banerjee and Joy Govinda Shome felt about their networked identity and voiced it in the *The Bengal Christian Herald* in 1870: "We have embraced Christianity, but we have not discarded our nationality. We are as intensely national as any of our brethren of the native press can be."[11]

The concepts of "Hindu Christians" or "Hindu Catholics", floated by some prominent Christians of the Bengal region is one of the variants of the dialectics of being Christian and being Indian. Kali Charan Banerjee said: "In having become Christians, we have not ceased to be Hindus. We are Hindu Christians, as thoroughly Hindu as Christians"[12] and called upon the Christian missionaries to "become Hindus just as St. Paul became all things to all people."[13] Brahmabandhab Upadhyay, a creative but controversial Catholic

[9] Bayly, 250-257; Cf. Susan Viswanathan, *The Christians of Kerala* (New Delhi: Oxford, 1993).

[10] Pachuau, *Indian and Christian*, 54.

[11] Ibid., 55.

[12] Ibid., 55.

[13] Ibid., 55.

nationalist, theologised on the concept of being a "Hindu-Catholic."[14] He argued that the teachings of the Old Testament of the Bible in the Indian context should be replaced with the Indian wisdom as found in Vedas and Upanishads. K. T. Paul, another important Christian leader to participate in the nationalist movement, wanted Indian Christianity to be enriched with the rich folklore, distinct music and the community values of India.[15] Down south in Tirunelveli, a group of Christians formed a church known as the 'Hindu Church of the Lord Jesus' in 1958.

Furthermore, the birth of the National Missionary Society in the year 1905 was yet another creative variant of the dialectics of being Indian and being Christian. K. T. Paul and V. S. Azariah, the two Christian leaders who founded this society, "made distinguished contributions in nationalizing Indian Christianity and Christianizing Indian nationality."[16] The society was a forerunner in inculcating the sentiments of patriotism to Christian missions, and the eventful inauguration of the Church of South India is an important instance of the maturation of this new manner of integration.

The era of indigenous liberation theologies like Dalit theology brought about occasions for engaging nationalism from the perspective of Dalit Christians. Theologians spoke of 'Dalit Jesus', 'Dalit Matha', etc., and an emancipatory intent was deeply integrated to this creative existential of Christian subalterns. Several Dalit Christian movements and associations within the mainline denominational churches gave expression to a socially liberative manner of being a Indian Christians.

It is quite revealing to see that it was either persons with elements of western Christian background (for example, Alan Octavian Hume) or that Indians influenced by Christianity (e.g. Rajaram Mohan Roy) played a significant role to awaken the spirit of renaissance or independence among the Indians. The life-itinerary of M.K. Gandhi took a turn towards nationalism due in a major part to his living in a Western "Christian" habitat. Joseph Baptista (1864-1930), a native Indian Christian, was the first president of the Indian Home Rule League, in the founding of which he played an important role.[17] All these and many more such intersectional personalities vouchsafe for the valuable integration of aspects of faith and nationalism in the Indian context.

During the contemporary times, conversion has been made a thorny issue in India, impacting upon the experience of nationalism, producing a political discourse around it. Studies from sociological, cultural, religious, psychological,

---

[14] Sebastian Painadath, SJ and Jacob Parapally, MSFS, eds. *A Hindu-Catholic – Brahmabandab Upadhyay's Significance for Indian Christian Theology,*

[15] Pachuau, *Indian and Christian*, 63.

[16] Ibid., 60.

[17] Leo Fernando and G. Gispert-Sauch, *Christianity in India* (Haryana: Penguin Random House, 2004), 250.

political, and theological perspectives abound. Studies also on the implications of conversion to the question of nationalism too are on the increase. While "genuine" conversions, purportedly of individual persons, were not anathema to some of the tall leaders, including M. K. Gandhi of the classical "secular" nationalist era, conversion by collectives or communities of people became suspect and conflict-ridden. The political right that is in ascendance now has spewed antipathy towards the very phenomenon of religious conversion, branding those involved in it as anti-nationals and as causes of threat to the sovereignty and even to the very security of the Indian nation. Needless to say, religious conversion has been much maligned today.

The Christian involvement in conversion begins with its core religious experience of *metanoia* – the central call of Jesus to every individual and community "to repent and believe." It is an integral part of the Christian belief system, its spirituality, sacramentality, and theology. It is certainly an inner experience, but also transformative of communities and social systems. Being a Christian, one cannot but value the goal of conversion, both of oneself and of others. However, this call is not anti-national, much less of an intention to secede or isolate or carve out a group from the national mainstream. That the Christian community in India has remained a miniscule minority of the general population for millennia together attests to the fact that the experience of conversion is more of a spiritual phenomenon than of a demographic intent. Indian Christians wish to practise conversion and the post-conversion life on the premise of the dictum, quoted earlier, by bishop Samuel Azaria, "my faith, my country." Over and above the constitutional right to conversion, which Indian Christians certainly value, conversion as a religious experience is a theological desideratum for Christians. The constitutional right, as part of the global democratic freedom of religion, is only a legal guarantee but that alone neither legitimises nor discredits the Christian religious experience of conversion. Neither does the fact that the mega resistance to conversion coheres with the structural "impossibility" of a change from one caste to another, undermine the religious import of conversion!

Being Indian and Christian in Public Sphere

While the foregoing narration has indicated some salient historical instances from the life of Indian Christians to indicate the kind of relationship they forged between their faith and patriotism, their presence in and contribution to the public life of India stands out in their relationship to the Indian nation. Christians have been a miniscule minority for centuries together, but their presence is very insignificant for the public life of Indians. As Nandini Chatterjee, in her book titled *The Making of Indian Secularism: Empire, Law and Christianity 1830-1960*[18] has argued 'Indian Christianity has come to wield an influence, disproportionate to its numerical strength, in the public life of Indians'.

Christianity's relationship with the Indian public sphere, a prototype of the civil sphere, has indeed been complex, characterised by processes of involvement, contestation, differentiation, and distinction. These dynamics indeed resonate with the dialectics we have been speaking about. Christianity's relationship with the Indian public sphere became more pronounced during the modern era. Aided by the availability of the inchoate print media, Christian missionaries began to interact with the wider public from the sixteenth century onwards. Catholic missionaries in the southern Tamil region - starting with Henrique Henriques (1520-1600), who introduced the printed Christian literature, to Robert de Nobili (1577-1656) and Joseph Constantius Beschi (1680-1747) who produced varieties of literatures, prose and poetry, had embarked upon public conversations and disputations on religious and philosophical matters. Disputations on religious themes went hand in hand with adaptations of Indic language, symbols, and traditions to express and shape up a native Christian tradition. Literary creations like epics, tales, commentaries, dictionaries, and translations of Indic classics into European languages created a base for early public discursive practices emergent during the sixteenth-seventeenth-eighteenth centuries. This is not to deny the existence of discursive forums prior to their introduction by Christian missionaries; the vibrant debating forums of the last Tamil Sangam (circa 400 BCE – 200 BCE), the interreligious dialogical forum run by Akbar as recent as mid sixteenth century CE, the "intensifying religious interactions" during the Mughal period,[19] are good examples of their earlier existence. However, while the latter debating spheres existed more among rulers and experts, the former began to include wider sections of people.

The Protestant missionary presence, beginning with the first Protestant missionary Bartholomew Ziegenbalg who had installed a printing press at Tranquebar and the Serampore trio who had established a printing 'industry' at Serampore during the eighteenth century contributed to the emergence of a printed-literature-based discursive field in the Indian public. The subsequent eventful missionary activities of the classical missionary societies and of the Anglican churches during the nineteenth century contributed multi-dimensionally to the relative strengthening of the discursive public sphere. Translations of Bible into native languages and printing them, and undertaking the 'mission' of imparting modern education to wider sections of

[18] Cf. Nandini Chatterjee, *The Making of Indian Secularism: Empire, Law and Christianity 1830-1960* (New York: Palgrave Macmillan, 2011).

[19] Cf. Vashua Dalmia and Munis D. Faruqui, eds. *Religious Interactions in Mughal India* (New Delhi: Oxford University Press, 2014).

Indian population, along with making efforts to do away with discriminatory and oppressive practices in the Indian socio-cultural systems, went a long way in enhancing the Indian public sphere, which, along with the rule of law and the relatively more rationalised administration of the British India, began to grow steadily. Founding of various institutions by 'orientalists' for study of native literatures and printing the Indological classics to circulate them among the public markedly changed the demography of readership in the Indian subcontinent. A process of democratisation of Indian classics, along with the spread of modern mass education, contributed significantly to the emergence of the structures of public communication. It is no less significant a fact that Indian Christianity was a singular contributor to this process.

All these contributions to the cultural, social and political terrain of India made them unique public personalities, whose impact continues to endure until this day. Their contributions, put forth amidst untold sufferings and sacrifices, were multi-dimensional in character and could not be reduced to a restrictive understanding of "religious conversion." They valued their contributions as leading to the common good of this country, which, for many of them was the only "home-country" they ever lived in.

The post-colonial era has brought forth a different scenario as regards the presence of Indian Christianity in the Indian public. A phase of post-independent national integration, combined with the project of Five-Year plans for development, saw Indian Christians involved enthusiastically in welfare schemes, programmes of poverty alleviation, literacy programmes, disaster management, sanitation, health, and primary / higher / professional education of the Indian population. Spread of the modern education to further layers of Indian population set in a 'silent revolution' as in the words of Christophe Jeffrelot mentioned above,[20] and Indian Christians came to constitute and bear a distinctively subaltern social identity. Advocacy for civil liberties of the subaltern people, involvement in movements for various social goals, voluntary initiatives for amelioration and eradication of social evils, etc., became important sites of Christian presence. In terms of relationship with other religions, they undertook inter-religious dialogues, study-centres, and ashrams for inter-religious experiences.

All these done in an ambience of relative spontaneity and freedom! The scenario changed with the political ascendance of the far-right, with its religio-cultural nationalism. As studies show, violence against Christians[21] has rapidly increased, and conversion has become a thorny issue between those who affirm their Constitutional right for conversion and others who oppose

[20] Cf. Christophe Jaffrelot, *India's Silent Revolution – The Rise of the Low Castes in North Indian Politics* (Delhi: Permanent Black, 2003).

[21] Cf. Sarbeswar Sahoo, *Pentecostalism and Politics of Conversion in India* (Cambridge: Cambridge University Press, 2018).

it not merely in debates but also through acts of violence. Majoritarianism in politics has given a hegemonic power to the religious majority in the domains of culture, knowledge, education, and even civil rights, and it has been adversely instrumentalised by a small section that has self-assumed the religious leadership of the majority, by collating an ideology with religion, and this religion with patriotism. Indian Christians, as a result, seem to develop tendencies to 'in-grow', become self-conscious, etc., rather than participating in the public life of the nation. Religio-cultural nationalism of the self-assumed leadership goes to the extent of implicating the Indian Christian identity to be culturally conflictive and politically divisive, with an implied accusation of preventing the Indian nation from emerging into the global world as a united political power; it is as if the patriotism of Indian Christians, along with that of other religious minorities, needed to be proved on a day-to-day basis. One could think of the isolation of Indian Christians also as one suffered by a subaltern identity in a ritual framework of purity and pollution characteristic of the Indian caste-system.

Challenges to the Theo-Political Existential

The awakening of the Indian national consciousness among a section of the elites of India during the later part of the nineteenth century, as Paul Heehs observes, had much to do with their spiritual / religious quest. Some of the prominent right-of-the-centre nationalists like Bankimchandra Chatterjee, Bipinchandra Pal, Aurobindo Ghose, and Vivekananda almost identified the 'devotion to the nation' (*desa bhakti*) with religious or spiritual piety. For Ghose, religion was the 'soul of the nation'. In a speech delivered in 1907, Ghose said: "Nationalism is not a mere political programme; Nationalism is a religion that has come from God. Nationalism is a creed which you shall have to live."[22]

And for Vivekanada it was the abiding spiritual quest which made the Indian nation what it was and what it could become of universally. He said: "If there is any land on this earth that can lay claim to be the blessed *Punya Bhumi*, ... the land of introspection and of spirituality, it is India."[23] India attained this greatness because, he said, it turned its mind away from "acquisition of immense wealth poured in by trade, of the power and spread of commercialism", and held on "to God, to the treasure-house of religion and spirituality."[24]

[22] Cited by Paul Heehs, "Bengali Religious Nationalism and Communalism", *International Journal of Hindu Studies*, Apr., 1997, Vol. 1, No. 1 (Apr., 1997), pp. 117-139, 121).

[23] Swami Vivekananda, *My India – The India Eternal*, Calcutta: The Ramakrishna Mission Institute of Culture, 1993 (Reprint), p. 13.

[24] *Ibid.*, p. 17.

An element of this stream of spiritual / religious nationalism got integrated with the political project of M. K. Gandhi, who mobilised the political consciousness of the people by invoking the religious imaginary of *Ramrajya*. He was religiously sensitive enough to feel the vitality of religion for political mobilisation, but he was also politically sensitive to not mingle religion with the statecraft and to treat different religious communities with fairness and equality. He did think of politics as his religion, but to the extent that it could cultivate the inner qualities of being political; and, he did consider the religious truth as the political truth, but only to the point of forming the character of the people for a civic polity. He was acutely aware of the danger of mixing religion with the statecraft, its power and the running of the government.

Nation is Religion!!!

Going much further, what has occurred during the phase of the present-day Hindutva politics in the post-independent India is a strong move towards identifying the statecraft, the running of the government, with a religion. In fact, the already existing tendency in the ex-colonies in South Asia to collapse the nation and the state into one[25] facilitates the further move to identity both the state and the nation with a religion. With much ease, therefore, nation and the religion are collapsed into one, and both nation and religion are identified with the state. This move does not even reckon the specificity of the formation of the post-colonial states like India to be nation-states, i.e., two distinct identities, networked with their distinctiveness, allowing multiple nations - religio-cultural communities, to exist with their autonomy within a state. Such a consciousness of the hyphenated character of the Indian nation-state is totally lost upon the political right. Consequently, the impartiality of the state is lost, and different others are treated as aliens in their own soil. Religion is instrumentalised here to fetch political dividends at the reckoning. Religious rituals are pressed into the service of constructing a political sovereignty. Burton Stein, the well-known historian, argued that constructing a ritual sovereignty was the modus operandi for any ruler who wished to maintain an autocratic political hegemony.

The Christian Theo-Political Existential in India Today

"My nation *is* my faith" seems thus to be the reigning dictum of religious nationalism, especially of the religious right in the contemporary Indian context. This poses one of the major theological challenges to Indian Christians. This identification of religion and nation, according to the Christian mind, seems to lead humanity towards an act of indulging with nations / political units and

---

[25] T. K. Oommen, "Demystifying the Nation and Nationalism", India International Centre Quarterly , WINTER 2002-SPRING 2003, Vol. 29, No. 3/4, India: A National Culture? (WINTER 2002-SPRING 2003), pp. 259-274, 264.

as a result lose the ability to situate life in a horizon of transcendent faith. This misadventure, in the Christian theological vocabulary, is named as "idolatry", i.e. an experience of closures with respect to the future and an inability to take life beyond a "temporary" historical religio-cultural configuration. Contrasting the idols against icons, Jean-Luc Marion, a philosophical phenomenologist, observed that icons mediate our gaze beyond a medium while idols foreclose them and enclose us from within us.[26] In the reflection of Jean-Luc Nancy, idols freeze our ability to experience the ongoing "dis-enclosures."[27] In the face of the threat of such obfuscating nationalism, "M. M. Thomas made clear in his writings in the 1940s and 1950s, (that) Christians should maintain critical distance especially because nationalism has the potential of turning idolatrous."[28]

How do we face the idolatrous brand of nationalism is the most crucial theo-political challenge to Indian Christians today. This brand, with the support of populist religious nationalism, is poised to dwarf the democratic political potential for our country and foreclose our future of an egalitarian polity and society. Christians therefore are called upon to become theologically more creative and active to respond to the situation. The long standing Christian theological dialectics of 'being Christian and being Indian' needs to be creatively explored today.

It is time the Indian Christian community stood up, without being despondent about its vulnerability, but as a catalyst that can participate in more substantive and enduring ways in the wider Indian public, in the expansive civil sphere of the nation. K. T. Paul, making a mention in his speech about the 'spirit' of Indian Christians during the first Roundtable Conference held in Briton, said:

> ... Nor do we feel isolated in point of culture and tradition. We drink from the same founts of literature, art and music, and in fact the most modern tendency of even our religious thought and expression is to relate them, in all loyalty to its past history and tradition, to the categories that are derived from what is characteristically Indian lore... The attitude of our community is thus one of trust and confidence... Our religious life brings us into intimate relations with the life of many nations of the West, and our community is in a peculiar position to appreciate the enormous importance of our

[26] Jean-Luc Marion, *In Exces – Studies in Saturated Phenomena* (New York: Fordham University Press, 2002); Marion, *God Without Being* (Chicago: The University of Chicago Press, 1991).

[27] Jean-Luc Nancy, *Dis-enclosure – The Deconstruction of Christianity* (New York: Fordham University Press, 2008).

[28] Pachuau, *Indian and Christian,* 57.

> country maintaining international relationships on as many lines as possible. We shall fail in our duty if we do not here and now emphasise, what indeed is no new idea to our national leaders, that our Motherland has everything to gain by every tie she makes with other nations, East and West.[29]

Though much removed in time and context from ours, K. T. Paul's capturing of the Indian Christian spirit at the time of the surge of nationalist sentiments in the 1930s seems very relevant today. Paul was a Christian nationalist, did not support the communal electorates, and gave expression to an idea of interactive and integrating existence for Indian Christians. Though duly acknowledging the challenges of being a minority, Paul went ahead to imagine that the Christians were in a unique position, rooted in the Indian cultural heritage on the one hand and opportuned to mediate with the international communities on the other. This is a meaningful viewpoint even today, when extreme cultural nationalist forces have gained power in the Indian political horizon. Extremely challenging situations do not make Indian Christians less Indian, in spite of the concerted inimical portrayal to be one; and, no acute pain inflicted on them make them less connected with others nationally and internationally. This unique position, imbued with the depth of the Indian 'spirit', is the vantage point from which Indian Christianity has to look upon its identity, religion, culture and its commitment for the Indian democratic nation. It is with this spirit that Indian Christianity is called upon to explore its public role today. Developing a sound 'public theology' is nothing but a meaningful way of living out this public role in the Indian nation.

Firstly, they would do well to theologically rethink about their presence and role in the public sphere for the contemporary times. With a meaningful initiation into the public sphere made by earlier generation of Christians, they can pro-actively continue the tradition to effectively converse with different others for common good. Their theology needs to turn public, by way of widening the vistas of their theological horizon and striking deep roots in the religio-cultural terrain of this land. They need to know, understand and imbibe the wisdom present, especially in the traditions of the subaltern people of this land. In addition, they need to become skilful in public conversations. It is strange that in spite of their relatively better education, their presence in the public discursive sphere is abysmally low! They need to balance the theological consciousness of their Christian tradition with the historical consciousness of being Indians, and thus create a vibrantly networked consciousness to sustain an Indian Christian theo-political existential. Spiritual or religious power certainly is an important ingredient of becoming mature political agents, and

[29] H. A. Popley, *K. T. Paul – Christian Leader* (Madras: The Christian Literature Society, 1987 [originally published by YMCA, Calcutta 1938]), 193-194.

that needs to be integrated in a dialectical manner so that one does not collapse into the other.

Secondly, they would do well to inspire a process of doing inter-religious public theology on public life. Different religious traditions of India have their own theo-political wisdom which needs to emerge into the public through a process of conversations and mutual collaboration. Inter-religious public theology, though integrating the positive potentials of inter-religious dialogues, is characterised by its concern for the nurturance of civil values, ultimately helping a democratic polity to mature. Civic virtues like human dignity, citizenship, conversations, non-domination, social justice, care for the marginalised, patriotism, and common good need to be cultivated drawing resources from the wellsprings of different religions.

3

Indian Christianity, Civil Society, and the Democratic Process in India

Introduction

Giorgia Meloni, the Italian Prime Minister, was euphoric the other day about the salience of the conservative political right in countries like the USA, India, Italy, Argentina and even Germany. Critiquing left-of-Centre and Leftist parties for not being adequately responding to contemporary situation, Meloni said the political right is remaking the world in newer ways. Let her euphoria be what it may, what we do see is that the salience of the political right today feeds on the salience of political religions across the globe. While we may find varieties of political religions in human history, through its different epochs like the feudal and the capitalist ones, what we witness to today is political religions aligning with majoritarian or racial supremacist regimes trying to pass for democracies, and that too grassroots democracies.

The salience of this combination of the political far-right and majoritarian political religions seems to thrive on several popular concerns of nation-states. In the western zone, the primary concern seems to be protecting their nations from the migratory population, especially the one that enters their countries seeking asylum apparently through illegal routes. Even those who legally enter seem to pose threats to them in terms of sharing their job market and political leadership, and setting in a very challenging situation of multiculturalism. In the Eastern zone, especially in countries of South Asia like India and Sri Lanka, concerns of cultural and racial nationalism seem to play vital roles, even while re-emergence of feudalist forces and populist democracies undergird the combination.

What seem to be a common thread in all these developments is the dismaying of secular and liberal politics in many countries of the world. The political policies adopted during the modern centuries to separate state and religion for the wellbeing of both have dismayed today. There are those who interpret secularism not so much as separation of state and religion, but as equal treatment of different religions by the state, while failing to do so under the heavy weight of cultural and racial majoritarianism. Religion is being mindlessly instrumentalised to manufacture political consent to set up brute powers which trample upon the fundamental freedoms which had been cherished nationally and globally. Ultimately, a political civilization, centring round the goal of democracy, by which the grassroots sections of humanity gradually began to participate in the political processes is being reversed or corroded today. Authoritarianism, dictatorship, majoritarianism, and corporate feudalism seem to further stifle the veins of the civilization of democracy. In countries like India, what is called 'fratured modernity' is aiding and abetting the instrumentalistion of religions as well as democracy. It is unfortunate that narrow communal forces are on ascendency by using the inchoate democratic platforms and policies.

In this context, what can Indian Christianity, a minority religious tradition, do to contribute to prevent the continuing erosion of the substantive dimensions of democracy is the central question reflected in this article. Can Indian Christianity, with its religious resources, still contribute positively and liberatively to the democratic process? If yes, how so? – are the questions. It proposes that doing public theology is one of the most meaningful ways to make its contribution in the best way possible today. The proposal goes with certain assertions: 1. Doing public theology makes Indian Christianity to build upon some of its already existing positive potentials, and adapt them to the newer context; 2. Indian Christianity rejuvenates itself in the light of public theology and becomes a publicly creative tradition; 3. It becomes a catalyst to inspire other religious traditions to join in the process of doing public theology; and, 4. It revisits the relationship of state and religion and adapts to a relevant approach which takes the civil sphere as the site of creative contributions for social transformation. These assertions will be analytically unpacked in the following sections of the article.

Renewing the Positive Potentials of Indian Christianity

Public theology is a contextual theology that springs forth from contemporary context wherein human beings increasingly become involved in the processes of making decisions for common and public good. In a historical gaze, we may perceive that unlike the past centuries when vertical and hierarchical processes of decision making by a monarch, king, chief, etc for wider sections of human populations were at work, our contemporary context is characterised by horizontal and participatory processes which involve increasingly widening sections of human population for decision making. While this trend was set in with the birth of modern nation-states, what is happening during our global era is a very emphatic push towards widening of the circles of democratic participation.

The participation that we witness to in our context is multidimensional. First, many a country today wish to or does implement the electoral democracy, and therefore wider sections of people get to cast a vote and participate in the process of electing their representatives. This is an act performed by individuals as members of a given political society. Second, parallel to this process, we also find increasing sections of humanity involved in conversations of the public sphere.[1] As different from the political sphere constituted by political representatives like members of State Assemblies or Parliaments and their support groups like political parties, public sphere is constituted by those who can create public opinions at various forums like the academia, writers' forums, public debating clubs, chat shows, and the like. Researchers, writers, debaters and opinion makers of a given field are the prominent contributors to the public sphere. Though an independent sphere, public sphere is the most proximate to the political sphere and generate opinions which influence the political sphere leading to decision making. Third, parallel to the political and public spheres, there is the civil sphere which serve as the primary field to germinate creative ideas and motivate ethical actions for common good. This is a sphere which serves as the very fulcrum of a political sphere.

In each context of life, a human person encounters at least two types of spheres – one the "natural" society and the other the civil society. Natural society, which is a given context of life to any individual, is constituted by families, tribes, clans, castes, and other ascriptive or hereditary communities, and their customs, lores, traditions, etc. which serve as the glue to constitute these communities as the natural society. As different from this natural society, we have the civil society which human beings create by their participation in various free associations like Churches, religious organisations, ideological groups, art and aesthetic groups, performing cultural groups, and various other voluntary organisations. What marks out the civil sphere from those of the natural society is the freedom with which human persons expresses their creative ideas and energies; this singular factor of freedom, unpacked in terms of "freedom of speech", "freedom of religion", "freedom of expression", "freedom of association", etc., is what makes something "civil" and is continuously nurtured in any democratic polity. As Alexis Toqueville, a French Political philosopher

---

[1] We have today a rich literature on the processes of the public sphere. Cf. Alan McKee, *An Introduction to the Public Sphere* (Cambridge: Cambridge University Press, 2005); Craig Calhoun, ed. *Habermas and the Public Sphere* (Cambridge: The MIT Press, 1996); Jim McGuigan, *Culture and the Public Sphere* (London: Routledge, 1996).

pointed out, it was a vibrant civil society which made democracy vibrant in North America during the nineteenth century, and his insight applies to our context as well.

Indian Civil Sphere and Indian Christianity

For our concern here, civil sphere provides the starting point to consider the contribution of Indian Christianity to the democratic process in India. Indian civil sphere can be meaningfully associated with Indian Christianity at least at two broad levels: One, at the level of contributing to create the basic facilities for the functioning of civil society in India; two, at the level of public activism.

At the first level, the contribution of Indian Christianity needs be looked at both historically and contemporaneously. Historically speaking, the contribution is quite significant. In a context where ascriptive exclusive communities like the caste – based communities, the Indian *gemeinschaft* (to adopt the phrase of Tonnies Ferdinand) had a stranglehold in the Indian natural society and therefore had inhibited for centuries the emergence of a public space wherein individuals could be treated with equality and freedom, Indian Christianity made an opening towards inclusivity and freedom. It did so by introducing modern and mass education to Indian population and opened the floodgates of social assertion and mobility from wider subaltern sections of humanity who were otherwise reeling under the caste-based hierarchical and segregating structures. In the event of modernisation of consciousness as well as introduction of infrastructural facilities like transport and communication, wider sections of Indian population began to participate in public events, administrative capabilities, and even in inchoate representative bodies. It was through these facilities that the intimations of democracy reached the Indian shores. This is not certainly to deny the existence of some form or the other of participatory leadership in some traditional Indian political units, but only to say that this was the beginning of an open sphere across the regions and that too based on civic principles of equality and freedom for everyone. Along with the introduction of modern education, Indian Christianity has also played significant roles in the reform of the Indian society through various measures. In addition, the creative contributions to the writing of scripts for several indigenous languages and production of mass literature (literature for the wider public) in several prominent Indian languages have contributed their undeniable share in the shaping up of pro-active participatory consciousness in several Indian generations for over four centuries.

While these are some of the historical contributions to the birthing of modern democracy in the Indian soil, Indian Christianity has also gone on to contribute to nurturing of democracy through its "public activism." Involvement in nation building programmes undertaken by the independent India through its five-year plans, participation in disaster managements on occasions of famine, natural calamities, etc., and involvement in social movements and advocacy for human rights and civil liberties by prominent Christian individuals and voluntary agencies keep contributing their share to the nurturing of democratic values.

These are the ways Indian Christianity has contributed and continues to contribute to the nurturing of rudiments of civil society and thereby Indian democracy. But the question could be whether the historical and the present-day pro-active contributions have any contemporary relevance in the context of democracy turning majoritarian, a danger inbuilt into the democratic ideal itself, which was alerted to by philosophers like Plato and Aristotle right from the beginning of its birth in the Greek city-states. The remaining part of this article will reflect about how Indian Christianity can still contribute to the democratic processes so that an egalitarian society may blossom in the way social reformers like Ambedkar wanted Indian democracy to be.

Rejuvenating Indian Christianity

To continue to contribute to the transformation of Indian democracy, Indian Christianity need to locate its mission in the Indian civil sphere. As narrated above, the association of Indian Christianity to the Indian civil sphere is not anything new, and, in fact, it has contributed to the making of the basic facilities needed to constitute the civil sphere or civil society. In addition to this, Indian Christianity, as a religious tradition, has also the religious resources in terms of theological insights and motivations that are facilitative of creating a healthy civil society. For instance, the corpus of social teachings of the Catholic Church, known generally as the Catholic Social Teachings (CST), is a wellspring of values appropriate to any civil society. Beginning with its emphasis on the transcendental character of the human, the corpus dwells upon human dignity, freedom, respect for the other, civilization of love, commitment for social justice, concern for the environment, etc. which are very vital for constituting a healthy civil society. Similarly, the social teachings of the World Council of Churches too have rich teachings as well as commitments which empower the poor and the marginalised. Furthermore, we have rich Indian Christian theological oeuvre which has been shaped up for about two centuries by theologians from all denominations, and they have a creative section which deals with Indian Christianity's commitment to civil society and social transformation. With all these rich heritages, we need to learn to do public theologies for the sake of transforming Indian democracy today.

As a first step, Indian Christianity must rejuvenate itself according to the vison of public theology.[2] The primary goal of public theology is creating

---

[2] There is immense material about public theology today. For a deeper understanding, one may refer to: Sebastian Kim and Katie Day, eds. *A Companion to Public Theology* (Leiden: BRILL, 2017); John W. de Gruchy, "Public Theology as Christian Witness: Exploring the Genre",

participatory, non-discriminatory, and egalitarian procedures for decision making for a given community, and its core dynamics is constituting a public sphere through public reasoning and conversations. Indian Christianity, constituted by innumerable churches under various denominations, should emerge as a worthy public body by developing the characteristics of a healthy civil society within itself.

The Inner Life

Civic virtues could become more pronounced in the inner life of Indian Christianity. It could cultivate within its bodies the art of public reasoning, which is one of the benchmarks of civic participation. Civil society is an arena of the culture of encounter, articulated through discursive performances. Skills of listening, presenting a view-point, arguing, debating, discerning, arriving at consensus, respecting differences, etc., need to be cultivated with due care.

Membership in the Church can be discussed in terms of an "ecclesial citizenship." A baptized member, analogous to a citizen of a constitutional polity, need to be treated with rights and duties which derive from the ecclesial communion. The rights to an ecclesial citizen to participate fully in the life and mission of the church must be respected. Hurdles emerging from gender, caste, and rites need to be eradicated.

The embedded presence of ascriptive ties in the various Churches, in terms of kinship and caste needs to be eradicated to bring up the characteristics of civil society more effectively and inspiringly. The Indian Catholic Church is still encumbered by caste and kinship preferences, and they shape up an invisible ambience to practice endogamy to create a niche in the caste-based hierarchical web.

Ecumenically

Participatory bodies between denominational churches for spiritual solidarity, economic cooperation, political solidarity, and social harmony could be created at local, regional and national levels. The Indian Catholic Church, being the numerically strong communion among others, has a responsibility to take the lead in this regard. A sphere of solidarity and collaboration beyond theological, liturgical, and spiritual layers is a must for today.

There was a time when the Catholic Church attempted to constitute itself to be a civil society against the challenges posed by the liberal modern

---

International Journal of Public Theology, DOI: 10.1163/156973207X194466; Gavin D'Costa, *Theology in the Public Square – Church, Academy and Nation* (USA: Blackwell Publishing, 2005). More pertinently, we also have several publications with respect to Christian public theologies to the Indian context. Following are some among them: Gnana Patrick, *Public Theology – Indian Concerns, Perspectives and Themes* (USA: Fortress Press, 2020); Raj Bharat Patta, *Subaltern Public Theology: Dalits and the Indian Public Sphere* (UK: Palgrave Macmillan, 2003).

society. It founded several civil society institutions like educational institutions, social service organizations, political forums, etc. to contribute to the common good of humanity. These have come to the present-day Catholics as valuable patrimonies, with which it can be substantively active in the wider civil society today.

Christian presence in the domain of education, an important component of civil society, is facing up to increasing challenges: first of all, the process of "commercialization" of education, a global phenomenon though, is posing a big challenge to the Christian mind. Promoting literacy, higher education and scientific pursuits have always been promoted by the Catholic Church as necessary pathways to develop the potentials as well as the moral character of the human person as ordained by God. But the present-day challenge of commercialization, sailing on the impulses of the technocratic paradigm and profit-making, is tempting us to walk a path of immanentist anti-witness. It creates a typical "tensive" moment for the Church. Deep analysis and discernment among the Christian agents of education is a necessity today.

Moreover, some major shifts in educational polices introduced by the Government do not resonate well with the Christian values. For example, if there is a project of homogenization of cultures written into some educational policies, how can Christians collaborate with it? Right from the beginning of the Catholic Social teachings, homogenization of the civil sphere by the industrial forces has been severely critiqued on the ground that it damages the dignity and freedom of the human person. How can we, therefore, go in support of such projects?

Social service and health ministry, which are also parts of the civil society, too are facing up to challenges. A deep suspicion is cast upon the Christian project of social service under the label of 'conversion'. Starting from the local fanatics, to doctrinaire scholarship, and to sections of prejudiced judiciary, the Christian agency becomes victim of the suspicion. Conversion as a religious experience gets lost in the din of partisan political discourses, and the human right associated with it becomes suspect. "Social service is welcome, but not conversion" is the slogan heard today. Though not in any way instrumentalising social service for conversion, disconnecting the social service from a religious inspiration paralyses the Christian mind, personality and the collective body. How do we face this crucial challenge?

Facing up to these challenges and questions need deeper discernments and participation in wider circles of conversations. As Pope Francis would have it, we need to participate in a "dialogical culture of encounter." Polyhedron is the image he uses to bring radically different others around the table of dialogue or conversation. This image gives the inner strength to take on these challenges and questions as part of our participation in the culture of encounter.

Interreligious Dialogues in Public Square

Indian Christianity has endeavoured to encounter or relate with other religions in interreligious sites – dialogue centres, ashrams, study centres, research institutions and publications. These sites have been, more often than not, created and maintained by Christian agencies while different others are invited to participate in processes and dynamics of encounters. To the extent Indian Christians have involved in these sites, to that extent they have contributed to civic spaces of mutuality and harmony; they have also contributed to the generation of "social capital", i.e. resources of social trust.[3]

Times are changing. Interreligious sites created by Christian agencies are increasingly becoming isolated and even deserted. They are no more appreciated by different others as bipartisan centres of mutuality. There is a need to open up interreligious efforts to the demands of the radical publicness that is emerging. We need to join in doing public theology along with different religious others in common public sites like the civil sphere. It would mean creating public sites of religious dialogues for the common good especially of Indian democracy.

'Public sites of religious dialogues' can emerge only with participants who are capable of undertaking public dialogues on different religious traditions. It would imply that public educational agencies take up the responsibility of educating the Indian citizens right from their school days on the tenets of different religions. A curriculum on religious education needs to be introduced into the educational stream from the primary to the higher educational levels. It is a pity that a country known as a land of religions has not embarked upon studying the religious traditions systematically. Such an education will help the Indian mind to learn not merely the basic tenets of different religions but also be formed to approach the religious traditions (their rituals, myths and institutions) with an attitude of respect and encounter for greater learning and deeper experiences. India, then, needs to embark upon the project of 'religious literacy', as it did for basic literacy programme some time ago for the entire population. Such a preparation will help participants of public dialogues on religions to enter the zone of dialogues with more information and greater level of maturity. What Raimon Panikkar suggested in terms of undertaking intrareligious dialogues before interreligious dialogues will become possible due to the religious education offered to every Indian citizen.

Fruitful public religious dialogues will contribute to the maturation or strengthening of ethical personalities, because every religious tradition has a strong ethical core. These dialogues will, in an unassuming manner, counsel the personalities along ethical sensibilities and goals. Confluence of different

[3] Corwin E Smidt (ed), *Religion as Social Capital: Producing the Common Good* (Waco, TX: Baylor University Press, 2003).

theologies emerging from different religious traditions in a public dialogical site will certainly be oriented towards goals of common good. As a result, they will also religiously identify values of common good for the Indian nation and will come to value Indian democracy with an ethical commitment.

Revisiting Indian Secularism

We need to also re-envision Indian secularism from the perspective of public theology. While the Eurocentric variant of secularism, originating in the context of conflicts between religions on the one hand and antagonism of religions towards the state on the other, has played its due role in helping us recognise the autonomy of the different spheres of state and religions, an Indian variant of secularism needs to help us recognise the space for different others in a political framework. This recognition will foster religious mutuality, even while jointly constituting spaces of impartiality. It will radically interrogate intentions of dominance over the public space in the name of any one religion. Similarly, it will adopt a preferential option for the minority others, to respect and preserve what are called minority traditions.

Furthermore, the Indian variant of secularism, far from being scientistic in its orientation, will certainly foster the spirit of enquiry and self-critical reflexivity, which perhaps are the fine pearls of a scientific quest for human knowledge and understanding. It will promote deeper and systematic research on questions of common good.

Secularism as Political Ethic of 'Principled Distance'?

Rajee Bhargava, a votary of liberal democracy, dwells in detail through several of his publications, upon the promise of secular democracy in our country.[4] He opines that secularism is under attack today, not because it has failed, but because it has succeeded to a large extent in our country. He says the critics have not understood the specific character of Indian secularism, which, according to him, is not a neat and simple import from the west. Indian secularism showed its uniqueness in undertaking to wrestle with the tension to emerge due to the way it has combined the individual and community rights and to the way it has distanced itself from the affairs of particular religions but at the same time kept the right to intervene for reform.[5] This version of secularism, he calls as

[4] Rajeev Bhargava, *The Promise of India's Secular Democracy* (New Delhi: OUP, 2010); *Politics and the Ethics of the Indian Constitution* (New Delhi: OUP, 2009).

[5] Bhargava: "A political movement for a united, liberal, democratic India had to struggle against hierarchical and communal conceptions of community but without abandoning a reasonable communitarianism. Besides, the state had an important contribution to make in the transformation of these communities; for this reason, a perennial dilemma was imposed on it. The state in India walked a tight rope between the requirement of religious liberty that frequently entails non-interference in the affairs of religious communities, and the demand for equality and justice which necessitates intervention in religiously sanctioned social customs. Secularism in India

'contextual political secularism' with its own ethics of 'principled distance'[6] of the state from religions. It is not a mechanistic separation of state from religion, but a principled distance, which operates in accordance with the particular case in question. As he says, "the secularity of the state does not necessitate intervention, non-interference, or equidistance but rather any or all of these, as the case may be."[7] This principled distancing differs from the principle of neutrality in that it

> rests upon a distinction explicitly drawn by the American philosopher, Ronad Dworkin, between equal treatment and treating everyone as an equal. The principle of equal treatment, in the relevant political sense, requires that the state treat all its citizens equally in the relevant respect, for example, in the distribution of a resource or opportunity. The principle of treating people as equals entails that every person or group is treated with equal concern and respect. This second principle may sometimes require equal treatment, say, equal distribution of resources but it may also occasionally dictate unequal treatment. Treating people or groups as equals is entirely consistent with differential treatment.[8]

This principled distance respects the religious liberty duly. Religions are not to reel under the unilateral actions of the state, but, in turn, they too can make their critical intervention for the promotion of equality of citizenship and communities. He reflects: "Does principled distance also entail that religion intervene in the affairs of the state? In some contexts, it may certainly do so. Religion may intervene in the affairs of the state if such intervention promotes freedom, equality, or any other value integral to secularism."[9] "… [U]nlike mainstream western secularism that appears to impose on us a choice between active hostility or benign indifference, Indian secularism brings to bear on religion an attitude of critical respect."[10] Bhargava clarifies his theory further saying that there is a necessity for 'depoliticization' of religion in a secular state, but this should not be equated with depublicization. "Indeed, the constitution even allows a contextual politicization of religion, for example, if such politicization advances the cause of equality and freedom. If justice

---

simply had to be different from the western liberal model that does not recognize communities, and dictates strict separation between religious and political institutions" (*The Promise,* 86).

[6] Bhargava: "The idea of principled distance unpacks the metaphor of separation differently. It accepts a disconnection between state and religion at the level of ends and institutions but does not make a fetish of it at the third level of policy and law" (*The Promise,* 88).

[7] Bhargava, *The Promise,* 28.

[8] Ibid., 89.

[9] Ibid., 91.

[10] Ibid., 91.

ever required the local politicization of religion, then any defensible version of secularism must support it."[11]

Bhargava takes care to point out that secularism is not identical with religious tolerance: "Indian secularism must not be confused with a generally professed Hindu tolerance. It is frequently claimed that Indians have a natural, traditional affinity with secularism. In view of our traditional obsession with subtle and not so subtle hierarchies, this claim must be taken with a pinch of salt, if not pepper."[12] And, he is equally critical of such concepts as 'religious co-existence', 'inter-religious' understanding, etc. He says, "I take religious coexistence to be equivalent to peace but to identify the secular state with a state that maintains peace between religions, that allows different religions to coexist, does little justice to the rich history and conceptual structure of secularism as a multi-value doctrine. Much the same is true of the interpretation of Indian secularism as inter-religious toleration.... It is equally inappropriate to identify secularism with equal respect for all religions."[13]

Bhargava underlines the core of Indian secularism as: "the core idea of secularism then is: separation of religion and state for the sake of religious liberty and equality of free citizenship."[14] He makes a distinction between 'passive' and 'active' citizenships. While the former entails the right to physical security, material wellbeing, etc., of an individual, the latter refers to the protection of a citizen as he/she emerges as an active participant in a public domain. Both types of citizenships must be ensured to an individual in a secular state.

Rajeev Bhargava has a positive and dynamic understanding of secularism. However, his theory of principled distance can also engender arbitrary exercise of power, depending on the rulers of the state. That is indeed a serious challenge to this theory. But, it breaks the dogmatism of secularism and finds sound bases for community rights, public role of religions, etc. It would do well to draw inspiration from his writings for the defence of secularism.

Conclusion

There is a retreat of liberalism which undergirded democratic practices during the classical modern era. In our post-liberal times, religions have come to the fore both positively and negatively. Positively religious resources are positively valued for personal growth and social relationships. Negatively, certain political establishments across the globe have instrumentalised religions for constituting power at various levels. In India, we find majoritarianism masquerading under the name of democracy. How do we prevent further corrosion of democracies is the crucial question today. And, as Christians in India, what could we do in

[11] Ibid., 104.

[12] Ibid., 83.

[13] Ibid., 102-103.

[14] Ibid., 79.

terms of our religious tradition is the most important question. While reflecting about it, we find the congeniality of Indian Christianity with the Indian civil sphere, both historically and contemporaneously. Indian Christianity can pro-actively enter the civil sphere with a praxis of public theology. It can reform its own self to become a public body, worthy of a civil society. Simultaneously, it can also play a catalytic role in bringing together different religious traditions to do public theologies from their religious resources for the common good of our Indian nation. In the process of it can renew its understanding of secularism to make the latter a value-based political goal to transform the Indian nation.

4

Being a Minority 'Other'
The Case of Indian Christians Today

Introduction

Not one but several factors of the contemporary global world bring up the concern and debate on minority identity to the fore. Migration that started growing faster from the last quarter of the twentieth century is indeed a crucial factor to the emergence of the now-prominent identity discourse. During the 90ies of the twentieth century, faced with the advent of different migrant communities in their liberal political polities, the Canadian and North-American Governments were discussing 'multiculturalism' as their standard liberal political practice so as to do justice to different identities. If we go back a little further in time to the post-World War II era, we find yet another important factor in the formation of independent nation-states in southern and eastern hemispheres, freeing themselves from the erstwhile colonial powers. Different cultural identities had to contend with the nation-states which were constructing unified national identities for their states.

We find the minority identity discourse emerging into the fore in this context. As Will Kymlicka observes, the post-colonial and post-cold war era brought to the fore questions of relationship between States and minorities, between minorities, and within minorities themselves.[1] He identifies two broad categories of minorities: one, 'national minorities' who had pre-existed the colonial States and continue to exist inter-generationally in post-colonial States too with certain common denominators of language, religion, culture, etc.; and the other, 'ethnic minorities', most often immigrants, who have formed into

[1] Will Kymlicka, ed. *Multiculturalism in Asia* (Oxford Scholarship Online, 2005, doi:10.1093/0199277621.001.0001), 3.

minorities in their countries of settlements. What is a relevant point to draw out from Kymlicka's large oeuvre on the liberal theory of multiculturalism and minority rights is the emergence to the fore of the question of minorities – their identities, rights, cultures, etc., within the framework of the contemporary post-colonial democratic States. Immediately after the attainment of independence from colonial powers, the newly emerging democratic States drew together the different cultural communities into the common project of nation-building. Now, after about half a century or more, these States have to deal with problems arising from identity politics, majority-minority conflicts, and so on.

Against this background, the discipline of *minority studies* has emerged as an important field of research today,[2] and minority identity discourse has obtained significance in these studies. It is heartening to see that several higher educational institutions, especially in the western hemisphere, have established centres for minority studies. Unfortunately, the Indian academia is yet to reckon with it and contribute to the understanding of the phenomenon with substantial research and debates.

Indian Context Today

Indian context, however, is debating the issue vigorously at the practical realms of politics. India, as an independent nation-state, is emerging today to play a prominent role in the global world, based apparently on its expansive consumerist base (in terms of the huge population), and constructs, overtly and covertly, its specific identity in the international arena. Major political players feel that India has to emerge not only as a unified powerful political and economic entity, but also as a cultural and religious universe, having its specific identity cut out for negotiations at various global fora.

In this context, India is has to grapple with 'majoritarianism' in political, cultural and religious fields; and it goes with a hegemonising dynamic by the dominant sections in the Indian hierarchical society. Those who construct majoritarianism adduce several reasons for their project: a) India has been under foreign or alien rule for centuries together, and it is but legitimate that the majority of Indian population aspire for their own nationhood; b) India has a spiritual and religious core which has withstood the vicissitudes of history (as proposed by Vivekananda, Radhakrishnan and the neo-Hindu philosophers) and this should become the core of Indian polity, if not the global polity for the benefit of humanity. With these and other reasons, the political players are endeavouring to construct a majoritarian religio-cultural identity for a sub-continent that has 1.46 billion people, speaking 22 official languages, 122 major languages and 1599 minor dialects, and following such distinctly diverse religious traditions as Saivism, Vaishnavism, Sakthaism, Jainism, Buddhism, Zorastrianism, Christianity, Islam, Sikhism, along with

[2] Cf. Rowena Robinson, ed., *Minority Studies* (New Delhi: Oxford University Press, 2012).

hundreds of Guru-specific and folk religious traditions. An attempt is being made, as aptly pointed out to by Manjari Katju, a professor of political science, to refashion the secular democracy into that of a 'Hindu'[3] democracy, with its own specific philosophy of nation, citizenship, ethical ideals and so on.[4]

Indian Christianity

Indian Christianity is feeling its feet through the challenges posed by the situation today. As per the 2011 Indian census, Christians in India constitute 2.34 % of the Indian population, which in absolute numbers would be about 31.66 million, which supersedes the total population of some European countries. Christians are the second largest minority in India, after the Muslims. Their number has not shown any increase during the last two decennial censuses.[5] While their presence in southern and North-Eastern States are significant, the northern region of India has only a thin presence.

Indian Christianity, though it stands out as a single religious tradition in relation to others, is internally diversified in terms of denominations, rites, and cultures. It consists of the Catholic Church, which is constituted by the three Rites (Latin, Syro-Malabar and Syro-Malankara), Protestant Churches, Oriental Orthodox Churches, and Pentecostal Churches (mainline and

---

[3] A name that has come handy for this project is what is being addressed today as 'Hinduism'. Etymologically a word that stood for the geographical region beyond the river Sindhu, as addressed by the Persians, the word 'Hindu', with a very gradually evolving usage through the centuries, has come to stand for a religious universe today, and there is a strenuous political effort being made to construct this unified religious identity to go in support of Hindutva, an ideology of political Hinduism. As perceptively pointed out to by Romila Thappar, a noted Indian historian, there is an effort at work to construct a 'syndicated Hinduism', after the model of the Semitic religions. For more on this debate, cf. Romila Thappar, *Cultural Pasts* (New Delhi: Oxford University Press, 2003); Vinay Lal, *Political Hinduism – The Religious Imagination in the Public Sphere* (New Delhi: Oxford University Press, 2009); Geoggrey A. Oddie, *Imagined Hinduism – British Protestant Missionary Constructions of Hinduism, 1793 – 1900* (New Delhi: SAGE, 2006); Christophe Jaffrelot, ed. *Hindu Nationalism – A Reader* (Raniket: Permanent Black, 2013).

[4] Manjari Katju, *Hinduising Democracy – The Vishva Hindu Parishad in Contemporary India* (New Delhi: The New Text Publications Pvt. Ltd, 2017).

[5] The reasons for the stagnation of Christian population are many. Though India has a liberal secular Constitution which underscores the freedom of religion, there are laws which indirectly dissuade the people from converting to Christianity. The Hindu Marriage Law, for example, denies the right to inheritance to someone who has converted to a religion other than Hinduism; moreover, a few States have positively brought about anti-conversion laws which act as deterrent against conversion. In addition, the Christians, generally being educated, prefer to have smaller families, a factor that inhibits the growth of the number of Christians. There are some unofficial accounts which claim that the numbers of Christians in actuality are much more than the number given by the census data. Because, several Christians do not divulge their religious identity to the census enumerators, fearing the denial of benefits of certain affirmative action implemented for the socially backward sections of the Indian society.

independent). Historically speaking, one could speak of several 'springs'[6] of Christianity which emerged across the centuries. From the very early centuries of the Christian Era, India had the presence of those who are called today as St. Thomas Christians. As per a vibrant tradition, this spring of Christians came to exist with the mission of St. Thomas,[7] an apostle of Jesus, and was further augmented by the arrival of a contingent of Syrian Christians during the fourth century. Since they used the Syriac language in their liturgy, and were united with the ancient churches in Syria, they were known also as the Eastern Syrian Christians. These Christians, mostly traders, seem to have gotten integrated with the native 'higher caste' communities of the southern western Malabar region and continued to live on as the only Christian community in India for about sixteen centuries.

The next spring arose at the instance of the *padroado mission* of the sixteenth century. This mission was eventful in different ways: first of all, there were 'mass conversions' to Christianity due to the missionary activities of the Jesuits in the Coromandel coast; secondly, these missionary activities, supported by the Portuguese power, spread to areas other than those wherein Christianity remained confined until then; and, thirdly, the Roman Catholic Christianity spread by these missionaries came into a conflict-ridden relationship with the existing Eastern Syrian Christianity, and the integration or otherwise of the latter with the former has become an enduring part of history until this day. As of now, there are two Syrian Christian communities (Syro-Malabar and Syro-Malankara) existing within the Roman Catholic fold, while a relatively lesser number of Syrian Christians formed under different Churches like Orthodox, Jacobites, Mar Thoma, etc. exist by themselves. The Roman Catholics of the *Padrado Mission* continued to spread from the coastal regions to the hinterland of the southern Tamil region, encompassing different strata of the Tamil society under its fold through the fervent missionary efforts of the Jesuits down the centuries. There were also other Catholic missionary agencies who entered

[6] Cf. Leonard Fernando and G. Gispert-Sauch, *Christianity in India* (New Delhi: Penguin Random House India, 2004).

[7] The exact period from which this community came into existence is a point of dispute existing for a long time among historians. The popular 'belief' here in India is that the community came into existence with the evangelization of Thomas, one of the apostles of Jesus, who arrived here in the year 52 AD. Historians have held differing and contradicting views as regards this 'belief'. However, a conclusion to which majority of Church historians from India veer around is that, due to multiple cumulative indications, the arrival of Thomas the apostle to India cannot be denied, and it is high probability. For a recent work that discusses comprehensively about the issues involved, cf. George Nedungatt, S.J., *Quest for the Historical Thomas Apostle of India – A Re-reading of the Evidence* (Bangalore: Theological Publications in India, 2008).

the field at various times and have together contributed to the formation of a Catholic Christian community in South India.[8]

The third spring of Christianity emerged from the early part of the eighteenth century with the efforts taken by the Protestant missionary agencies. Lutheran missionaries landed here first to be followed up by Baptists, Anglicans, Presbyterians, Methodists, and others. Their missionary agencies, consisting of some European powers and independently formed missionary societies, created Protestant Christian communities in South and North Indian territories. Bartholomew Ziegenbalg, the Protestant missionary to India, landed and worked at Tarangambadi, a Danish settlement along the south eastern coast. Ziegenbalg translated the New Testament of the Bible into Tamil so as to enable the native converts read, understand and preach the Gospel. He ventured also into an understanding of native religious traditions, and brought to light the deep religious visions present among the native people. His publications[9] initiated a deep exploration and dialogue between Christianity and native religious traditions. Subsequently during the end of the eighteenth century, the setting up of a mission at Srirampur, near Kolkata, by the trio – William Carey, Joshua Marshman and William Ward, took up the translation of the Bible into several Asian languages and strengthened the presence of Christianity in India. During the nineteenth century, the works of missionaries sponsored by the London Missionary society took Anglican Churches to the southern tip of India. And several other missionary agencies followed up with their endeavours. It must be noted that their missionary endeavours, coinciding with the rule of the British in India, contributed very significantly to the making of the modern India.

The next spring of Christianity is what the twentieth century has witnessed to: spread of the Pentecostal Churches. These Churches, emergent in the North American soil from the early part of the twentieth century, began to cross over and exist as mainline and independent Pentecostal Churches in the Indian soil. Mainline Pentecostal Churches are federated with international networks of leadership, while the independent Churches exist independently, though a broader network of solidarity is present among them too. It needs be noted that a considerable section of people attending Pentecostal Churches are drawn from the economically poor and the socially marginal communities of India.

Sociologically speaking, Indian Christians hail from different 'caste' groups, whose relationship with one another is not so egalitarian as one would expect. There are instances of discrimination, denial of civic rights, jostling

---

[8] Cf. E. R. Hambye, *History of Christianity in India, Vol. III Eighteenth Century* (Bangalore: The Church History Association of India, 1997).

[9] Cf. Daniel Jeyaraj, *Bartholomaus Zieganbalg: The Father of Modern Protestant Mission* (New Delhi: ISPCK & Chennai: Gurukul, 2006).

for power, and even of violent manifestations of 'caste pride' between different groups. The caste composition of Indian Christianity has been explored much,[10] and it is a general consensus that about 65 per cent of the Indian Christian population hails from the subaltern communities of Dalits and Tribals; the rest belong to the most backward, backward, other backward and forward 'castes'. In spite of constant rhetoric and well-meaning efforts being made, the religious leadership does not yet represent the composition of the people, and there are discriminatory practices still existing within the Churches as regards occupation of ritual spaces. While such is the reality within Indian Christianity, the treatment meted out to Christians by the external others is no less characterised by an isolating tendency.

In terms of gender justice, there is a long way to go before the Indian Christian community experiences freedom and justice to every gender. Patriarchal domination is the ruling ethos within the Churches, although Indian Christians fare better in sex-ratio (1023 women per 1000 men according to 2011 census)[11] and conscious efforts are being made to address the question of gender justice.

Educationally, thanks to the missionary efforts made during the nineteenth century for mass education, Indian Christians have become the community with high literacy (Indian Christians have about 80 per cent literacy according to 2011 census) and with the ability for individual capabilities in terms of life-skills and occupations.

Politically speaking it would not be beside the truth to say that Indian Christians make a rather quiescent community, and their political assertiveness and visible participation are yet to emerge on to the horizon. They do not have politically active individuals proportionate to the levels of education they have obtained during the recent centuries. This could be due to several factors: one could be that in the traditional Indian context wherein economic power had been the salient factor behind the rise of politically assertive individuals, Indian Christians, in general, are on a disadvantage; another reason could be that a strand of world-negating theology and spirituality which have been propounded within Christianity for a long time has possibly inhibited the Christian individuals from participating actively in the political sphere; yet another reason could be that Indian Christians had, at least during the colonial era, got so used to becoming dependent upon the 'protective' colonial powers that they have lost for a while the prowess for their independent political assertiveness. There could be many more such reasons. However, it should be noted that

[10] Cf. James Massey and T. K. John, eds. *Christians of Scheduled Caste Origin in India – A Study of their Socio-Economic, Cultural and Political Status* (New Delhi: Centre for Dalit / Subaltern Studies, 2013).

[11] Cf. https://timesofindia.indiatimes.com/india/Christians-have-best-sex-ratio-in-India/articleshow/50312741.cms accessed on 09-09-2018.

Indian Christians are indeed beginning to be politically assertive today against the obtaining reality of anti-Christian violence and majoritarian democracy. It is in place to note that several ecclesial leaders are out in the public domain voicing their concerns upon their security and freedom. Emergence of this voice has to do not only with the incidents of violence against Christians being reported today, but also with the corrosion of religious freedom guaranteed in the Indian Constitution. Indian Christians have now come to realise that they must defend the spirit of freedom enshrined in the Constitution.

Contours of Indian Christians' Religio-Cultural Interactions

Indian Christianity, though embodying a religious tradition distinct from native ones, was less preoccupied with constructing a different identity, while interacting creatively with other traditions in an ambience of spontaneity and freedom. In its early days, Indian Christianity of the Syrian Christian tradition seems to have merged relatively more easily with the native religio-cultural traditions. Being a mercantile group, having been accommodated into the 'high' castes by marital ties, the Syrian Christian tradition interacted and entered more deeply into the religio-cultural terrain of the people living in the south west coastal region. These Christians seem to have taken in several cultural elements like aesthetics, architecture, art-forms, and, folklores; they had taken in also the lineaments of the caste-system; however, they seemed to have continued to be non-vegetarians, as distinct from the vegetarian 'high castes' who lived in joint families. Moreover, they nurtured the Christian faith through a worship or liturgy, which was conducted in Syriac language and which centred round a sacramental theology of human regeneration through the death and resurrection of Christ Jesus. Practice of this religion went with several features of socio-cultural accommodations, and the Christian community was apparently 'respected' by others, and enjoyed freedom to be on their own, in their own way. The religio-cultural face of this early Christian tradition, therefore, was a unique formation.

During the early modern era, an event-filled missionary era, beginning with the Portuguese missionary endeavours of the sixteenth century (as mentioned above), Indian Christianity inaugurated, so to say, a new phase of interaction. Headquarted in Goa, the *padroado* mission agency, supported by the Portuguese colonial power, undertook its mission along the western as well as the eastern coast and witnessed to a good number of native people becoming Christians. Along the western coast, it met with the existing Syrian Christians whom it befriended for a while before breaking off, even violently, on account of an attempt at co-opting them into the Roman Catholic fold headed by the Pope.[12] The zeal of Francis Xavier, a prominent Jesuit missionary of the time,

[12] Cf. A. M. Mundadan, *History of Christianity in India, Vol. 1 – From the Beginning up to the Middle of the Sixteenth Century* (Bangalore: Church History Association of India, 2001).

took Christianity to the people living along the Coromandel Coast and the southern tip of the erstwhile Travancore kingdom. Liturgically, architecturally, theologically, and cosmologically, it was a version of Portuguese Catholic Christianity that began to exist in the Indian soil. The then missionary paradigm, informed by an overarching religious zeal to save the souls of the entire humanity, went also with an exclusive ecclesial-centric soteriology of 'No salvation outside the Church', and it introduced a discourse of radical difference, hurtingly though to different religious others. There were reactions from the native people, who appreciated less the religion of the meat-eating and wine-drinking food habit of the Portuguese. But for an initial bout of conversion to Christianity, the natives kept aloof from the missionising religion, tagging the latter with an ambiguous but apparently derogatory term '*Paranghi* religion' (*paranghi margam*),[13] which attributed a very lowly identity to Christianity.

The label, and the resistance to Christianity, became a major concern for an upcoming missionary of the *padroado* mission. Robert de Nobili, a Jesuit of Italian origin, who came to serve the Madurai Mission, was intrigued by the labelling of Christianity as *Paranghi Margam*, and endeavoured to present a respectable picture of Christianity as a religion followed by dignified people in Europe. He initiated a method of adaptation of Christianity to the socio-cultural behaviours of the Brahmin Sannyasis. While proclaiming the Christian religion in terms of doctrines and beliefs, in dialogue with Agamas, Upanishads, and other Indian theistic traditions (which he studied rather deeply in Sanskrit and Tamil), he presented himself in the attire and other markers of a Brahmin Sannyasi (Brahmin ascetic, generally considered to be learned), taking to strict vegetarian food, prepared by a Brahmin cook. All these efforts were to make himself and his religion acceptable to the 'learned and religious' sections of the Tamil region. A very small section of people showed interest in De Nobili's endeavours, and the method of adaptation did not bear much fruits. The perceived identity as *Parangi Margam* was not to be erased so easily. It remained in the consciousness of the local people for a very long time to come.

The Jesuits then embarked upon a new path to reach Christianity to the people. They adapted themselves to the religious world of the people beyond the Brahmins, at further layers of the Indian caste system. They identified that those who were catering to the religious needs of these people were known as *Pandarams*,[14] and therefore, they presented themselves as *Pandarasamis*. Starting with Balthasar da Costa, the first *Pandarasami* to be initiated in the year 1640, Jesuits missionaries adopted the attire and markers of *Pandarams*

[13] The term *paranghi* stood for the Portuguese, who, according to the perception of the high caste natives, "did not wash or bathe frequently, who ate beef, drank liquor, and communicated freely with persons of the most despised castes." Joseph Thekkedath, *History of Christianity, Vol. II* (Bangalore: The Church History Association of India, 2001 [1982]), 212.

[14] Religious leaders of the castes, next in ladder after the Brahmins.

to preach Christianity. Their efforts seemed to have brought in more people into Christianity, but not without further conflicts and resistance. Those at the next layers of the caste system (beyond the Brahmins) were not ready to accept those who were further down the lane or those beyond the boundaries of the system of caste to worship together with them, lest they too 'defiled themselves'. The ensuing struggle seemed to have made the Jesuits introduce yet another category of *Pandarasamis* who served further sections of people in the layers of caste. Handling the caste factor in relation to the identity of Christianity was a continuing struggle for the Jesuit missionaries. They had to face it even during the period of the new Madurai Mission.[15]

It should be noted here that the Jesuits' missionary efforts branched off to other domains as well. We find, and a vast majority of Tamil people recognise until today, that the Tamil literary contributions[16] made by the scholar Jesuits from the sixteenth century onwards have a lasting impact and abiding value. Though the corpus of Tamil literature that they produced went beyond the framework of the typical Christian mission of the day, some of their writings have introduced the Christian faith-tradition to the Tamil literary field in an effective way. The corpus of Tamil Christian Literature is being studied and inspiration drawn from until this day, not only for literary interest but also for inter-religious and even political solidarity. Thus, the literary strand of Tamil Christianity has had an enduring impact upon the consciousness of the Tamil people. It may well be stated that the stiff against Christianity on account of its being a *parangi margam* was 'compensated', so to say, by the reception of the literary output of the European Christian scholars.

While the Portuguese missionary efforts continued, the Protestant missionary era began in the early part of the eighteenth century, as mentioned above, with the Lutheran mission founded by the first Protestant missionary Bartholomew Ziegenbalg in a south Indian Danish colony along the eastern coast at Tarangambadi. Later during the end of the same century, again as noted above, the founding of yet another mission by the Baptist missionaries at Srirampur near Kolkata introduced the Protestant Christianity to north India as well. And the subsequent eventful missionary work during the nineteenth century by missionaries sponsored by the then emergent European missionary societies like London Missionary Society, Church Missionary Society, Society for the Propagation of the Gospel, etc., contributed much to the introduction of the Christianity among the subaltern people of Indian society, and made

---

[15] The old Madurai Mission came to a halt due to the suppression by the Pope of the Jesuits Congregation in the year 1773. When it was revoked again after forty years, the new Madurai Mission by the Jesuits came into existence.

[16] For more reading on the contributions of the European scholars to Tamil literature or Tamil Christian literature, cf. K. Meenaskshisundaram, *Contribution of European Scholars to Tamil* (Madras: University of Madras, 1974).

an enduring presence in political and civil spheres of India in terms of its much disputed 'civilizing mission.'[17] The Protestant mission, unlike the earlier Catholic missionary efforts, focussed upon the reading and understanding of the Bible, as a prerequisite of which they embarked upon the project of educating the people in modern education, providing them with health care, sensitizing them upon their civil liberties, etc., which as a whole came to be addressed later as the 'civilizing mission'. The Protestant missionary presence was active among the subaltern sections of India, and it gave subaltern identity to Indian Christians. It empowered them to assert their rights and even undertake struggles to do away with certain unmeaning social evils of the time.

The British colonial power was more interested in trade which could go on well without 'disturbing the political stability' of the country. And so, they adopted a policy of religious neutrality, though an evangelical section in the British Parliament sought to rationalise the colonial presence in India in terms of the 'civilizing mission'. The Protestant missionaries heartily involved in the civilizing mission, presuming it necessary for the Indian mind to grasp the message of the Gospel. The salvation offered through the Gospel was presented to be far superior to the liberation offered in any Indian religion. Their work, however, combined with the modern education, engaged several spiritually inclined Indian intellectuals of the time, and it inspired the emergence of the socio-religious movements like Brahma Samaj, Prarthana Samaj and Arya Samaj. The Christianity of the time inspired also a corpus of writings which attempted to integrate the Indian philosophical-religious vision into Christian theology.[18] The result was what came to be known later as the Indian Christian theology, and it was, unlike the earlier effort to adapt to the native socio-cultural systems, an effort at the plane of theologising with Indian categories. Such an integrative initiative could be pursued in an ambience of relative freedom.

From the beginning of the twentieth century, in the context of the struggle for Indian independence combined with a discourse on Indian nationalism, Indian Christianity increasingly became conscious of its Indian identity. Indian Christian missionary societies, the Ashrams model of inculturation and dialogue, participation in nation-building with socio-economic contributions, etc., became the new initiatives. Indian Christians were shaping up an identity of a religious community, self-confident and open-minded, interacting with and contributing to the wider society through their service-oriented institutions and initiatives. Minority rights enshrined in the Indian constitution recognised the need of the religious and linguistic minorities to nurture their distinct cultural identities and provided for freedom to run educational and welfare

[17] On the contributions of the civilizing mission, cf. J. C. Ingleby, *Missionaries, Education and India – Issues in Protestant Missionary Education in the Long Nineteenth Century* (New Delhi: ISPCK, 2000).

[18] This constitutes a large section of what is known today as the 'Indian Christian Theology'.

institutions.[19] Indian Christian leaders seemed to have argued for these rights in lieu of the communal award that had been granted earlier by the British power.[20]

Indian Christians began also to address some of the age-old internal issues, like that of the prevalence of caste-based discriminations and exclusions within the body of Indian Christianity. With the growing realisation that the majority of Indian Christians were drawn from the Dalit and Tribal communities, Christianity in India, existing in its different denominational Churches, was addressing the questions of social justice within the Churches.

The preoccupation with being a 'minority religious community' did not gain salience in the Indian Christian mind until the onset of the discourse on Indian nationalism. Since the religio-cultural terrain had remained open and expansive, relatively less bounded, - and not the least around a single organising political idea of nation, the sense of being a majority or a minority did not emerge into the consciousness of the people until the time of nationalism. Indian nationalism was the project of the time, serving a meaningful cause of Indian independence from foreign colonialism, and eventually, through sacrifices and trauma, gave birth to the political entity of an independent nation called India. Needless to say, that the political nationhood of the post-colonial era, as Kymlica pointed out, brought in the discourse of minorities and their rights too.

Contemporary Challenges

Today, Indian Christianity is facing up to the politics of majoritarianism and its cultural nationalism. The issues and concerns that they are facing today are changing them over from being a 'religious community' to a 'communally conscious minority', with increasing concerns over security, freedom of religion, cultural rights, rights to partake of the civil society, etc. Indian Christians are treated in terms of multiple not-well-meaning identities: colonial, western, proselytising, 'low caste', culturally alien, politically divisive, and so on:

1. Colonial – Western: In spite of the fact that Christianity in India has existed from very ancient times, and has been part of the Asian religious landscape; despite the fact that those who practise Christianity in India are people of the Indian types (Dravidians, Dalits, Tribals, etc); and in spite of the fact that the cultural dimension of Indian Christianity has to do more with native indigenous cultures than the western ones, Christianity in India is still being identified with the colonial powers and western cultures.

---

[19] Article 30 of the Indian Constitution.

[20] Cf. Leonardo Fernando and G. Gispert-Sauch, *Christianity in India.*

2. Proselytising Agent: Indian States have gone about legislating upon 'anti-conversion' laws, under the pretext of banning conversion by 'force, coercion and fraudulent means'. Some of them have had such legislations right from the very early days of independent India. The reasoning behind these legislations was that conversion is unduly disturbing the fabric of Indian society and playing a divisive role in the wider society. Though this reasoning has been prevalent for a long time, it has become very vocal today. In an ambience of majoritarianism and cultural nationalism, conversion is countered with violent outbursts today. Since 1990 when religious nationalism emerged boldly, the number of violent acts against the Christians has increased. Christian personnel – pastors, nuns, priests, etc., are humiliated publicly, tortured, and even killed by rightist fanatics.
3. Unacknowledged contributors! There is a certain 'untouchability' that goes with the Christian identity, when looked at from the optic of purity and pollution that goes with the caste-system of India. The failure the recognise in the National Education Policy 2020 the historical contribution of Indian Christianity to the education of the Indian mind is a case in point. Ther is hesitation, combined with a 'wilfully induced amnesia', to acknowledge the significant role played by Christianity to the Indian public. The service rendered by Christians is treated as something, after all, incumbent upon a 'servant' class of people!
4. Culturally Alien: For a very long time in the Indian films, Christian characters are depicted as villains, womanisers, and drunkards. Why do Christians get such roles? It has a colonial legacy, coming from Portuguese times onwards. But do simple ordinary Christian folks today deserve to be depicted like this? Adding to such not so trivial instances, Christians continue to suffer the tag of being the cultural aliens.

A phenomenological study of these experiences of being a minority would unearth the pathos of living a life framed by a minority identity. A person of minority identity lives in a vulnerable position of being incessantly called into question, and that person is always required to 'prove his / her patriotism' in front of a self-righteous majority. Will Kymlicka made a fine distinction between patriotism, the feeling of allegiance to a state, from nationalism, the sense of membership in a group.[21] Recognition of such a distinction would indicate the quality of democracy that might exist in a given political unit. Unfortunately, in the Indian case, the national identity is wilfully being

[21] Kymlica's distinction dwells upon the distinction between an allegiance to the State, in terms of fostering citizenship, from nationalist sentiments which envelop the people in terms of their identities.

conflated with the majoritarian Hindu identity by a politically vocal section upon the ideology of Hindutva, and that conflation is further conflated with patriotism to reap political mileage. A minority has to prove oneself against these multiple yardsticks, and failing in one would be seen as failing in another.

Surrogate Victims!?!

I attempt to proffer one possible explanation on the basis of an insight provided by Rene Girard, the well-known analyst of, what he calls, 'sacred violence'. Girard's theory holds that violence emerges in a society within the context of 'mimetic rivalry', a fierce rivalry between a 'model' and an 'imitator'. Herein, "violence is the process ... when two or more partners try to prevent one another from appropriating the object they all desire through physical or other means."[22] "As an object becomes the focus of mimetic rivalry between two or more antagonists, other members of the group tend to join in, mimetically attracted by the presence of mimetic desire."[23] As a resolution of this antagonism, Girard finds the ritual sacrifice to be a social mechanism wherein 'transference of violence' takes place, by way of saving the society from its own mimetic violence. Offering a victim in sacrifice, "serves to protect the entire community from its *own* violence..."[24]

I suggest that the contemporary implication of religion in violence may well be understood with this Girardian insight. As a sample, when we try to see as to why the Hindutva right is so vehemently against the Muslims or Christians, this insight enlightens us of the fact that the religion of the Muslim-Christian Other becomes the sacred victim or object of scapegoat mechanism in the process of redressing the mimetic rivalry that has got generated because of the relative empowerment of the subaltern classes of people with the onset of modernisation. The subaltern people's 'emerging competition' in fields of economics, politics, and social dignity with the erstwhile beneficiaries of these systems generates a mimetic rivalry. Such a rivalry, as understood within the Girardian concept, looks for surrogate victims, so as to recover the smooth functioning of its traditional systems. The Hindutva right, by offering the Christian and Muslim religions as surrogate victims of sacrifice, is endeavouring to protect the so-called hierarchically constituted majoritarian community from its own internal violence. The so-called 'Hindu' world suffers deeply from cleavages and exclusions created by the workings of the caste, and the discontent generated in the social body of the oppressed seeks to burst out in violent forms. This simmering violence is a constant threat to the unity of what is put together as a "Hindu nation". It is within this context of the dire

[22] Rene Girard, *The Girard Reader*, (edited by James G. Williams), The Crossword Publishing Company, 1996, p. 7.

[23] Rene Girard, p. 11.

[24] Rene Girard, p. 8.

necessity of preserving it from its own violence that the Hindutva right finds a surrogate victim in the religions of Muslims and Christians, and they are sacrificed in the flames of communal hatred.

For Christians, being treated a sacrificial victim, after all, is nothing but an occasion to identify themselves with Jesus Christ, their Saviour, who suffered on the Cross to rise again!

5

Human Rights and Religion in India
The Communitarian Turn and its Challenges

The discourse of human rights, for a long time, based itself on universal humanism, which believed in the common nature of human beings, beyond race, colour, caste, language, religion, region, culture, gender, and so on. The thirty statements found in the universal declaration of human rights (1948), excepting for their sexist language (which certainly is a grave matter), speak of the rights and the freedoms as equally applicable to all human beings on earth without any exception whatsoever. This vision of the universal humanism undergirded the liberal values like liberty, equality, fraternity, and justice. And the human rights covenants and mechanisms to implement them went with full confidence on this concept of universal humanism.

However, we are at the crossroads now. With the help of the ongoing critical explorations of the human mind, the present era has questioned the so-called neutrality of the discourse of human rights and its universal humanism. 'Whose human rights?', 'whose justice?', 'whose liberty?', 'human rights or rights of the poor?', - are questions we hear for some time now. These questions come to the fore on the realisation of the impossibility of holding on to absolute, universally valid discourses while encountering provisional, 'fragmented', context-specific experiences of knowledge, truth, moral claims, religious doctrines, aesthetics, etc. The language-riddenness of the human experience of reality, brought to light by post-structural linguistic philosophies, accentuates further the latter experiences. Globalization is yet another historical phenomenon that has generated a sense of profundity as well as ubiquity of thick plurality which inform almost every dimension of human living on this planet.

It is in this context that a 'communitarian' approach to human rights is being proposed by political philosophers from the west. Human self or the essential human nature is irreversibly embedded in a community's tradition, language, culture, values, vision, and perspectives. There is no 'neutral humanity' apart from the spatio-temporally embedded subjects. That being the case, the universally absolute discourses should acknowledge their situatedness, and adapt to a new inter-subjective vision and mode of universality. This brings us to the crossroads now. Can we afford to give up the categorical nature of human rights discourses, especially in a context like ours where awareness of human rights is obviously very low? If not, can we afford to remain fortified against new realisations of truth, subjectivity, community, plurality, morality, and so on? Or, take up the challenge of reorienting our discourses along communitarian lines, without giving up the continuous efforts to reach higher and higher standards in human rights? How do we, therefore, re-do our human rights discourse and re-learn the values in the present context, are important questions today.

By way of discussing these questions, it would do well first to take a look at the trajectory of the human rights discourse in the western context, the provenance of its emergence, and then proceed to discuss the present scenario in relation to the Indian context.

Liberal Origins of Human Rights

The discourse on human rights had its origin in the western liberal consciousness, remotely set in motion by the Renaissance and the Reformation movements, leading to multiple revolutions, including the French revolution which centred round the values of liberty, equality, and fraternity, and the American Revolution that gave a constitutional face to them. An array of declarations or agreements starting even from the Magna Carta and the bill of rights (1215), the Glorious Revolution, and the Declaration of American Independence, the French Declaration of Rights of Man and Citizen (1789) – all played their role in the unfolding of the 'rights consciousness'. Further on, this consciousness was dialectically getting enshrined through such epochal crises like the 'wars of religions', 'Fascism', 'Nazism', and the 'World Wars' on the one hand, and through such positive experiences like workers' movements, labour unions, and civil rights movements on the other.

A tradition of liberal political thinking starting from the seventeenth century, developed by political philosophers like John Locke, Thomas Hobbes, Montesquieu, Rousseau, John Dewey until the twentieth century philosopher John Rawls, supported the liberal human rights discourse in the west. John Locke (1632-1704), the English political philosopher, who played a significant role in the separation of the Church and the State, highlighted the dignity of the individual person endowing them with 'inalienable rights' like the rights to life, freedom, conscience, and even private property. He considered these rights as 'natural rights' borne out of the very nature of being human and argued that the human person had the right not to be interfered with from outside. The American Declaration of Independence (1776) was much imbued with Lock's ideas as can be seen in its statement: "We hold these truths to be self-evident, that all men are created equal, that they are endowed by their Creator with certain inalienable rights, that among these are Life, Liberty and the pursuit of happiness – that to secure these rights, governments are instituted among men, deriving their just powers from the consent of the governed."[1] Immanuel Kant, the Enlightenment philosopher, enriched the idea of the right of the human person by speaking of formation of self-legislating autonomous individuals to be set as the goal of the Enlightenment process.

During the twentieth century, John Rawls (1921-2002) propounded a 'coherent' secular liberal theory of justice, i.e., justice done within a democratic constitutional framework to the universal individual person in terms of their inalienable rights. He sought to come up with the best coherent theory of individual rights which could be the benchmark for liberal democracy everywhere. Postulating a hypothetical original position of contract between perfectly equal human beings, he constructed a theory which could support the rights and freedom of human persons in every historical context. There was no place for any exception, except in the case of what he called the 'difference principle', a principle whereby discrimination could be legitimate, provided such discrimination went to the benefit of the least advantaged. Different visions of good born out of moral, religious, cultural, and philosophical comprehensive doctrines had no place in his liberal theory of justice. The core space of democracy, for him, was value-neutral, though it is to be built up by a secular vision of justice. Integration of different visions of good would, in his theory, prevent a democratic system from delivering fair justice to its participants - individuals being the primary participating agents. However, he, in his later revisions, began to take note of the role of different traditions in nurturing the democratic freedom, and therefore, considered the value of 'overlapping consensus' between different visions of good, provided they 'translated' themselves in terms of public reason, which was intelligible to the secular institutions of the state. Such political philosophical ideas have nourished the fundamentals of liberal human rights discourse in the west until this day.

With such a long tradition of reflection, a strong sense of individualism had come to be operative in the western context. It leads, like an invisible hand, the global market-economy, culture and even morality. In the field of biotechnology, weird instances of genetic engineering are examples of extreme

---

[1] Clemens N Nathan, *The Changing Face of Religion and Human Rights – A Personal Reflection* (Leiden: Martinus Nijhoff Publishers, 2009), 26.

libertarian freedom in the domain of culture. And in economy, development of neo-liberalism which induced the growth of mindless super-rich individuals who form very minuscule population of the earth (Joseph Stiglitz, a former chief economist of WB, wrote in 2011 an article entitled 'by the one percent, for the one percent and of the one percent'!). Such aberrations can take place due to skewed forms of economic liberalism, and it takes place in the Indian context as well.

The west, however, is witnessing today to a critique of liberalism *per se* from the perspective of communitarian political philosophies. Alasdair MacIntyre, Charles Taylor, Michael Sandel, and others have raised their criticism against the liberal orientation to human rights. MacIntyre has critiqued even the very concept of human rights as illusionary. "There are no such rights, and belief in them is one with belief in witches and unicorns" – says McIntyre. His criticism, as paraphrased by David Hollenbach, a present-day public theologian, is:

> ... the way I should treat others and the way they ought to treat me cannot be determined apart from ... traditions, social relations, and roles. Morality is a "practice" that one must learn much as an apprentice learns a skill under the tutelage of a master craftsman. The idea of rights assumes an entirely different view of morality. It maintains that all persons are entitled to certain forms of treatment independent of their communal bonds, social roles, historical period, and cultural traditions. The notion of human rights abstracts from these historical and communal dimensions of human existence. It rests on a concept of the person as an "unencumbered self" - a self whose personal identity is established prior to and independent of its ends, history, and communal relationships.[2]

It indeed is a scorching critique of human rights. MacIntyre and other communitarians are concerned about the excesses of individual liberty on the one hand and the dismaying of the liberal universal values of freedom on the other; and they propose communitarian visions of common good, basing on or in association with multiple 'visions of moral good' emerging from different religio-cultural traditions.[3] They speak, as pointed out above, of the value of communities, local traditions, embeddedness of individuals in communitarian systems, and collective visions of common good emerging in context-specific manners. They do take care to reflect upon the challenges involved in bringing

---

[2] David Hollenbach, "Communitarian Reconstruction of Human Rights: Contributions from Catholic Tradition", in *Catholicism and Liberalism – Contributions to American Public Philosophy,* eds. R. Bruce Douglass and David Hollenbach, 127-150 (Cambridge: Cambridge University Press, 1994), 129.

[3] Michael Sandel, *Liberalism and the Limits of Justice* (Cambridge: Cambridge University Press, 1998 – 2nd Edition).

together 'incommensurable' comprehensive moral doctrines arising from different communities or traditions and find such challenges creative and meaningful to be encountered with.

In retrospect, we are now able to see that even the secular liberal orientation of human rights discourse in the west had the backing of a culture that had been nurtured with religious resources for several centuries. Starting with natural law theories, originating from Aristotle, but adapted to Christian religious worldview by Thomas Aquinas and the subsequent scholastic tradition, the Protestant Reformation emphasing the privileged position of individuals to receive direct revelation from God through the scriptures, the Catholic social teachings which have invariably dwelt upon human dignity, freedom and inviolable rights on account of human being created in the 'image and likeness' of God, and the involvement of Christian agencies in the post-War era to remedy the problems of migrants, refugees, differently-abled persons, etc. have all already gone into the making of the human rights environment in the west.

Going by such realisations, today, there is a perceivable fervour seen among activists and scholars in the western context to integrate religious, cultural, and other symbolic resources in the maintenance and promotion of human rights. As Thomas Banchoff and Robert Wuthnow observe, "[T]he last several decades have seen a remarkable mobilization of faith-inspired actors and organizations around diverse political, social, and economic human rights agendas. … Religion and the global politics of human rights are now more intertwined than ever."[4]

Going a step further, Amitai Etizioni, a well known political philosopher, very confidently speaks of the emergence of a synthesis between the liberal values of the west and the communitarian values of the East. In his own words:

> I will present evidence to suggest that the world actually is moving toward a new synthesis between the West's great respect for individual" rights and choices and the East's respect for social obligations (in a variety of ways, of course); between the West's preoccupation with autonomy and the East's preoccupation with social order; between Western legal and political egalitarianism and Eastern authoritarianism; between the West's rejection of grand ideologies, of utopianism, and the East's extensive normative characterization of "dos" and "don'ts"; between Western secularism and moral relativism and visions of the afterlife and transcendental sets of meanings, found in several Eastern belief systems including Hinduism, Confucianism, and select African traditions. The

[4] Thomas Banchoff and Robert Wuthnow, "Introduction", *Religion and Global Politics of Human Rights*, eds. Thomas Banchoff and Robert Wuthnow (New York: Oxford, 2011), 2.

> synthesizing process entails modifying the elements that go into it; it is not a mechanical combination of Eastern and Western elements, but rather it is akin to a chemical fusion.[5]

Furthermore, taking a cue from Jonathan Rauch, Etizioni calls this synthesis a "soft communitarianism." According to Rauch, "A soft communitarian is a person who maintains a deep respect for what I call 'hidden law'—the norms, conventions, implicit bargains, and folk wisdom that organize social expectations, regulate everyday behavior, and manage interpersonal conflicts." It would be a synthesis, then, wherein the "open law" of a liberal state premised on the liberal values of individual rights and dignity with be effectively synchronized with the "hidden law" of the communitarian values and wisdom. Etizioni is confident that the world is moving towards such a synthesis.

Indian Context

The history of human rights discourse in the Indian context has a different trajectory, though it occurred through a dialectics of continuity and discontinuity with the western discourse. Its introduction had its remote origin in the process of modernisation, involving industrialisation, modern public education and the rule of law. Abolition of slavery, sati, child marriages, untouchability, restrictions on civil rights, etc. was achieved by, among other things, a modern consciousness, cultivated by the rule of law. The many socio-religious movements which emerged in India during the early modern and modern era played their role too. Some prominent individuals like Rajaram Mohan Roy, Rabindranath Tagore, Brahmabandhab Upadyay, Henry Louis Vivian Deroze, and others played their part as well. British colonial officials like James Mill and John Stuart Mill were instrumental in spreading the utilitarian strand of liberalism. The nationalist movement played its political role well to obtain one of the basics of freedoms – the political freedom. In the post-Independent India, Ambedkar played a significant role in bringing the human rights consciousness to bear upon the social and the political realms. Ambedkar, having been a student of John Dewey, one of the leading proponents of liberal education in the North American context, imbibed the liberal principles of equality, liberty and fraternity and sought to integrate them in the Indian Constitution. It is indeed a vibrant source of human rights discourse today.

Challenges

However, a meaningful experience of liberal democracy still remains deceptive. As a result, we see that the human rights consciousness has not been integrated into people's consciousness so as to create a 'human rights civic environment'

---

[5] Amitai Etizioni, *From Empire to Community* (New York: Palgrave Macmillan, 2004), 14-15.

in the everyday Indian life context. The kind of flagrant violations reported like 'honour killing', 'murders on account of choice of food', 'attacks on account of change of religions', 'denial of permission to women and Dalits to enter sacred places', 'boycott of symbols of public honour to subaltern people', 'a feudal environment of intimidation against assertion of civic rights by subalterns', 'sexual abuse of children and women', 'gruesome attacks against girls resisting male advancements', 'still prevalent denial of public utilities like streets, ponds, and public spaces', etc. indicate an abysmal record of human rights consciousness and implementation in the Indian context. That its performance status in a global human rights and rule of law index is 7.4 in a 0-10 descending order (0 being the best performance) proves the case. Why has India not fared well to cultivate the consciousness of human rights among the people?

Several reasons are being cited:

1. 'Communities' over individuals: Unlike the west, Indian, nay Asian, cultural climate privileges 'communities' over individuals. Kinships, jatis, families, tribes, and other similar bonds embed the individuals within them and the subject of human rights could well be the rights of these collectives rather than of individuals. In the 1990s, some Asian leaders argued that human rights were contrary to the Asian values of kinship-based communities.
2. Ascriptive hierarchy: The system of hierarchy in the Indian society is deeply entrenched and enduring. It is ascriptive, caste-ridden, and supported by indoctrination on ritual purity and pollution. Operation of such a hierarchy at village and rural levels will systemically prevent the emergence of individuals who could defend their individual rights.
3. Fragmented community: Indian society is systemically fragmented by castes and therefore, as Ambedkar observed, a common civic community to serve as the framework for human rights cannot emerge. The innumerable miniscule communities, federated on imaginative caste-ranking, are deemed to bestow and ensure hierarchically positioned honour to individuals in concrete life-contexts rather than on 'abstract' principles of equality, liberty, fraternity, freedom of conscience, freedom of expression and so on.
4. Salience of mythos over logos: the populace of India are motivated largely by mythic narratives, wherein space and time are a-historical, events are irruptive rather than initiated, goals are utopian rather than realistic and consciousness is imaginative rather than analytic. Heroes rather than ordinary individuals accomplish things for collectives. In such a context of mythic consciousness, reasoning related to human rights may not take roots

5. Dharma: It is an overarching moral law present among various religious communities in India. Both orthodox and heterodox religious traditions take recourse to dharma to explain their ethical principles. The major thrust of dharma is to instruct its adherents on duty and virtue, rather than rights and principles.
6. Illiteracy and lack of higher education: The relatively lower rates of literacy in majority of Indian states, and the consequent low rate of higher education, can also be causes for the absence or the weak performance of human rights.
7. The latest challenge of ethno-religious nationalism, the majoritarian politics: The latest obstacle to human rights has emerged in the form of majoritarianism, born out of ethno-religious nationalism. A majoritarian regime cannot be validated on democratic principles and much less on principles of human rights. It organises power along communalistic lines, and it not merely suppresses the voices of minorities, but paralyses the very civil society which is the backbone of democracy.

   What seems to be common among these hurdles is the overbearing control of restrictive non-civic communities over individuals. Whether a communitarian turn will further accentuate these controls and make creating a meaningful human rights environment a far distant dream is the pertinent question here.

We need to work out an Indian specific synthesis of the liberal and the communitarian principles of human rights today. A 'civic communitarian' orientation to human rights, integrating the transcendental dimensions provided by religious and spiritual traditions, would be in order in the Indian context.[6] Such integration can be cultivated through diverse public forums operative in the civil spaces of the country. Too general and unrealistic this might sound, but this is the sure orientation human rights discourse should take in India. It is not without some inner potential that India remains to be a liberal democracy, while some of the neighbours had many hiccups. That Indian opened up to liberal democracy in the first place itself strikes a confident note in us.

Prospects

Amartya Sen, for example, argued sometime ago that the gestalt of Indian personality is typically argumentative, which goes with a cultural sense of

[6] Rajeev Bhargava's idea of 'contextual secularism' or Cecile Laborde's idea of 'segregation of religion in relation to the state' are pertinent insights in this regard. While the civil sphere can involve in dialogues of traditions, the state apparatus should keep to standard normative principles in an 'impartial' manner.

democracy. Debates and disputations are part and parcel of Indian culture and that is a seedbed for human rights discourse as well.

Pratap Banu Metha, a scholar on Indian democracy, argues that Hinduism is positively oriented towards liberal democracy and human rights discourse.[7] He avers that Hinduism "has an idea of individuated authority from the beginning"[8] and therefore the human rights discourse can go well here. And he continues that, Hinduism does not have divinely instituted civil / political authorities or state power to control individuals, and the moral law of *dharma* acts as a transcendent force to which even the state power should submit.[9] All these are congenial to human rights in Hinduism.

Felix Wilfred treats the instrument of human rights as a 'converging point' between persons committed to religious and secular ideals to take on the challenges posed by forces of globalization. He avers that "Asia needs to draw from its own civilisational sources new insights, perspectives and motives for upholding the dignity and rights of every human person."[10] He places the human who is able to be compassionate to the other as the subject of human rights and goes on to argue that such an anthropology would take the victims of history like the poor, the refugees, the Dalits, the tribals and the women as preferred foci of human rights discourses. "To serve the cause of the poor" he says, "a spiritual approach to human rights is called for."[11] 'Spiritual' for him is "basically a centrifugal movement, that is a movement away from the world of the self towards the other ... a movement towards truth which necessarily calls for a continuous transcendence of the self and its interests."[12] In this perspective, he says, "the practice of human rights can be part and parcel of a vibrant spiritual realization."[13]

'Dalit Christianity' in India is a case in point for relatively better integration of religion with human rights discourse. Some fundamental human rights like right to life, shelter, security, dignity, equal treatment, freedom from torture, freedom of expression, right to education and work, right to association, etc., seem to have been better addressed by Dalit Christians when compared to non-Christian Dalits. Notwithstanding the inner church discriminations and marginalisations Dalit Christians continue to experience, it is a fact that they have acquired a better level of confidence to address such problems within and

---

[7] Pratap Bhanu Metha, "Hinduism and the Politics of Rights in India", in *Religion and the Global Politics of Human Rights,* eds. Thomas Banchoff and Robert Wuthnow (New York: Oxford University Press, 2011), 193-212.

[8] Ibid., 194.

[9] Ibid., 196.

[10] Felix Wilfred, *Asian Dreams and Christian Hope* (New Delhi: ISPCK, 2003), 80.

[11] Ibid., 89.

[12] Ibid., 89.

[13] Ibid., 89.

without Christian Churches. The level of intellectual capabilities they have obtained, the quality of public interactions they are able to make at national and international levels, and the economic power they have acquired through competitive jobs, etc., would testify to the other developmental attributes Dalit Christians have gained through their practice of Christian religion. Suffice it to say that this is one good example of integrating religion for addressing human rights in India, and similar instances within other major religious traditions too can be identified to witness to the positive interfacing of religion and human rights.

Part-II

Public Theological Potentials – The Catholic Wellspring

6

Faith and Reason
John Paul II's *Fides et Ratio* and Religious Studies in India

In an article titled, "John Paul II's Papal Encyclicals as Dialectic", Dennis D. Cali argues that the pope's encyclicals "evince a class of discourse" that could be "called *dialectic*, as contra-distinguished from rhetoric."[1] While developing the argument, Cali situates this form of discourse within the history of the Catholic theological attempt, especially within the Thomistic (combined with Aristotle) one, to bring together faith and reason in a creative and critical dialogue. The *dialectic* form, according to him, refers to a "mode of discourse characterized by dialogue, conversation, or disputation."[2] It comprises of a (1) *premise* to begin with, assumes a (2) 'determinate Being', i.e., a clearly stated view of reality, associates with a (3) 'normative categorical view', and (4) seeks to dispute and disprove opposing viewpoints, as against rhetoric discourse which opens with a 'thesis', assumes an indeterminate view of reality, goes non-normatively with traditions, and seeks to convince through the continuing discourse.

Cali's ideas bring up a good starting point to discuss John Paul II's encyclical *Fides et Ratio* (hereafter FR) and relate it to the Indian / Asian context of religious and philosophical studies. They throw up perceptions which help appreciate the inner dynamics of FR in a deeper manner. While acknowledging the insight embedded in Cali's perception, one may wonder how far one can stretch the binary between 'dialectic' and 'rhetoric', especially against the contemporary consciousness born out of the philosophical realisations of the language-riddenness of human experience of reality wherein every discourse is

[1] Dennis D. Cali, "John Paul II's Papal Encyclicals as Dialectic", in *The Rhetoric of Pope John Paul II,* ed. Joseph R. Blaney & Joseph P. Zompetti (UK: Lexington Books, 2009), 241.

[2] Ibid.

a narrative, a rhetoric in a substantive sense. It would imply that even *dialectic* is a form of rhetoric, a narrative, a discourse in a disputative mode. The very gestalt of FR as a 'dialectical rhetoric', if one may wish, situates itself within a long tradition of attempts to bring together Faith and Reason, and promotes a creative, critical and responsible interaction between them. While doing so, it endeavours to free human experience from extremes of fideism / traditionalism on the one hand and rationalism / ontologism on the other. A 'balanced' integration of faith and reason, according to FR, would take humanity to greater realisations of truths. I surmise that such a discourse can meaningfully converse with religious studies in the Indian / Asian context.

Religious Studies in India

Religious studies' is a knowledge-perspective which is still in the early stage of its development in India. The very genre of 'religious studies', embodying a reflective and critical approach to religion, in line with the disciplinary pursuits of knowledge, has not yet sufficiently informed the Indian mind. A heavy weight of traditions and the attendant fascination to *mythos* are yet to open up a space for religious studies in the subcontinent. A concept like 'religion' presents enormous complexity while being related to Indian reality.

This is, however, not to deny the rigorous pursuits of philosophical enquiries and reflections upon traditions that have been present in this subcontinent from time immemorial. Scholars like K. C. Bhattacharya, Sarvepalli Radhakrishnan, Surendranath Dasgupta, Eric Frauwallner, Karl H. Potter and others, through their voluminous writings, have brought to our awareness the emergence from ancient times of deep metaphysical reflections found in various orthodox or heterodox traditions, philosophical 'systems' and 'devotion'-based 'religious' traditions of this land.[3] These instances of deep reflections point not merely to the 'axiological reflexivity'[4] obtained by humanity in this region of the globe but also to the emergence of human reasoning, expressed in argumentations, disputations and differentiations, as part of a relentless search for 'truth', considered to be the ultimate reality. These forms of reasoning eventually flowed down to the making of the typical *Argumentative Indian* as in the words of Amartya Sen.[5]

---

[3] Cf. Karl H. Potter ed. *Encyclopaedia of Indian Philosophies* I-IX Volumes (New Delhi: Motilal Banarsidass, 1977); Radhakrishnan, S. *Indian Philosophy* (2 volumes). London: George Allen & Unwin Ltd., 1923; Eric Frauwallner, *History of Indian Philosophy* I-II Volumes (New Delhi: Motilal Banarsidass, 1973).

[4] Axiological reflexivity, as per Karl Jaspers, is a reflective consciousness emergent around the sixth B.C., due to which several meta-reflective traditions were born around the globe.

[5] Cf. Amartya Sen, *The Argumentative Indian – Writings on Indian Culture, History and Identity* (London: Penguin Books, 2005).

While a stream of such traditions continued to flow through the Indian sacred landscape, they did not yet constitute critical perspectives, characteristic of religious studies. A remote beginning of the latter, however, began with the scholars of comparative religion and not less so with the ethnographers of the British colonial dispensation. Max Muller[6] in an earlier period and Mircea Eliade[7] in a later period produced voluminous material on 'religions' of the East, and propelled multifaceted intellectual enquiries in the subcontinent, if not in the whole of Asia. Scholars, known as the Orientalists, through their strenuous efforts at collection, classifications and printing the available texts, brought up the philosophical heritage of India to the public gaze and contributed significantly to inform the Indian mind of ancient traditions.

Though this initial stage of 'comparative religion' did bring about insights, discussions, debates, and argumentations, they did not yet give birth to an academic study or disciplinary pursuit on religious studies. As Vasutha Narayanan observes, even the educational policy makers of the colonial times, such as Lord Macaulay, did not consider making religion a subject of academic studies,[8] while other modern subjects like language, literature, law, mathematics, etc were introduced. This apparently was a beginning of the absence of religious studies which continued for a long time until some higher educational institutions during the post-colonial era introduced them under Departments of Philosophies, Civilization Studies, Literature, and in some Universities under the name of Departments of Religious Studies.[9] But they are very far and few, in a country which has about 900 Universities! Moreover, the kinds of studies that are pursued in these academic institutions do not lend themselves to be classified uniformly under the genre of religious studies. In not a few institutions, what goes on under religious studies is 'religious instructions', along with memorising religious texts and traditions. However, this is not to deny the serious academic attempts being made in some quarters to study religion or traditions with rigorous methods.

What is very important to note is that besides these limited academic circles we find a host of voluntary, individual or institution centred, research initiatives to study religion and philosophy in India. First, we have native Indian

---

[6] Cf. Friedrich Max Muller, *On the Origin and Growth of Religion as Illustrated by the Religions of India* (London: Longmans, Greens and Co, 1878).

[7] Cf. Mircea Eliade, *Patterns in Comparative Religion* (New York: Sheed and Ward, 1958).

[8] Cf. Vasuntha Narayanan, "The History of the Academic Study of Religion in Universities, Centres, and Institutes in India." *Numen*, vol. 62, No. 1, Special Issue – *De-Orienting Religious Studies: Four Genealogies of the Study of Religion in Modern Asia*, 2015, pp. 7-39.

[9] The University of Madras, for example, has five religious studies departments and one department for Indian philosophy: Departments of Religious Studies for Vaishnavism, Saivism, Jaina Studies, Islamic Studies and Christian Studies, along with a Department for Indian Philosophy.

Professorial scholars like T. N. Madan, T. M. B. Mahadevan, Daya Krishna, J. N. Mohanty and others who have studied or study religion / philosophy and publish widely. While some of them do in the style of systematic expositions, others do it more interpretatively. Secondly, there is a host of scholars of Indian origin but placed abroad in universities or research Institutions, like Arvind Sharma, Vasudha Dalmia, Vasudha Narayanan, Ashuthosh Varshney, and others who study Indian religion and philosophy with high levels of specialisations. Most of their studies are textual in focus. Thirdly, we have a good number of scholars of Indian origin, placed either abroad or in India, who study the interfaces between religion, philosophy, politics, society, and so on. Ashis Nandy, Partha Chatterjee, and Rajiv Bhargava are some good examples. Fourthly, we have a host of foreign scholars, collectives and institutions who pursue studies upon Indian religions and philosophies. A good section among them follow textual studies, branching off into studies which fall within religious studies or philosophy frameworks, and, studies which combine sociological, cultural, and psychological perspectives; yet another good section does field-based empirical researches.

The profile of religious studies emerging from the foregoing account brings up certain important concerns as regards the status and role of religious studies in the Indian context today. The first and foremost of the concerns is to address the question of the academic status of religious studies in India. Can India, one of the most populous countries in the world, having about 900 Universities, bring religious studies in its mainline educational curriculum? Can religion be taught and studied at the higher educational institutions so as to cultivate the young minds with the wisdom of different religions and to enable younger generation to approach different religions in an informed and enlightened manner? What are the challenges and prospects facing such a project?

To the question 'why in the first place India did not come to have religious studies', several answers are being proposed. As noted above, Vasudha Narayanan, in her study about the status of religious studies in Indian Universities, observed that the colonial educational policy makers, who introduced the modern system of education to India, did not introduce religious studies in the curriculum, and the fallout of this decision continues to inform the educational curriculum until this day. Well, while this could be one of the reasons for the failure to institute religious studies in the first place, it cannot, however, continue to be reason as to why it has not been instituted subsequently. Given the fact that India, in its post-independent phase, has come up with new policies on education, it could well have incorporated religion in its academic pursuit. This could have been so, especially when some of the early education related committees appointed by the independent India openly expressed the need for religious and moral education for the youth of India.

For example, a committee constituted in 1959 by the Government of India on "Religious and Moral Instructions" stated that, "many ills that ... our society as a whole is suffering today, resulting in widespread disturbances and dislocation of life, are mainly due to the gradual disturbance of the hold of basic principles of religion on the hearts of our people."[10]

That being so, another reason, more in line with the previous one, could be that the policy of religious neutrality adopted by the British Government continued to exist in the independent India and that the latter consciously adopted a secular Constitution in which there was no place for public education on religion, i.e., religious studies in public educational institutions. This could certainly be a more substantive reason, given the fact that Indian Constitution specifically mentions (Art. 28) that publicly funded educational institutions could not have religious education in its curriculum. Moreover, the 'fathers' of the nation, either for reasons of their own secularist orientation or for practical reasons of avoiding conflicts and controversies in dealing with education on different religious traditions, did not even think of introducing religious studies in the mainline curriculum.

While this could be true to certain extent, it would still be a limited understanding if the reasons are confined only to the decisions of the 'fathers' of the nation and the Constitution makers, who, after all, were not individuals living in islands. Their understanding of secularism, the immediate concerns of handling religious strife and, above all, the general religious ethos of the country, combined with an enormity of diverse traditions, weighed upon their minds to inhibit a vision of religious education in public institutions. The Nehruvian era, first of all, went with a 'dogmatic' secularism, which sought to comprehensively separate state and religion, without however adapting the western secularism to the Indian context; secondly, the pressing need of handling religious strife made them to think of keeping religion away rather than getting to know them systematically; and, thirdly, the general religious or spiritual ethos, born upon a thick plurality of traditions of the people 'naturally' inhibited an attitude towards objectivising and studying them.

The last of the reasons mentioned above needs some elaboration. It has always been stated that India is a land of religions and that it privileges spiritual goals above 'material' pursuits. 'Land of religions' would mean a land where religious traditions proliferate as well as a land where religiosity takes priority over other concerns in the life and consciousness of the people. Some scholars have gone on to state that Indian mind is characterised by a religio-mythical consciousness in contradistinction to the logo-rational consciousness of the

[10] Quoted by A. R. Desai, "National Integration and Religion," *Sociological Bulletin*, Vol. 12, No. 1 (March 1963), pp. 55.

west. Vivekananda, for example, glorified the spiritual quest of India, which, unlike the west, forewent material benefits for eternal spiritual goals.[11]

However, others have refuted such a marked distinction and have pointed out to more qualified differences. Edmund Husserl, for example, would opine that even though both the Greek, the fountainhead of western philosophy, and the Indian philosophies would be involved in explorations of truth, the purpose of such explorations "is different on each side, ... Indian thinkers still belong to the so-called 'mythical-religious' mentality whereas only Greece reaches the pure philosophy that implies the autonomy of rational thought."[12] Philosophical reflections or explorations on the basis of human reasoning in India are aimed at end-time purposes of obtaining a release from the karmic cycles[13] and gaining 'ultimate' liberation, rather than being valuable in themselves or being concerned with temporal gains. As S. K. Maitra would put it, Hindu Philosophy and culture are not against human reasoning, but "against the values which reason generates, namely, what may be called pragmatic values, which concern themselves only with the economic, political, or social needs of man."[14] It is thus possible that the general Indian mind had inhibition towards academic methodological pursuit of philosophies and religion, because of its proclivity towards 'pragmatic' objectives.

Another probable hurdle in the academic spread of religious studies could have been the problematic of naming those realities which are usually addressed by religion and philosophy. Some variants of them had been addressed as 'parambara' (traditions) or 'shastra' (philosophy) or 'tarka' (debate) before the advent of the Anglicised categories of religion and philosophy. As Sonia Sikka opines, one does not "assume the modern Western categories of 'philosophy' and 'religion' in one's approach to Indian tradition within academic disciplines."[15] Several scholars have argued that the term 'religion' or its central concepts like 'revelation', 'creation', 'salvation', etc. do not apply to the Indian realities as

---

[11] Cf. Swami Vivekananda, *My India – The India Eternal*, Calcutta: The Ramakrishna Mission Institute of Culture, 1993 (Reprint), p. 13.

[12] As cited in Alexis Pinchard, "Does the Concept of theoria fit the beginning of Indian Thought?" in *Universe and Inner Self in Early Indian and Early Greek Thought*, ed. Richard Seaford, 118-133. Edinburg: Edinburg University Press, 2016. 118.

[13] As Adrados would opine that, "The great differences which exist between the philosophies of Greece and India, have their roots in the India's insistence on ideas like that of the *karma* of the *samsara*, and Salvation and Liberation, which in their turn are based on identification of the *Atma* and *Brahma*" - Francisco R. Adrados "Indian and Greek Philosophy." *Annals of the Bhandarkar Oriental Research Institute*, Vol. 58/59, 1977-78, 6.

[14] S. K. Maitra, "Reason in Hindu Philosophy: Classical and Contemporary." *Philosophy East and West*. Vol. 11, No. 3 (Oct., 1961), 141.

[15] Sonia Sikka, "Teaching Religion and Philosophy in India," *India International Centre Quarterly, Vol. 40,* No. ¾, 2013, 143.

they do in western contexts, though similar religious concepts or experiences are prevalent here. For example, Sonia Sikka would argue as follows:

> Krishna does 'reveal' his true form to Arjuna, who is then being granted an extraordinary vision of the truth of things, but this does not lead to the Gita being considered a revealed text in the way the Bible is for Christianity, or the Quran for Islam. What we have here is not 'religion' as a distinct sphere of existence involving a special way of believing, but a description of how things are, along with views about how one gets to know how things are, and how one should think and act, given that this is how things are.[16]

For Sikka, what are kind of quotidian events in India are analytically brought under certain special distinctive sacred realm of religion, with their semantic difference in the West and this does not cohere well with the Indian mind. The Durkheimian scheme of 'separation' of the sacred and profane does not take place in the Indian context so as to name something as 'religious' or as something outside the purview of argumentation, debates and disputation. That's why traditions, whether 'sacred' or 'profane', have been disputed in the past and counter-traditions were initiated in the Indian context with much freedom. Juxtaposing of sacred and profane or faith and reason are not germane to the Indian ethos, and this makes categories like religion not appealing. Sikka would argue as follows: "I would argue that one of the most serious problems with conceiving of Indian traditions as 'religions' is precisely that the term 'religion' has become largely synonymous with 'faith'. Faith, moreover, tends to be defined in terms of the various 'others' of reason."[17] While such a difficulty presents itself when naming categories known as religion and philosophy, it is also a fact that these categories have come to exist in academic circles and have gained currency in general usage, and therefore they may be adopted for their heuristic purposes if not for their essence.

Yet another factor to inhibit the spread of academic study of religion could have been that the Indian mind treats authority as a valid source of knowledge. Academic study of religion, influenced much by the western development of disciplines, might base itself upon empirical evidences or at the most take a phenomenological stance wherein authority or testimony of charismatic individuals do not count much. But as Saksena puts it, "Indian philosophy not only recognizes testimony amongst its sources knowledge, but sometimes even accords it a higher place of importance, inasmuch as by authority alone are certain facts supposed to be known which are not capable

[16] Ibid., 139.

[17] Ibid., 141.

of being revealed by other source... Modern Western philosophy, the contrary, is founded upon a revolt against authority."[18]

Need of the Hour: Project Goals

While these may be some of the probable hurdles on the academic pursuit of religious / philosophical studies, the need for academic studies on religion and philosophy can be never more urgent and relevant than today. The religio-philosophical terrain in India needs a creative fertilization today. What we do have now are mostly summations and repetitions than creative philosophical explorations. Though inheriting a substantive philosophical corpus, an ongoing philosophical hermeneutical exploration seems to be feeble in India. Daya Krishna, one of the leading post-Independent India's philosophers, observes that most of the philosophical studies in India stop with giving an account of liberation or *moksha* and do not engage progressively with unfolding realities of the times. A creative philosophical endeavour, as Mukherji rightly proposes, needs to engage in conversation with the leading knowledge-systems of the time, and renew the human consciousness continuously.[19] Every society, in order to be creative and forward-looking, needs critical self-examinations; and even when a philosophy becomes critical of others, as in the case of Indian philosophy becoming critical of the western religions and philosophies, it needs to be self-critical so as to be true to its vocation. As Mukherji opines, "in order for a philosophical tradition to be significantly critical of others, it must develop tools and discourses to be able to critically examine its own edifice of knowledge. Constant self-examination, leading perhaps to self-rejection at times, has been a liberating feature of philosophy in any tradition since antiquity."[20] Indian philosophy has to experience this liberating feature today. Needless to say academic studies of philosophy and religion can go a long way in this direction.

At this juncture, one needs also to think of the academic freedom which is a desideratum for free philosophical enquiries and religious studies. In the contemporary context of religio-cultural nationalism and identity politics, the casualty oftentimes is the philosophical freedom, i.e., freedom for human reason. Well-known scholars like Romila Thapar have gone to the public with the cry on a shrinking space for academic freedom. Amartya Sen is yet another well-known public intellectual who has demanded freedom before thinking of one's identity. Safeguarding the freedom for philosophy, especially from

[18] S. K. Saksena, "Authority in Indian Philosophy", Philosophy East and West," Vol. 1, No. 3 (Oct., 1951), 28, https://www.jstor.org/stable/1397171, Accessed: 26-12-2019 07:30 UTC.

[19] Nirmalangshu Mukherji, "Academic Philosophy in India," Economic and Political Weekly, Vol. 37, No. 10 (Mar. 9-15, 2002), 931, Stable URL: https://www.jstor.org/stable/4411839, Accessed: 28-12-2019.

[20] Ibid.

religio-cultural nationalism and oppressive identity politics, would imply that we study religio-cultural traditions with the light of reason and promote public conversations on religions and philosophies. Knowing different religious and philosophic traditions in the public creates a common discursive field for multi-religious and philosophical conversations. It would mean that systematic knowledge about Indian religions and philosophies are imparted to successive generations through public educational institutions.

Fides et Ratio

In such a context of the dire need of academic studies of philosophies and religion on the one hand, and the enduring prohibitive hurdles on the other, one would look for inspirations and motivations from different sources. The document *Fides et Ratio* (hereafter FR) I propose, could be a valuable inspiration or stimulant for getting involved in academic studies to bring together faith and reason in Indian / Asian contexts. While the inspiration can occur on several aspects of the document of FR, I wish to dwell upon some aspects which emerge out of the very gestalt or the thrust of the whole document rather than its individual themes and dynamics.

The way the document dwells upon the intent of 'dialogue of faith and reason' constitutes the very gestalt of FR. It shows how faith and reason can, and even should, come together, without dismantling the horizon of faith, the experience of Divine mystery, manifest in the consciousness of mythos. The very concern of reflecting about the relationship between faith and reason is timely, especially at a time when there is a perceived resurgence of religion all over the world today. Several studies point out to this reality of resurgence, along with emergence of what are known as 'new age religions', 'public religions', etc. Ours is a time, when the human experience of mythos is gaining salience even while that of the logos is taking unimaginable strides. Contemporary specialized areas of scientific disciplines take human knowledge to dizzy heights to the point of even causing vertigo of consciousness for humanity. Take for example, the possibilities of gene editing! One would be in for a shock of a millennial kind! Over against this context, the resurgence of religion and its variegated features seem to pose more perplexity than meaningful experiences. Think of the weird forms of religious practices emergent among some sections of the youth population today! It is against such a context, a text coming from the Catholic head on the need of harmonising faith and reason has a deeply inspirational and revitalising impact.

With its opening sentence, "Faith and reason are like two wings on which the human spirit rises to the contemplation of truth", the document discloses its intent of addressing some of the challenges of our time. With different discursive tropes like 'immanentism', 'uncertainties', 'weariness of reason', 'relativism', scepticism', 'nihilism', etc., it tries to point out that the challenge of the present time is that it suffers from an inability for transcendence, the hope for creative futures. Such an inability, according to the document, is due to a serious lack in the dialogue of faith and reason / theology and philosophy, due to which what we witness to are either fideism or traditionalism on the one hand, and rationalism and nihilism on the other.

The text speaks about a *weariness on the part of human reason* to search after the truth. The prevalence of relativism and scepticism, the causes, according to FR, of uncertainties and insecurities in the human mind of the present generation, is born out of a lack in healthy philosophising. Contemporary philosophers in India too observe that Indian philosophy too has been faced with certain weariness in the fields of philosophy. Daya Krishna, a leading post-Independent Indian philosopher, regrets that what is being presented as Indian philosophy today is not a living philosophy but a recollection of the memories of the past. Along similar lines, Mukherji too surmises that Indian philosophy stopped growing sometime before the British came to this soil, and today it lacks the vitality to respond to contemporary life-issues of people. If the human spirit has to spread its wings with hope, it needs to be therefore involved in healthy and genuine dialogue of faith and reason.

Faith, for the document, is, naturally, the Christian faith, because it addresses the Christian audience, through the bishops. It therefore dwells upon the revelation of God in Jesus Christ as the fullness of grace and truth, the embodiments of faith. However, the features of faith and Revelation as enunciated in the document may well share commonalities with other religious traditions as well. As the document says, "This truth, which God reveals to us in Jesus Christ, is not opposed to the truths which philosophy perceives." (§34) "Revelation", for FR, is that which "introduces into our history a universal and ultimate truth which stirs the human mind to ceaseless effort" (§14), and it serves as the "true lodestar of men and women as they strive to make their way amid the pressures of an immanentist habit of mind and the constrictions of a technocratic logic" (§15). Faith that is born out of this revelation is one that "sharpens the inner eye, opening the mind to discover in the flux of events the workings of Providence" (§16). It is "in a sense an "exercise of thought" (§43), and "It is faith which stirs reason to move beyond all isolation and willingly to run risks so that it may attain whatever is beautiful, good and true. Faith thus becomes the convinced and convincing advocate of reason." (§56) These understandings of faith and revelation can appeal well to Indian philosophies and religion, because, Indian philosophy is one which seeks not merely the truth born out of human perceptions and inference, but also the ultimate truth that is born out of intuition and revelation. It is in place to note that FR too acknowledges the presence of such metaphysical quest in the Indian soil: "A great spiritual impulse leads Indian thought to seek an experience which would liberate the spirit from the shackles of time and space and would therefore acquire absolute value. The dynamic of this quest for liberation provides the context for great metaphysical systems" (§72). And the document continues to state that in India "it is the duty of Christians now to draw from this rich heritage the elements compatible with their faith, in order to enrich Christian thought" (§72).

The understanding of reason, as presented in FR, also can share commonalities with philosophical quests everywhere. FR speaks of the innate capacity of human reason to search and arrive at the ultimate truth; it characterises this capacity as a capacity for transcendence. It is born out of a deep trust in the powers of the human person, because they are created by the transcendent God. It is an innate property that enquires into things as they are; it is a resource to search for the meaning and purpose of life; it is a human orientation towards truth, and it can search for the fundamental truths of life. It formulates the first / universal principles of life, and leads to the realisations of ultimate truth. Reason, as FR envisions, can search for truth at three levels: one, the experimental level wherein truth is sought through testing, evidence, proof, etc.; second, the philosophical level, wherein truth is sought speculatively, by speculating the first principles of life, the universal and ultimate truth; and the third is at the level of religious truth, understanding the mysteries of revealed truths.

FR surmises that the human reason today is focussed upon the experimental truth, in terms of generating knowledge on science and technology, neglecting the philosophical and religious. It has failed to gaze at heights, because it has wilted under the weight of knowledge; it has failed to explore the philosophy of being, but has engrossed in the philosophy of knowing. "In consequence, the human spirit is often invaded by a kind of ambiguous thinking which leads it to an ever deepening introversion, locked within the confines of its own immanence without reference of any kind to the transcendent. A philosophy which no longer asks the question of the meaning of life would be in grave danger of reducing reason to merely accessory functions, with no real passion for the search for truth" (81). On the other hand, when pursued as *recta ratio*, as a genuine rational search, human reason, according to FR, can be the propaeduetic path to faith. It is a path that acknowledges the validity and meaningfulness of Revealed truth through the power of human reason, without however, hurting or damaging the latter. In this way, human reason and faith get related to one another. Such a vision of relationship between faith and reason could be meaningfully applied to the Indian context, wherein there is a reluctance to study religion, because such a study would apparently damage the faith or tradition. A propaeduetic path, on the other hand, would ensure that reason is pursued, but yet remains to be a path to faith. A path wherein the human endeavour does not replace the transcendental experience would be welcomed in the Indian context.

Authority and Autonomy

Saksena, as mentioned above, argues that Indian philosophy treats authority as a valid source of knowledge. In addition to perception, inference, and intuitive knowledge, testimony that comes from an authority is given epistemological validity in Indian philosophy. It would imply that Indian philosophy accords equal, if not more, validity to testimony, authority and tradition even while admitting the validity of logic and epistemological relativism. An important relativist epistemological theory to emerge from Jainism is *cyadvada*, a theory which stands for the multilayered and multifaceted reality of truth. However, in practical terms, it has meant that testimony of sages and Gurus have wielded extraordinary influence upon the religious consciousness of Indians, probably also in the whole of Asia. Testimonies of authorities gain an acceptance which goes oftentimes beyond the scrutiny of independent human reason, logic and critical thought; or to put it otherwise, the philosophies of authorities, wherein philosophy and authority remain merged together, have salience over a philosophy that seeks autonomy of its own.

Very interestingly the document FR too speaks about the authority of the Magisterium in relation to the philosophical matters. It situates itself in relation to human reason / philosophy not so much as an authority over and above the latter, but a respondent or a critical partner to it. It speaks of "authoritatively exercise(ing) a critical discernment of opinions and philosophies" (§49), especially when philosophies "contradict" the revealed truth forming the core of Christian faith. This 'authoritative exercise' is not from a unilateral position of proclaiming truth, but from a concern of clarifying the Christian Faith, the 'simple faith' of Christian believers, in relation to emergent plurality of philosophies and opinions. One would thus see that the authority in the FR is more functional, a witness to truth, a service of recta ratio, and not ontological. It is to maintain the autonomy both of faith and reason. As it says, it is to be a corrective to "on the one hand, fideism and radical traditionalism, for their distrust of reason's natural capacities, and, on the other, rationalism and ontologism because they attributed to natural reason a knowledge which only the light of faith could confer" (§52). Again it says, "the Magisterium's interventions are intended above all to prompt, promote and encourage philosophical enquiry" (§51).

FR duly acknowledges the autonomy of human reason and philosophy for the sake of being at the service of truth, diakonia of truth. Right at the beginning of the section on the Magisterium, FR states that the Church does not have a philosophy of its own. Though this could be an equivocal claim, the documents goes on to say that it does not have a philosophy of its own precisely to acknowledge the autonomy of philosophy, which is necessary to seek after the truth, which is the primary goal of philosophy and even of theology. In its own words, "philosophy must remain faithful to its own principles and methods. Otherwise there would be no guarantee that it would remain oriented to truth and that it was moving towards truth by way of a process governed by reason. A philosophy which did not proceed in the light of reason according to its own principles and methods would serve little purpose. At the deepest level, the autonomy which philosophy enjoys is rooted in the fact that reason is by its nature oriented to truth and is equipped moreover with the means necessary to arrive at truth" (49). FR envisions that human reason / philosophy, if pursued with autonomy, has the capability to take humanity to truth, even to the ultimate truth. In the process it helps humanity to self-examine its traditions, purify it, and renew its energy for creativity.

Dialogue of Faith and Reason

The main thrust of FR, as we know, is to promote dialogue of faith and reason. Right from the beginning of the text, faith and reason are presented as two wings of human spirit, supportive of each other, containing one in the other, even while critically examining one another. One without the other, according to FR, would weaken each other. In the words of the text: "... each without the other is impoverished and enfeebled. Deprived of what Revelation offers, reason has taken side-tracks which expose it to the danger of losing sight of its final goal. Deprived of reason, faith has stressed feeling and experience, and so run the risk of no longer being a universal proposition. It is an illusion to think that faith, tied to weak reasoning, might be more penetrating; on the contrary, faith then runs the grave risk of withering into myth or superstition. The parrhesia of faith must be matched by the boldness of reason" (§48). A lively free expression of faith needs be matched with a bold reason! Every country has to learn much from this vision of FR. We are witnessing everywhere to extremes either in the form of curtailing the freedom of faith or the oppressive dominance of tradition. It is the dialogue of the parrhesia of faith and the boldness of reason which can serve as the remedy for such extremes.

As a fruit of the dialogue, it is not merely the extremes which get remedied, but also universal values that are cultivated. The FR states that Christianity, reaping the fruits of dialogue of faith and reason, has been endeavouring to dismantle "barriers of race, social status and gender", and has been proclaiming "the equality of all men and women before God" (§38). The fruits of the dialogue are, thus, to be seen in egalitarian ordering of human societies, which itself is the result of the way faith and reason dialogue within a "sapiential horizon within which scientific and technological achievements are wedded to the philosophical and ethical values" (§106).

Conclusion

The paper thus argues that FR, a substantive rhetoric embodying a dialectic gestalt, could be a conversational partner to inspire philosophical and religious studies, especially in academic circles. It shows how a genre of religious studies failed to emerge in the Indian context for various reasons, especially on account of the apprehension of the Indian mind upon the pragmatic orientation of the western-inspired academic studies. The paper shows that there could be a holistic way to pursue philosophical and religious studies by way of promoting a dialogue between faith and reason, within the horizon of faith, manifest in the consciousness of mythos.

7

Post-Vat II Catholic Theologies in India
A Bird's Eye View

The Second Vatican Council, the most important event that took place in the life of the Catholic Church during the twentieth century, was a watershed in the journey of Indian Catholic theology. The Council inspired many Catholic theologians to confidently explore the theological world, and opened up the Catholic theological creative potential in a manner not seen for centuries earlier. Theologies began to emerge in relation to the modern world, social-cultural-economic and political realities, religious plurality, secular ideologies and movements. Growing in solidarity with Catholic theologians in other parts of the world, many Indian theologians undertook to do 'contextual theologies' which were being propounded all over the Catholic, if not the Christian world, during the second part of the twentieth century. Hermeneutical explorations were their forte, so to say. Most of them sought not just to *apply* the Christian Faith to the Indian context, but to *interpret* it in the light of Indian social, cultural, religious and economic realities, and of the religious-philosophical systems. The present paper is an attempt to get a 'bird's eye view' of these creative initiatives by Indian Catholic theologians.

1. Continuing with the Catholic *Ashram* Tradition

Jules Monchanin (Parama Arubi Anandam) and Dom Le Saux (Abhishiktananda) – two Benedictine monks had initiated the Catholic *Ashram* tradition by founding the *Saccidananda Ashram* in Thanneerpalli along the banks of Kaveri river near Tiruchirapalli in the year 1938. Their theologies, based on a deeper reading of Indian philosophy of *Advaita Vedanta*, endeavoured to see where and how the revelation in Christ could find its meeting point with the 'Sanskritic Hinduism' and lead to the latter's fulfilment in Christ. In so doing the Benedictine monks drew inspiration from the Thomistic philosophical theology on the Holy Trinity, in terms of form and substance or essence and existence, and related it with the Sanskritic Hindu doctrine of *Sat-Cit-Ananda*, in terms both of the *Nirguna Brahman* (attribute-less ultimate reality) and the *Saguna Brahman* (personal God with attributes). Raimon Panikkar, a philosophical-theologian, with his profound knowledge of Indian Sanskritic philosophy and Christian philosophical theology, put forth reflections around the theme of the hidden Christ, who was present as the unknown Christ in Hinduism, nay, in all 'cosmic religions'. Christian mission of dialogue, he said, was to contribute to the unveiling of this hidden Christ.

During the second part of the twentieth century, Bede Griffiths (1906 – 1993), known as Swami Dayananda, originally an Anglican who had embraced Catholicism at the age of 25 and had become a Benedictine monk, founded Kurisimala Ashram in Kerala, but later shifted to the Trinity Ashram in Thanneerpalli to spend his life as a contemplative *Sannyasin*, and continued with the *Ashram* model of theologising. His important theological concern was, like his predecessors, to relate the Christian revelation of Trinity to the *Advaitic* vision of unity of reality. During his initial years, when he held to the view that Christianity 'fulfilled' other religions, he thought of cosmos, conscience, and Christ as three levels of Divine revelation. The cosmic revelation, according to him, was what the Bible witnessed to in the persons of Adam (representative of the universal humanity), Noah a 'pagan' representative and Melchizedek a 'pagan' priest; then came the revelation at the heart and conscience of the human person, as found in several religious traditions; and finally, the revelation in Christ fulfils all other revelations. Griffiths, however, later changed over to a view of 'complementarity' between revelations found in different religions, even while treating the Christian revelation as 'unique'. It was unique in that it presented the ultimate reality to be 'love', which was a radical relationship. While the *Advaitic* vision, for example, centred round monistic view of reality, it was Christian revelation which engaged the radical unity of God, but in Trinity, i.e., in relationality.

We see this *Ashram* tradition being continued by Indian born D. Amalorpavadoss, called as Amalorananda, who had founded the Anjali Ashram at the outskirts of Mysore, Karnataka. He was theologizing in the post-Vatican II context and he approached other religions with relatively more openness. He was particularly involved in inculturation in liturgy, catechesis and evangelization. He understood evangelization as a response to the "total situation of the country which includes its past cultural and religious heritage as well as its future hopes to be realized through its present historical struggles."[1] It implies that the Church dialogues with cultures, religions and socio-political

[1] Felix Wilfred, *Beyond Settled Foundations* (Chennai: Department of Christian Studies, University of Madras, 1993), 113.

realities of this country to do effective evangelization. Amalorpavadoss held that this evangelization began with the "experience of God-realization and the contemplation of the Gospel within the heart of the individual and within the Christian community...;"[2] it then extended to other religious and cultural communities through dialogue. He saw Christ working in other religions and cultures. He saw the Christian tradition together with Indian traditions as one whole, which mediated God's revelation and grace. In his words:

> Each Indian Christian experiences within himself (sic) two streams flowing and merging into one: the stream of Judaeo-Christian experience communicated through the biblical Word and continued through twenty centuries of Christian experiences and then the stream of 4000 years of Indian religious life articulated by Indian scriptures. These two streams do not flow in parallel lines as two separate streams but both merge at the depth of our being as a single river and become an ocean of single experience. Christians benefit from the Indian Scriptures for a deeper understanding of the biblical World and the Hindus benefit by the biblical Word to re-interpret their Scriptures and to discover the unknown riches and facets.[3]

Another Indian theologian of the time who reflected theologically on dialogue of Christianity with Indian philosophical system was John Britto Chethimattam, a professor who taught philosophy, theology and comparative religion at Dharmaram Vidya Kshetram, Bangalore. During his initial years, he attempted to explore Indian categories and insights which could best express the Christian faith; but later, he adopted a more experiential and open-ended approach, in which he considered theology to be an interior experience of the Spirit that moved on to the exterior manifestation. He observed: "[T]he internal experience of the Spirit acting in us as the *Aham* (our real 'I'), and the encounter with the world as the *Tvam* (Thou, the true Word) become unified in the supreme reality of the Father, the real *Tat*."[4]

Others who contributed to the Ashram tradition in notable ways were Sara Grant (1922 – 2000) and Vandana Mataji (1924 - 1988). They had attempted, through their contemplative life and spirituality, to relate the Christian faith with the mysticism of *Advaita*. Unity of life, or a non-dualistic mysticism, mediated through *Advaita* appealed to them greatly. It is in place to point out that Vandana Mataji took care to relate the *Ashram* living with the concern for social justice too.[5] During the recent years, Sebastian Painadath

---

[2] Ibid., 114.

[3] Ibid., 117.

[4] Ibid., 123.

[5] Cf. Sr. Vandana, S.R.C.J., *Social Justice and Ashrams* (Bangalore: ATC Publications, 1982).

(1942 -), who founded the *Sameeksha* – Centre for Indian Spirituality, Kalady, has endeavoured to relate Christian spirituality to those of other religions so as to promote the mystical sensitivity to life and thought. Treating all spiritual traditions as co-pilgrims towards the Divine, Sebastian calls for an inter-religious hermeneutics, wherein 'scripture' of one religion would interpret that of the other, challenging as well as complementing one another. Along similar lines, Jacob Theckanath (1942 - 2021) reflects that an Asian reading of Bible "should follow a contemplative intuitive style and give greater emphasis to the mystery dimension of the Word, letting it echo within oneself and allowing oneself to be claimed by the Lord."[6] Speaking of the need to study other religious scriptures, Subhash Anand (1943 - 2022), an Indian philosopher-theologian, holds the view that "Jesus is God's very special gift, a gift so profound that to understand Jesus we need the wisdom of all nations and all times."[7] Thus, cross-fertilisation of scriptures, through inter-religious dialogue, emerged as a salient theme among the Catholic theologians during the phase of Ashram tradition.

While this *Ashram* model of theologising sought to inculturate Christianity through the Sanskritic culture and religion, an effort to integrate the indigenous folk and tribal cultures in Christian theology became more visible during the last quarter of the twentieth century. For example, the Ishvani Kendra – Institute of Missiology and Communications, Pune, established in 1976, under the initiative of Engelbert Zeitler, made a significant effort to collect, document and study the indigenous cultures by way of doing mission theology. Jacob Kavunkal (1943 -), Director of this Institute (1993 – 1996), gave fresh understanding of mission as being 'salt' of the earth, and not as a triumphant faith with its paternalistic attitude towards other religions. Francis Barboza (1958 -) integrated the role of Bharata Natyam to communicate Christian faith, by innovating *deva-hastas* (hand gestures) for Christian symbols and themes. Sylvanus Sngi Lyngdoh, a tribal theologian, popularly known as 'Sngi', encouraged the Khasi people to "return to their culture and tradition in order to understand Christ and the Good News of salvation more deeply."[8] He was part of the initiative of Sebastian Karotempral who established the Don Bosco Centre for Indigenous Cultures (DBCIC), which, with a journal on Missiology and a museum for indigenous cultures, is involved in doing mission theology drawing insights from the indigenous cultures of the people of North-East India. Today there are several other theological initiatives from all over India to incorporate the folk and tribal cultures in Christian theology of mission.

---

[6] John C. England, et.al. *Asian Christian Theologies – A Research Guide to Authors, Movements, Sources*, vol. I [Asia Region, South Asian, Austral Asia] (New Delhi: ISPICK, 2002), 326.

[7] Ibid., 329.

[8] Ibid., 262.

2. Indian Liberation Theology

Sebastian Kappen

A socio-cultural and political orientation in Indian Catholic theology was pursued by Sebastian Kappen (1924 - 1993) who proposed an Indian liberation theology, drawing inspiration from the Latin American theology. *Jesus and Freedom*, one of his early works (1977) in English and his theological tracts known as *Anawim*, along with his other publications like *Negations* and *Jesus and Cultural Revolution – An Asian Perspective* (1983), presented the vision of Jesus for a new society as embodied in his proclamation of the Reign of God, and called for a practice of liberation theology. Methodologically, he integrated socio-cultural analysis with theology, with special reference to Christology. His publications like *Liberation Theology and Marxism* (1986), *Marxian Atheism* (1983), *The Future of Socialism and Socialism of the Future* (1992) were aimed at helping to bring about a healthy dialogue between Marxism and Liberation theology.

Kappen proposed a 'foundational theology', a theology which 'cuts across the barriers of religions and ideologies, and critically reflects on 'the historical self-manifestation of the Divine as gift-call and on the human response to it.'"[9] This theology brings together the experiences of the divine as found in various traditions, and sees how human beings across the traditions can respond to the Divine in a transformative way. "His conviction was that the resources belonging to all religions, cultures, ideologies, sciences and technology are to be channelled and harnessed for the social transformation and humanization of our world."[10] He prefers to use the word Divine, rather than God', first of all, to stay clear of the layers of meaning this word had obtained over the centuries, secondly, to be open towards genuine humanist ideologies which too are on a search for the 'ultimate' reality. By 'gift-call' he means the encounter of the Divine as a gift as found in genuine experiences of truth, love, and fellowship, and as a challenge mediated through the historical situation in which we live.[11] He calls these twin dimensions of the encounter as *theandric praxis,* and finds it relevant especially for the Indian context. He speaks of a hermeneutical circle between the Gospel and the theandric praxis (gift-call), in the sense that, Gospel can inspire a theandric praxis, and in turn be understood meaningfully through a theandric praxis.

Christianity is unique, according to him, not in the sense of being superior to other religions, but by being a corrective to the magical religiosity

[9] Felix Wilfred, *Beyond Settled Foundations – The Journey of Indian Theology* (Chennai: Department of Christian Studies, University of Madras, 1993), 140.

[10] Kuncheria Pathil, *Trends in Indian Theology* (Bangalore: Asian Trading Corporation, 2005), 45.

[11] Cf. Ibid.

found in some forms of religiosity. As a prophetic religion, with its critical sense characterised by social justice, Christianity can find partners among the Indian religions of dissent like Buddhism and Bhakti traditions. Kappen classifies Indian religiosity as cosmic, Gnostic and prophetic. While the pre-upanishadic form of religiosity is cosmic in the sense that it is something primordial and ubiquitous, upanishadic religion is Gnostic in the sense that it deals with knowledge as its tool of liberation, and the Bhakti religion is prophetic in the sense that it integrates an ethical vision in its religiosity. Along with the latter prophetic religions of India, Christianity can create a counter-culture for integral liberation. Jesus' movement, for Kappen, was a counter-cultural movement. In his book, *Jesus and Cultural Revolution*, Kappen "considers the contribution of the Jesus tradition to the revolution of consciousness required for the restructuring of Indian society through a new, humane and humanizing culture."[12]

3. Theology as Transformative Art

Samuel Rayan

Samuel Rayan (1920 - 2019) combines active commitment, as a chaplain to the Kerala region of the All India Catholic University Federation (AICUF) from 1960 to 1972 and as a member of the Faith and Order Commission of the WCC from 1968 to 1983, with theological reflection, put forth in teaching systematic theology and missiology at various theological institutions run by Jesuits in India. He brings in an element of poetic imagination to his theology, as he was a good poet himself.

As the volume on *Asian Christian Theologies* put it, "[F]or Rayan theology ... is the light that sparks when faith and life interact, disclosing new levels of faith's historical significance and new forms of transformative intervention to better the human condition."[13] Rayan brought forth a theology of co-relation, which deeply interfaced the experience of faith with a transformative intervention in bettering the human condition. Theology for him was, simultaneously, an articulation by experts of the theology implicit in the life, work, yearnings and relationships of people, and an inspiration for transformative action. To be an effective inspiration, theology, he thought, should integrate the knowledge of social structures, and can express itself better in art, symbols, and parables.

Rayan's theology, to use his own imagery, produced a theological spark, lighted with Christological, pneumatological, ecclesialogical and contextual themes, along with methodological insights. According to Kurien

---

[12] Michael Amaladoss, *Life in Freedom – Liberation Theologies from Asia* (Anand: Gujarat Sahitya Academy, 1997), 151.

[13] John C. England et.al (eds), *Asian Christian Theologies*, vol. 1 (New Delhi: ISPCK, 2002), 259.

Kunnumpuram,[14] a Professor of theology who edited his works, Rayan worked with two main concerns: "one, interpretation of the Christian Faith in the multi-religious context of India, and, two, to develop a theology for the creation of a just and more humane society in our land."[15]

Jesus, for Rayan, is both a history and a mystery. Jesus' humanity needs to be genuinely acknowledged. "An important task of theology" he would say, "is to convince the faithful that God's Son is truly a man among men and not God merely appearing as a man."[16] Acknowledging the humanity of Jesus is, for Rayan, to convince us of the possibility of the 'passibility of God', and begin our faith not with formulaic statement about his divine sonship, but with "human life, its events, experiences and vicissitudes... (and) attend to their significance, and to the further, deeper realities they reveal."[17]

For Rayan, Jesus, as a human person, had his limitations. Only when we know his limitations, do we share with his humanity meaningfully. There were things Jesus did not know. Jesus had a "limited human mind, culturally conditioned and relativised... Jesus had no knowledge or foreknowledge of everything... he was not acting out a drama all written in full."[18] But, "[I] t is the only way for the divine to become manifest in history. If God comes to us, it must always be in a limited, time-conditioned, human fashion." [19] Encountering the humanity of Jesus leads us to an experience of Christ, the divine son. In Christ, as Rayan puts it, "we do not have to 'reconcile' the divine and the human. In him the divine and the human make one single mystery of faith. Jesus the man is the expression of God."[20] Jesus was a historical person, however, a person who leads us beyond history. He was "crucified, died, and was buried", was "no longer merely history's victim, ... but its leader and fashioner as well. He is with humankind, guiding and moulding our history, leading it,

---

[14] His writings have been brought together by Kurien in four volumes titled as (1) *Jesus – The Relevance of His Person and Message for our Times,* (2) *In Spirit and Truth – Indian Christian Reflections on Spirituality and Worship,* (3) *Nature, Women and the Church – Indian Christian Reflections on Ecology, Feminism and Ecclesiology,* and, (4) *Doing Theology – Indian Christian Reflections on Theologising in India Today.*

[15] Kurien Kunnumpuram, SJ, *In Spirit and Truth – Indian Christian Reflections on Spirituality and Worship,* Selected Writings of Samuel Rayan, SJ, vol. II (Mumbai: St. Paul's, 2012), 9.

[16] Kurien Kunnumpuram, *Jesus – The Relevance of His Person and Message for our Times,* Selected Writings of Samuel Rayan, SJ, Vol. 1 (Mumbai: St. Paul's, 2011), 199.

[17] Ibid. 199.

[18] Ibid., 206.

[19] Ibid., 205.

[20] Ibid. 200.

in ways we cannot comprehend, into the Mystery of the Father."[21] His presence in history was one of solidarity with the struggles of the people for freedom, dignity, community and peace. Their "struggles are inspired and sustained by him in mysterious ways. By him are they invisibly led, encouraged, blessed and given meaning and hope."[22]

For Rayan, to be spiritual is "to be open and responsive to reality,"[23] and to be "carried by the Spirit and be profoundly transformed by her."[24] "[V] ivified and led by the Spirit, we become God's children and heirs of God and coheirs with Christ (Rom. 8:9-17)."[25] "The Holy Spirit is the Centre and Horizon of our life and openness and response to Her in terms of justice, mercy and solidarity constitute spirituality."[26] Rayan explores the aspect of mission inherent in this spirituality. For him, not just the text of Mt. 28:19 which gives the mission command, but several other episodes of the Bible dwell upon mission. The parable of Good Samaritan, for example, comes up with the command of 'Go and do likewise', which is nothing short of a mission command. So, mission command is present in many acts and utterances of Jesus. It is ultimately God's mission. "God sends the Son and the Spirit, and through the Son in the Spirit God sends forth creation. The overall mission of the created universe is to be a translation, in the language of matter and motion and energy and beauty, of the eternal word of God."[27] God's mission, according to Rayan, reflects in every religious tradition, and cannot be contained in one particular religious tradition alone. "The Spirit's activity overflows the bounds of the Christian community. The Spirit fills the whole earth and all history. *She* is new-creatively present in the lives of the followers of other faiths as well as in secular movements and struggles for justice, freedom and unity, and for the creation of the beautiful, whether physical or social. Not only the Church but humankind is endowed with a variety of Spirit-gifts (1 Cor 12:4-11).

Rayan's reflections upon eco-theology are inspiring: 'Earth is the Lord's, for it is the Lord's self-manifestation'. Earth "is something God is saying and doing. An ongoing revelation: an unfolding Word of God in which something of God's thought and heart are disclosed, and much of God's attitude to us is

---

[21] Kurien Kunnumpuram, *Jesus – The Relevance of His Person and Message for our Times,* Selected Writings of Samuel Rayan, SJ, Vol. 1 (Mumbai: St. Paul's, 2011), 317.

[22] Ibid., 234.

[23] Ibid., Vol. II., 20.

[24] Ibid., Vol. II. 21.

[25] Ibid., 21.

[26] Ibid., 25.

[27] Ibid., 92.

conveyed."[28] Even while the earth is the Lord's, it is also ours, because God has given it to us. "It is meant to serve the needs and the creative possibilities of all God's children. It is a song of glory and love God gives for all of us to learn to sing after God. It is our common home..."[29] The belongingness of the earth to God comes to "complete truth in Jesus Christ. In him the Earth does indeed become the Face of God and the place of saving encounter. In Jesus' resurrection, the Earth, which has seen and borne in its bosom so much death and dying, finally transcends death and attains abounding and endless life. In Jesus the Earth has become supremely honoured, seated as it is at the right hand of God."[30] We, humans, have polluted the earth, not only in its geographical and physical aspects but in bio-spiritual one as well. "It is the total quality of life and relationships, the whole human environment necessary for joyful and creative existence that has deteriorated and decayed."[31] The ideology of modern development, along with its instrumentalist science, has played no less a role in deteriorating the nature. The ecological crisis can be best met with a theology of nature. The bible, contrary to the accusation that it has promoted the human project of 'dominion' over the nature, sees nature as God's self-revealing and self-witnessing, temple of God, and sacrament of the Divine. Therefore, a "new perspective is to (be) developed which can see nature as a mystery, as an integrated whole, as an organic community and as endowed with rights."[32]

Theology, for Rayan, is "the meeting point of the Mystery of Man and God and History,"[33] and its vocation is "to be Womb for Jesus to continue effectively his entry and birth into our history."[34] This incarnational understanding of theology, according to Rayan, is more heart-centred than head-centred, because "the Word became flesh in a Woman's Womb and not words in someone's head."[35] Rayan makes out a case for weaning theology away from being a cerebral word-centred exercise, with its presumed legitimacy from a reason-based explanatory process, to an artistic expression through stories, images, myths, songs, symbols, etc., which embody our response to God like that of a child and the poor, who "grasp reality and respond to reality's call not

[28] Kurien Kunnumpuram, ed., *Nature, Women and the Church – Indian Christian Reflections on Ecology, Feminism and the Church*, Collected Writings of Samuel Rayan, vol. 1 (New Delhi: ISPCK, 2013), 5.

[29] Ibid., 9.

[30] Ibid., 12.

[31] Ibid., 49.

[32] Ibid., 71

[33] Ibid., 13.

[34] Kurien Kunnumpuram, *Doing Theology – Indian Christian Reflections on Theologizing in India Today,* Collected Writings of Samuel Rayan, Vol. II (New Delhi: ISPCK, 2013), 4.

[35] Ibid., 5.

with their brain but with their Whole Being, with the Centre and Depth of their Being, with their Heart, their Womb"[36] so as to become human before God. It "means that the language of theology has to be a total language in which the highest suggestive and connotative possibilities of speech will be allowed ample scope."[37] This can happen only when we take theology to be an art, rather than a logically argumentative process. Speaking further on the language of theology, Rayan has this fine statement to make:

> What kind of language and bodily reality shall we seek for our theology? A language that corresponds to our Life and our Faith. Our Faith circles round the rich Mystery and ineffable Wonder of God. It circles within our person and our history, of which the Depth and Centre is the Divine Inscrutability. It moves within the tortuous and obscure process of our becoming human. The Mystery of our Faith and the Mystery of human existence warn us against any facile adoption of formal rational logical language for theology.[38]

This non-rational dimension of theology makes it an art – an art which can be sacramental, and thereby transformative. "Art, then, is sacramental, and that precisely is what theology is meant to be and hopes to become."[39] "Theology can be neither art nor theology if it is not committed likewise, if it is not capable of discerning the real issues and raising the questions that matter for the masses."[40] This artistic language of theology should "facilitate the dismantling of the class structure of society since the primordial image with which theology works are those of an egalitarian Divine Community (God as Trinity) and of Humankind as God's Family on earth (the Our Father) in which there can be no division into upper and lower classes, into privileged and disprivileged groups, into underdogs and topdogs."[41] It makes a theologian a faith-based transformative artist.

4. Indian Biblical Theology

Indian biblical theology has put forth several foliages, taking the manure of the Indian soil. Many a Catholic Biblical scholar and theologian have endeavoured to bring forth these foliages. Herein I would like to present the works of George M. Soares-Prabhu as a representative of Catholic Biblical theologians of India.

[36] Ibid.

[37] Ibid. 7.

[38] Ibid.

[39] Ibid., 9

[40] Ibid., 11.

[41] Ibid., 8.

George M. Soares-Prabhu

George M. Soares-Prabhu's (1929 – 1995) writings have been collected under four volumes with the titles: 1. *Biblical Themes for a Contextual Theology*, 2. *A Biblical Theology for India*, 3. *Biblical Spirituality of Liberative Action*, 4. *Theology of Liberation: An Indian Biblical Perspective*. The titles of the volumes themselves point to the major themes he dealt with in his attempt to do Indian biblical theology. Situating liberation theology in the Indian reality and doing contextual theology had been the central concerns of Soares-Prabhu. In so doing, he dealt with such important theological themes as mission, inculturation, Indian Church, understanding Jesus Christ in the Indian context, biblical ethics, prophetic spirituality and the like. His insights on 'Indian interpretation' of the Bible are very meaningful.

Soares-Prabhu did his biblical studies during a period when Biblical interpretation had passed over from the modernist historical critical method through a text-centred linguistic structural method to a reader-response method, wherein the text opens itself up to the reader even while the reader opens herself / himself up to the text. Though acknowledging the value of the historical critical method to understand the 'original, historical / authorial' meaning of the Biblical texts, Soares-Prabhu found it "not really adequate for interpreting a text which is not scientific but religious, which deals not with quantitative but with qualitative realities."[42] This inadequacy of the method made it 'ineffective, irrelevant, and ideologically loaded.'[43] "The ineffectiveness of the historical critical method is shown by its chronic inability to arrive at conclusive results."[44] The irrelevance of the method is shown in its objectivism, which "deliberately ... pursue(s) objective knowledge (not wisdom) for knowledge's sake ... rather than responding to concrete personal and societal needs."[45] And, the supposed objective scientific neutrality of the method is not free from its ideological underpinnings, especially its 'class prejudices' as has been exposed by the Latin American Liberation theology.

He found the hermeneutical method more relevant. From within this method, he explored the pole of the reader from the perspective of the Indian reader, so as to enable a hermeneutical engagement with the prophetic meaning emerging from the historical Jesus, mediated through the authors of the biblical books, and from the linguistic structure of the very biblical text itself. The 'Indian mind', according to him, has certain unique world-views and are

---

[42] George Soares-Prabhu, "Towards an Indian Interpretation of the Bible," in *Biblical Themes for a Contextual Theology Today*, ed., Isaac Padinjarakuttu (Pune: Jnana-Deepa Vidyapeeth, 1999), 208.

[43] Cf. Ibid., 207-214.

[44] Ibid., 208.

[45] Ibid., 209.

characterised by certain Indian-specific realities. The unique world-views are: i) an inclusive world-view, which goes more with synthesis rather than analysis, or identity rather than contradiction; ii) cosmo-centric world-view according to which a person is part and parcel of the cosmic reality; iii) symbolic world-view which ultimately treats the world as a symbol of the Absolute; and, iv) pragmatic world-view, which reads a text with a transformative concern.[46] And these world-views are, on the other hand, characterised by the realities of poverty, plurality of religions and the oppressive casteism. Against these concrete realities, an Indian exegesis of the Bible, Soares-Prabhu avers, would take place. It would not be, as he suggests, "an exotic plant growing in isolation out of the humid soil of traditional Indian methods of interpretation. Rather it will result from the cross-fertilization of modern methods of biblical exegesis with contributors from Indian exegetical tradition, coming to flower in the stormy climate of the socio-cultural reality of India today."[47] Its indicators are that it should be a religious and a social reading. The religious reading need to employ the methods available in the Indian religious traditions, like for example, the Dhvani reading, and the social reading should read the Bible in the light of the liberating praxis of the socially oppressed people of India.

He attempts to understand the relevance of Jesus Christ amid the religions and ideologies of India today. India suffers poverty and caste discrimination in spite of its vitality of religiosity and of its secular ideologies. How come poverty and untouchability can go with the vitality of religious experience? How come that the secular ideologies are not able to solve these problems? Soares-Prabhu avers that the religions of India are either privatized, as may be the case with the elites of India, or pursuing other-worldly goals, ignoring the social evils; similarly, the secular ideologies cannot bring about social transformation bypassing the religiosity of the people. In this context of apathy of religions to social problems and inability of secular ideologies to bring about social change in India, Soares-Prabhu opines that Jesus Christ as the symbol of unity between the Godly and the human can be very relevant. "The relevance of Jesus lies precisely in his ability to hold together in an intimate and indissoluble unity man's God-experience and his Man-concern. He is in fact the living embodiment of their oneness. Christian theology has from its beginnings expressed the significance of Jesus through the symbol of incarnation... its root meaning surely is that God has somehow become 'man'

---

[46] Cf. Scaria Kuthirakkatel, "George M. Soares-Prabhu's Contribution towards an Indian Biblical Theology," in *A Biblical Theology for India* [Collected Writings of George M. Soares Prabhu, Vol. 2], edited by Scaria Kuthirakkatel, svd, (Pune: Jnana-Deepa Vidyapeeth, 1999), xxii.

[47] George Soares-Prabhu, "Towards an Indian Interpretation of the Bible," in *Biblical Themes for a Contextual Theology Today*, ed., Isaac Padinjarakuttu (Pune: Jnana-Deepa Vidyapeeth, 1999), 215-216.

in Jesus."[48] This unity of the divine and the human, as found in Jesus Christ, will be a relevant religious wisdom to 'unleash the social concerns' locked up in the Indian religious traditions and secular ideologies. This unity is not just contemplative and pious, but translated into activities of agape, acts of love towards one another. This act of love, springing from the faith in the love of God (God who loved us first, rather than we loving God), can ultimately bring about the social change.

Soares-Prabhu's understanding of mission is biblical and contextual. According to him, mission is three-dimensional: cosmic, social, and personal;[49] the cosmic dimension is found in the creation from chaos looking up to the creation of new heaven and new earth; the social dimension found in the liberation from bondage as in slavery (Egyptian) and exile (Babylonian) looking up to the realisation of the Reign of God, as indicated in a new community of table fellowship by Jesus; and the personal dimension found in salvation from sin to become a child of God, as found in the transformative experience of the resurrection of Jesus Christ. The Church has to carry out this three-dimensional mission not primarily by 'building up' an institutional Church as by helping the growth of the Reign of God on earth. The great mission command as given in Mt. 28:16-20, according to Soares-Prabhu, has to be read in relation to Mt. 5:13-16, to come to the realisation that "[M]ission ... is not just Christocentric (making disciples of the risen Lord) but theocentric (giving glory to God by building up God's Kingdom); and the way to this mission is not so much individual proclamation as community witness. Unless the Church lives as Church, that is, as the symbol and event of the Kingdom, it cannot engage in authentic mission."[50] The mission is not so much the verbal proclamation as 'infectious witness' by "doing good", as told in Mt. 5:16 "that they may see your good works and give glory to your Father in heaven." 'Seeing the good works and giving glory to God' is more congenial to the Indian mind which "'sees the divine image' (darshan) rather than 'hears the word of God'" and has been sensitive to "visual manifestations of religious experience in the life of individuals and communities, than to mere words about it."[51] He writes:

---

[48] George Soares-Prabhu, "Jesus Christ Amid The Religions and Ideologies of India Today," in *Biblical Themes for a Contextual Theology Today*, ed., Isaac Padinjarakuttu (Pune: Jnana-Deepa Vidyapeeth, 1999), 198.

[49] Cf. George Soares-Prabhu, "Expanding the Horizon of Christian Mission – A Biblical Perspective," in *Biblical Themes for a Contextual Theology Today*, ed., Isaac Padinjarakuttu (Pune: Jnana-Deepa Vidyapeeth, 1999), 1-13.

[50] George Soares-Prabhu, "The Church as Mission – A Reflection on Mt. 5:13-16," in *Biblical Themes for a Contextual Theology Today*, ed., Isaac Padinjarakuttu (Pune: Jnana-Deepa Vidyapeeth, 1999), 16.

[51] Ibid., 22.

> This understanding of mission is, I believe, specially appropriate in India today. Because of its plurireligious horizon, an Indian missiology will tend, like all Indian theology, to be centred on God rather than on the Church or even on Christ. Such a theocentric focus is nothing to be embarrassed about, for it is completely faithful to the Bible. The biblical story begins and ends not with the Church nor even with Jesus Christ but only with God who is all in all (Rom 11:36; 1 Cor. 8:6). It may be the task of an Indian theology to restore this theocentric focus to a Western Christianity, which, because it tends to stop short at Jesus (who is the way not the goal); or, worse, because it tends to sacralise the Church (which is a symbol and the servant of the Kingdom, but not the Kingdom itself), may have lost its sense of the overwhelming reality of God.[52]

Soares-Prabhu makes this argument persuasively in yet another essay on mission by pointing out that the mission command of Jesus is for a 'missionary discipleship', for *following* Jesus. "It is realised not merely through verbal proclamation, but equally through liberative action, indeed most of all (as is explicitly affirmed in the third great mission text of Mathew, the 'mission command' of the Sermon on the Mount in Mt. 5:13-16), through the enduring witness of the Christian mission."[53]

Besides Soares-Prabhu, there are several other catholic biblical theologians who have contributed or are contributing theologically. Lucien Legrand is a well known scholar of scripture, who has given good biblical reflections on themes related to 'the biblical doctrine of virginity', 'mission in the bible in the context of plurality', 'bible and culture', and so on. Mathew Vellanickal ... Joseph Pathrapankal, another biblical theologian, interprets the Bible in the multi-religious context of India. Cruz Hieronimus is yet another biblical scholar who contributes much through regional translations and commentaries. Maria Arul Raja and Antony Baptist interpret the bible from Dalit and feminist perspectives. There are many other Catholic biblical theologians whose work we are not able to bring up here due to want of space.

5. Theology as Dialogue of Cultures and Religions

Michael Amaladoss

A religio-cultural orientation in Indian Christian Theology, focussing upon inter-religious understanding and dialogue, has been pursued by Michael Amaladoss (1936 -). Theology for him is not just an intellectual assent to

---

[52] Ibid., 22-23.

[53] George Soares-Prabhu, "Following Jesus in Mission – Reflections on Mission in the Gospel of Mathew," in *Biblical Themes for a Contextual Theology Today*, ed., Isaac Padinjarakuttu (Pune: Jnana-Deepa Vidyapeeth, 1999), 41.

formulated truth claims, but a reflection upon faith, which is a response to God who is our creator. It should be contextual, indigenous, dialogical, personal and critical. He points out that when, in the history of the Church, faith was taken to be the light that illumines the intellect (as implied in 'faith seeking understanding'), theology was seen as a science; when faith was understood to be commitment to action (praxis), theology became a transformative, political and critical reflection-action dialectics; when faith is understood today, "as a total response to God's Word, involving not only transformation of the world and society but also conversion and self-realization of man, theology would become an integrated, multi-dimensional wisdom... The response is the whole of life in a continuing and discerning commitment, realizing the self and building up a new humanity, inserted in the historical process... Theology will then become more than a critical reflection, offering an ideology for involvement; it will also be an inspiring vision. It will lead not only to transforming action, but to celebration."[54] Celebration involves symbols, rituals, culture, music, and so on. All these can become valid forms of theology. Incidently, supported by his knowledge of classical music, Amaladoss evolved a theology of music. It is, for him, *sadhana*, a path to the absolute reality. "Theology is for life" – said Amaladoss, wanting theology to be an 'applied' theology, to be relevant to actual life. To this end, he wrote theological pieces, named as 'theological musings', and 'theology and life' series which have been published in the Catholic national magazine, *The New Leader*.

His theology of religion plays an important role in his theologizing. Religions are "relative symbolic expressions of the experience of the Absolute,"[55] and they cannot be reduced to any common experience or included into one another. Doing so would go not merely against the nature of religion, but against the limitlessly expansiveness of God. Plurality of religions is characteristically essential to the nature of religions, because religion is God self-disclosing or revealing in complete freedom, and human persons responding too in complete freedom, and therefore, plurality is built into the very nature of religion. "The diversity of experience and the plurality in the commitment to the Absolute have an inscrutable place in the overall plan of God that moves towards the fullness."[56] As he puts it, "[E]ach religion is capable, in its own historic-cultural situation, of giving expression to an absolute relationship. Therefore religions are relative to this absolute relationship and not to one another."[57]

---

[54] M. Amaladoss, SJ, "Towards an Indian Theology: Some Methodological Observations," in *Theologizing in India*, ed. M. Amaladoss et al, (Bangalore: Theological Publications in India, 1981), 44.

[55] Felix Wilfred, *Beyond Settled Foundations ...* 132.

[56] Ibid., 133.

[57] As cited in Ibid., 133.

What is necessary, therefore, is fruitful dialogue and cross-fertilization between them. He proposes a community model of relationship between religions. Rejecting the rainbow model suggested by Raimon Panikkar because it seems to treat different colours as part of a whole, i.e., the white light, Amaladoss opines that religions are what individuals are in a community, each unique, but related. As a community of persons, we grow together towards the experience of the fullness of God.

Religions, according to Amaladoss, have a dialectical relationship with culture, in the sense that both challenge one another and renew one another. Culture "has to do with a worldview and a value system that give meaning to life in community and orient individual and social behaviour."[58] This meaning is inculcated in a person or a community through ritualised behaviours. Religion comes into play as something that inculcates an ultimate meaning in the individual or community. In his words, "[W]hile culture provides an overall meaning system, religion is that element in culture which deals with ultimate or limit questions like the significance of birth and death and of the problem of evil. It may be said to be the deepest element of culture."[59] Religion as the deeper element, and culture as the general behaviour of meaning making, relate to one another in a prophetic tension, challenging and changing one another. This dynamic sense of culture and religion leads Amaladoss to rethink on the earlier project of 'inculturation'.

He wanted the Church to go beyond the project of inculturation, which, he said, had many questions to answer. For example, when Gospel is inculturated in a particular culture, then the pertinent question is whose culture is it? How about several other cultures which are left out? Can an encounter between Gospel and culture be thought in terms of 'embodiment' of Gospel in a culture? Trying to answer these questions, Amaladoss came to realise that the encounter between Gospel and culture can only be a dialogue, cast in an incarnational paradigm. Incarnational paradigm makes us be involved in the dialogue in a 'self-emptying' manner. It is by this dialogue that the Gospel can transform the culture, and ultimately transform the lives of the people. In his words, "[T]he focus of the gospel-culture encounter is the transformation, not only of culture, but of society as a whole, in the process of its becoming the Kingdom of God."[60] Therefore the encounter is an on-going reality, and it cannot be thought of in terms of static projects of 'inculturation'. He pointed out also that by the encounter between Gospel and culture, what is resulted is not a creation of a Church but an unfolding of the Reign of God, and a

---

[58] Michael Amaladoss, *Beyond Inculturation – Can the Many be One?* (New Delhi: Vidyajoti & ISPCK, 1998), 61.

[59] Ibid., 62.

[60] Ibid., 50.

resultant new society. All these, for him, are implied in the dialogue of Gospel and cultures.

Amaladoss grapples with the religious conflicts which are caused by, among others, reasons related to the absolutist claims of different religions during the contemporary times. Religions are conflictual not merely because of their absolutist claims, but also because of the ways in which they get assimilated to identity formation and identity-competition. It is sad that religions get associated with war too. "Social and Political conflicts are prevalent in many parts of the world today. Some of these use religion as a prop so that they are experienced also as religious conflicts. One of many methods of conflict resolution in such situations is dialogue between religious groups."[61] Dialogue is the only meaningful way in our context of religious pluralism. Dialogue can take place at different levels. It can take place at a level where representatives of religions meet together. It can take place when followers of different religions meet together with the aim of getting to understand the beliefs of each other. It can also take place when people meet as believers. All the three, according to Michael, are important for effective dialogue of religions.

6. Theology as Inter-Disciplinary Dialogue for Liberation

Felix Wilfred

Felix Wilfred (1948-2025), a well-known theologian, takes the Asian reality as the context of his reflection. His contribution to the theological field continues to expand. Titles like *Emergent Church in a New India, Theological Education in India, Sunset in the East, Beyond Settled Foundations, From the Dusty Soil, Leave the Temple, On the Banks of Ganges, The Sling of Utopia, Asian Dreams and Christian Hope, Margins: Site of Asian Theologies, Dalit Empowerment, Asian Public Theology, Theology to Go Public, Christians for a Better India,* an edited volume of *The Oxford Handbook of Christianity in Asia, Theology for an Inclusive World,* and *For a Socially Engaged Faith* along with the number of theological journals he has edited constitute his rich scholarly oeuvre. Right from the early phase of his theological reflections, Wilfred worked with an understanding of theology 'as a way of opening humanity to the mystery of the Divine, implying a transformation of the individual and the society from their oppressive factors'. He was critical of the rationalistic positivist language of the Enlightenment to represent reality comprehensively. He wrote: "It should not be forgotten that the rational, discursive approach intersects the reality only at a certain point and many more important areas and dimensions remain concealed and inaccessible to it."[62] Therefore, he observed that "theology that

[61] Michael Amaladoss, *Blessed are the Peacemakers – Theological Reflections* (Chennai: The New Leader Publications, 2012), 193.

[62] Felix Wilfred, "Faith without 'Faith'? – Popular Religion: A Challenge to Elistist Theology and Liturgy," in *Popular Devotions* ed., Paul Puthanangady (Bangalore: NBCLC, 1986), 599.

is wedded to rational discourse and systematization of concepts, and does not heed the fact that religious experience is best transmitted by symbols, would fail to respond to the experience of the people and their religiosity."[63] He understood the language of theology to be analogical - a language characterised by symbols, myths, legends, and rituals, serving as the 'icons' of the divine. And he appreciated the positive potentials of this analogical language to accomplish the transformation of the Church and the society.

Methodologically speaking, Wilfred approaches theology as an explorative science. His writings are interpretative, rather than enunciative and prescriptive. Theology, for him, is hermeneutics of the manifestations of the Divine in our socio-cultural, political and economic realities, and therefore, he started his theology with societal experiences, rather than with dogmatic truth-claims. He interpreted the vision and mission of the Church, always relating them to contextual and current issues faced by the people, the poor and the marginalised. In a titled, *From the Dusty Soil,* he observes that the "guiding principle in all these (his) researches and reflections has been *contextuality.*"[64] Theology was therefore a 'transformative hermeneutics', which interfaced the actual realities of the people with religio-cultural resources on the one hand, and the secular sciences on the other. He hesitated not to enter into other disciplinary fields so as to bring about a meaningful theological insight.

Wilfred speaks of two functions of theology: one, *overall integrative function*, and the other, *critical role*. The 'overall integrative function' stands for the holistic and integral vision theology can give in our world characterised by fragmentations. In his words, "[R]esponding to life calls for a holistic and integral vision in which the human nature and the Divine are harmoniously inter-related. The importance of an integrative approach stands out in bold relief when we set it against the present-day experience of fragmentation, to which science and technology have contributed."[65] Providing a holistic vision is not building a theological conceptual system in an architectonic way, but one which can be an integral part of reality in an 'organic' way. This organic way of theology can emerge, as he points out, only when theology "centres around the experiences of the poor and the suffering."[66] Secondly, the critical role of theology, as Felix envisions it, goes beyond the 'secularist' critical role introduced into theology by such streams of thinking as European Enlightenment; it becomes critical in the way it critiques substantively whatever is opposed to life. As he puts it, "[I]f life is the centre of theology, critique begins from life inasmuch

---

[63] Ibid.

[64] Felix Wilfred, *From the Dusty Soil – Contextual Reinterpretation of Christianity* (Chennai: Department of Christian Studies, University of Madras, 1995), vii.

[65] Felix Wilfred, *On the Banks of Ganges – Doing Contextual Theology* (New Delhi: ISPCK, 2002), 24.

[66] Ibid., 25.

as whatever is opposed to life is anti-theological. In other words, if theology is based on the experience of the divine mystery as life, the primary *critical function of theology relates to the experience of the absence of the divine.*"[67] And the basis for this critical function of theology is the Gospel which embodies "Jesus' own prophetic critique of all that diminishes and corrodes life", and this cannot be "substituted by the forms of critique deriving from critical reason."[68]

One can find, in a very broad sense, three important aspects in the development of theological reflections by Wilfred. First aspect focuses on interpretation of the nature and mission of the Church in the contemporary world. Second aspect focuses on the relationship between theology and social sciences in an inter-disciplinary way. Third aspect seems to focus on relating theology to public life and reality.

Wilfred does much reflection upon the nature of the Church, mission, inculturation, religious pluralism, and dialogue with religions and secular ideologies. The new ecclesiology, put forth by the Vatican Council II, envisioning Church not so much an institution as a communion became meaningful to him. Along this new thinking, he presented a liberative understanding of the church. Church, for him, was a community of the faithful, who, empower and liberate the *antyodaya*, the least of the society. He writes:

> The Church understands itself as a mystery of communion; its mission is to create fellowship. Therefore the Indian Church is called upon to contribute to the creation of a free and fraternal community, society, by releasing its moral and spiritual resources in the mid-stream of Indian life. The Indian Church can fulfil a meaningful role when it relates to peoples and groups as a builder of the community, while remaining deeply committed to the issue of justice... The real proof for the Church as an agent of unity and communion is precisely in its ability to respond to the situation of bondage and injustice. The Church cannot promote communion, amity and harmony among the various groups without itself being committed to justice and liberation.[69]

Inculturation, for him, "means solidarity and identification with the brokenness of the people and sharing in their cup of sorrow; it means hoping with them for the dawn of a new day of love, truth, freedom and justice. It is a question of being rooted to be able to offer spiritual fruits."[70] Considering plurality to be a "gift of God to the human family for its enrichment", Felix foresaw that

[67] Ibid., 25-26.

[68] Ibid., 26.

[69] Felix Wilfred, *Sunset in the East – Asian Challenges and Christian Involvement* (Chennai: Chair in Christianity, University of Madras, 1991), 257.

[70] Ibid., vii.

"without a political and economic framework attuned to the Asian situation, pluralism (would) simply be a matter of folklore."[71] So the focus, according to him, had to shift from *inculturating* Christianity in alien cultures to exploring the role of Christianity for social transformation in a religiously pluralistic world. It means re-envisioning the value of other religions beyond the frameworks of exclusivism, inclusivism and even pluralism. He writes: "The mystery of incarnation is a mystery of servanthood (Mk. 10:45; Mk. 10:43-44), of self-emptying (Phil. 2:8-9; 1 Cor 8:9) and suffering (Heb 2:17-18). In the task of relating to our neighbours of other faiths, the Church is challenged to follow Jesus who emptied himself (*kenosis*), and free itself from all kind of triumphalisms vis-à-vis other cultures and religions."[72] Shedding the elements of triumphalism is necessary for a 'living dialogue' with other religions and cultures. "The participation of Christians in living religious dialogue is but a concrete expression of their faith in the universal salvific will of God, in the action of the Spirit, and a manifestation of their hope in the coming of the fullness of God's kingdom."[73]

Wilfred reflects much upon the relationship of Christian theology to social sciences. According to him, both Christian theology and social sciences are in a new paradigm of knowledge. The traditional paradigm of knowledge, basing itself upon universal epistemological principles, sought for eternal and universal truth. But, today, it is increasingly being realised that knowledge is contextual, and unless it works with an emancipatory concern, producing knowledge would be a futile exercise for him. For example, in a rigorously argued essay titled, "The Struggles of Liberation Theology for a New Paradigm,"[74] Wilfred explored how liberation theology, in the light of the critical social sciences, began to consider its validity not in terms of universal claims but in terms of its praxis for liberation; and similarly how the social sciences needed to shed their 'value-neutral' objective positions in order to bring about the emancipation of the poor and the marginalised. "Knowledge even when it is systematized and organized into science cannot abandon its inherent orientation to liberation."[75] Both theology and social sciences, according to him, need to ask the question, 'how they could transform themselves from being the tool of domination to being the 'weapon of the weak'.

Integrating this liberative dimension of social sciences, Wilfred brings forth much reflection upon Indian liberation theology and contextual theology. He thinks of a multi-dimensional dialogue as the methodology for

[71] Ibid., 20.

[72] Ibid., 151.

[73] Ibid., 153.

[74] Cf. Felix Wilfred, "The Struggles of Liberation Theology for a New Paradigm," *Development & Change*, vol. IV, No. 1, 1999.

[75] Ibid., 143.

liberation and contextual theologies. Theology has to, first of all, dialogue with the overall situation, the situation of suffering and pain of the poor; secondly, it has to undertake an inter-religious dialogue in order to respond to the situation effectively; thirdly, it has to dialogue with other sciences, because, "the promotion of life, which is the vocation of theology, calls for the support of all the sciences that can throw light on the reality of life and help respond to its contemporary exigencies"[76] and "no science can shirk the responsibility of promoting life. Though sciences may have autonomy in their respective spheres, their orientation needs to be such that they positively promote life and its quality."[77] These three dialogues are the ways by which, according to him, theologizing takes place.

Indian liberation theology begins with its response to the 'limit-situation' of the poor in India. "[L]imit-situation of food or lack of food is ... a situation in which one is brought face to face with the Ultimate Mystery, even though this may not be expressly articulated by the people involved."[78] Suffering, *dhukka*, is an "important locus of theologizing in India,"[79] and "[S]uffering is that which throws light on the reality and reveals it."[80] God as the ultimate reality and mystery is revealed amidst the experience of suffering as the source of empowerment, and theology has to articulate this experience. As he writes, "[T]he question of what is life and who is God, begins for the victims from such experiences and it is here that theology as the logos on God begins."[81] Accordingly "[T]he most immediate and striking source for theology is the unrelenting quest for life we find among the people in the midst of so much poverty, misery and struggle."[82]

Comparing and contrasting with the Latin American liberation theology, Wilfred gives the following elements as characterising the Indian liberation theology: Unlike the Latin American liberation theology, Indian one is an *inter-religious* project. "In the pluralistic Indian society, the poor cut across the various religious affiliations. Therefore, any liberative endeavour should be attuned in its very dynamics to this *inter-religious* character."[83] This inter-religious character requires that liberation becomes a common project, wherein the resources of different religions are integrated for liberative projects. Accordingly, "[W]e need to seriously take into account the various ways

[76] Felix Wilfred, *On the Banks of Ganges – Doing Contextual Theology* (New Delhi: ISPCK, 2002), 13.

[77] Ibid., 15

[78] Ibid., 6.

[79] Ibid., 7.

[80] Ibid.

[81] Ibid.

[82] Ibid., 19.

[83] Ibid., 96.

the scriptures of our neighbours have responded to poverty, oppression and injustice."[84] When it comes to the content of liberation, the Indian vision has to integrate the 'interior liberation', along with the search for socio-political liberation. We need therefore to cultivate a 'spirituality of liberation', which integrates action with contemplation, which, in turn, ensues "a process of liberation of the self, society and nature – all organically linked together by common bonds of unity."[85] Bonds of unity, in the Indian context, necessarily implies "acceptance of diversity, difference and pluralism" and becomes a dynamic unity. Yet another crucial concern of Indian liberation theology is "the recovery by the oppressed and subjugated peoples of their authentic selves – the tribals, Dalits, women and so on."[86] While the Latin American liberation theology dwelt upon the economic liberation, in the Indian context, there can be no integral liberation without the social emancipation of the subaltern people. Understanding the dynamics of society in the Indian context cannot be undertaken only on the basis of the logocentric European Enlightenment rationality; but the mythos, the symbolic, plays a vital role in the social dynamics in India and therefore the power of the mythos need be integrated into the project of liberation in India. Similarly, along with the historical and dialectical dimensions of knowledge as emerged from the western context, compassion and harmony need to be integrated, as for example, Gandhi resisted the colonial power through compassion and inner harmony.[87]

Wilfred reflects on a relevant approach to Jesus Christ for the Asian context. He advocates a creative understanding and interpretation of Jesus Christ so as to be relevant to our context. He opines that "the Asian experience unmistakably shows that Jesus has been the object of devotion and interpretation by neighbours of other faiths"[88] too. He takes a look at the existing Indian approaches to Jesus Christ: "there is an approach in the *advaitic* experience of the Divine which has stimulated Hindu as well as Christian thinkers to speak of Jesus Christ as the *Cit* (consciousness) of the Divine"[89] understood as *Sat-Cit-Ananda*, in a Trinitarian model of divinity. "Unlike in the *advaitic* interpretation where there is little room for love, in the theistic tradition, ... devotion and attachment of Jesus to the Father is to such an extent that he can say that he is one with the Father,"[90] and in this theistic tradition, Jesus Christ is considered an *avatar*. Going beyond these *advaitic* and theistic traditions, Jesus

[84] Ibid., 98.

[85] Ibid., 98

[86] Ibid., 100.

[87] Cf. Ibid., 104.

[88] Felix Wilfred, *Margins – Site of Asian Theologies* (New Delhi: ISPCK, 2008), 189.

[89] Felix Wilfred, *On the Banks of Ganges – Doing Contextual Theology* (New Delhi: ISPCK, 2002), 144.

[90] Ibid., 147.

Christ has also been understood as an ethical teacher, proclaimer of a unique *dharma*. Beyond all these existing approaches, Wilfred looks at Jesus Christ as the poor and the marginalised look at him. They do so from a prophetic point of view:

> To be able to understand the interpretation of Jesus Christ by the poor of India, especially the Dalits, one has to place it against the background of the strong confrontation of the lower and backward castes and classes against the continuing political, cultural and religious hegemony of the Brahmanic and other upper castes and classes. According to Ambedkar, the resistance on the part of upper castes to Christianity is not so much on the basis of doctrine as the challenge it represents to the *social order*. At least, in its ideals – if not in practice – Christianity has been a message of equality. And this is precisely what the poor and the Dalits see embodied in Jesus Christ.[91]

The poor understand Jesus Christ not purely in a historical manner, as a person of the past, but as a trans-historical mystery, a contemporary reality. And this, for him, is the relevant approach to understand Jesus Christ in India and Asia.

Wilfred has contributed significantly not merely to understand Asian Christianity, but also to inspire Asian Christians to commit themselves for the liberation of the poor, oppressed, and marginalised as part of their practice of Christian Faith. Asian Christianity, for him, is not so much a continuity of the western Christianity as an indigenous religious tradition with its challenges and opportunities. He has integrated the role of social sciences to describe and analyse Asian Christianity, even while integrating the insights of other religions from Asia to interpret the life and mission of Asian Christianity. The emphasis that he lays on the way Asians have received and live out Christianity in their lives brings up Asian Christianity on its own, so to say.

During the present times, Felix reflects much about the relevance of public theology for Asia and India. Relationship between secularity and religion has been one of the important themes of his theological reflections for a very long time. He spoke of the 'sacredness of the secular'. Now, when the secular sphere has been wrecked by corruption, domination, exploitation, fundamentalism and communalism, the relationship between the secular and the religious, he thinks, has to be revisited. "Can religions sit idle and watch these things happen? How can religion and theology address public issues affecting the people, especially the poorest of the poor? How can theology respond to the aspirations of the poor? The existing forms of theology need to transform

---

[91] Ibid., 156-57.

themselves into public theology..."[92] – he observes. It is a meaningful way of continuing our common journey along with other religious traditions to realise our quest for the mystery of the Divine in a post-metaphysical world. He holds that Asian public theology, with its own specificity, will concern with 1) defence of freedom against state despotism of various kinds and grades; 2) defence of the poor from the tyranny of the market; 3) creation of harmonious and non-exclusive communities; and, 4) protecting the environment. While these will be the public concerns of theology, potentials of faith found in different religions will become the common resource for public theology. Religions can theologise upon one another's faith claims. For example, "even Christology could be so interpreted and explained that a person who is not a Christian by religious belonging will find the discourse meaningful."[93]

Thus a multi-dimensional approach to theology, deeply embodying a dialogue of sciences – treating theology too as a science in a post-metaphysical sense, for the sake of seeking the Divine amidst the societal realities of the sufferings of the poor and marginalised as the source of freedom and life, continues to emerge from Felix Wilfred.

7. Theologies of Dalit and Tribal Liberation

P. Arockiadoss, a systematic theologian, began to contribute meaningfully to theology of Dalit liberation. Inspired by the positive estimation of the Second Vatican Council on the 'spiritual and moral good' found among other religions and cultures, Arockiadoss showed deep interest in exploring the spiritual and moral resources found among the religions and cultures of the subaltern people for doing contextual theology. Unlike the previous Indian theologians who integrated themes, symbols and rituals from the Sanskritic Hinduism, Arockiadoss sought to integrate the religious and cultural resources emerging from the subaltern people of India. Theologizing upon the narratives of the liberative struggles and sacrifices of the Dalit heroes who evolved to be their deities, Arockiadoss wrote:

> Delving deeply, we see some resemblance between these Dalit deities and Jesus Christ in his Paschal Mystery. The folk heroes and heroines behind these folk deities have sacrificed their own lives in their battle against the powers of death and darkness. Like Jesus, they also have suffered and died in order to uphold the just Reign of God. God has vindicated their noble sacrifice by their mysterious presence that lingers even after their cruel death, investing them with divine powers to protect and promote the life and dignity of

[92] Felix Wilfred, *Asian Public Theology – Critical Concerns in Challenging Times* (New Delhi: ISPCK, 2010), vi.

[93] Ibid., xxiii.

> the poor. ... The memory and celebration of their life and sacrifice mediate to the wounded humanity the healing and enabling grace of God.[94]

Thus Arockiadoss had opened a new terrain for doing the theology of Dalit liberation. Maria Arul Raja, a biblical scholar, followed suit, by integrating with his theological reflections active involvement in the struggles of the subaltern people for liberation. Starting with his Ph.D. thesis written on the topic, "Dalit Encounter with their Suffering: An Emancipatory Interpretation of Mark 15:1-47", Raja has come out with voluminous literature on interpretation of Bible from the perspective of Dalit Liberation. Commentaries written by him on the Books of *Genesis, Job, Psalms, Isaiah,* and *Revelation*, and the commentary on the *Gospel according to Mark,* as part of the series of Dalit Biblical Commentaries, are milestones in his contribution to biblical theology of Dalit liberation. As part of his effort at contextual reading of the Bible, Raja has made inter-textual readings, relating Bible to religious texts, especially of subaltern religious traditions. Antony Baptist is yet another upcoming biblical scholar who pursues subaltern reading of the Bible, contributing notably to theology of Dalit liberation. His books, *Together as Sisters* and *Unsung Melodies from Margins* are good contributions in this regard.

Similar to their contribution to the theology of Dalit liberation, catholic theologians have contributed to theology of tribal liberation as well. One of the central themes discussed in relation to the contribution of Christianity to the liberation of Tribal people in India is the interaction of Christianity with the cultures of the Tribal people. While there are critics who hold the view that Christianity has 'damaged' the traditional wholesome culture of the Tribal people, Catholic theologians generally view the relationship as one of mutuality and cross-fertilization. Joseph Marianus Kujur, for example, endorses this view in the following words:

> The contact between Christian faith and tribal culture has mutually enriched each other. The liberative aspects in the *sarna*[95] undo the 'oppressive' in the Church, and the positive elements in Christianity remove the 'negative' in the *sarna.* To preserve the traditional faith and enable it to cope with modern conditions in India should be the aim of the tribal Church. Christ must be presented to people in a relevant manner, addressing the main issues they are grappling with in their daily lives. At the same time he must be allowed to transform

[94] P. Arockiadoss, "Apotheosis of Dalit Martyrs: An Exploration into the Faith Dynamics of Dalit Soteriology of Tamil Nadu," in *Seeking New Horizons,* ed., Leonard Fernando (Vidyajoti & ISPCK, 2002), 158.

[95] A generic name for the traditional religions of the tribes, mainly in Jharkhand.

> society from within. There is, in this process, an opportunity for tribal culture to transform the Church from within.[96]

From this concern of cross-fertilization, several other theologians have explored the theological riches of tribal religions and cultures for a contextual Christian theology, and, similarly, related the tenets of Christian theology to the tribal world-view and life-world.

8. Theology of Indian Women / Feminist Liberation

Number of catholic theologians like Stella Balthazar, Margaret Shanthi Stephens, Pauline Chakkalakal, Kochurani Abraham, Evelyn Monteiro, Pushpa Joseph, Shalini Mulackal, Astrid Lobo Gajiwala, Metti Amirtham and others pursue theology of women liberation in India. They adopt a hermeneutical approach to their theologising in the Indian context. Pushpa Joseph, for example, clarifies the Indian specific feminist hermeneutical approach in her publication *Feminist Hermeneutics – A Contextual Reconstruction* as a way of deconstructing the myth of ideal womanhood and reconstructing the silenced feminity, especially of Indian women.[97] And, they situate their theology in the context of involvement in the struggles of the poor and the marginalised. For example, Stella Balthazar "believes that theology must emerge from our involvement with people in their struggle for self-determination, dignity and control over their destiny."[98] The sinful structures of caste and patriarchy have become major concerns of their theology. For example, the research of Shalini Mulackal on 'Women and Rituals: A Critical Inquiry into the Religio-Cultural Practices of Catholic Women of Dalit Origin in Tiruvalluvar District, Tamilnadu,' focuses upon the oppression the Dalit Christian women undergo in their life-worlds; and, the research of Kochurani Abraham on 'An Inquiry into the Impact of Socio-Religious Aspects of Patriarchy in the Life of Catholic Syrian Christian Women of Kerala', focuses critically upon the way religion inscribes patriarchy. Metti Amirtham explores theologically how the female body is both the victim of patriarchal oppression as well as a source of empowerment of women especially in the Indian context.

Though situated within the Indian context, they do not fail to dwell upon themes common to feminist theology everywhere. Margaret Shanthi (1943-2013), for example, opines that feminist theology is necessary not

---

[96] Joseph Marianus Kujur, "Christian Faith and Tribal Culture: Crisis, Negotiations and Convergence," in *Seeking New Horizons,* ed., Leonard Fernando (Vidyajoti & ISPCK, 2002), 180.

[97] Cf. Pushpa Joseph, *Feminist Hermeneutics – A Contextual Reconstruction* (Siliguri: Salesian College Publication, 2010).

[98] John C. England, et.al. *Asian Christian Theologies – A Research Guide to Authors, Movements, Sources,* vol. I [Asia Region, South Asian, Austral Asia] (New Delhi: ISPICK, 2002), 348.

merely for the uplift of women, but even to 'free' theology from its gender bias, which treats male as a universal principle. According to her, "[T]he very concept of 'God as male patriarch', and the theology of sin and grace, which scapegoated 'woman as the source of sin', needs to be transformed by the feminist perspective of 'women as bearers / nurturers of life' and by recovering the respect and sacredness of women which was earlier imaged in the Mother Goddess – God as Mother."[99] Stella Balthazar (1952 -), combing feminist and liberation theological orientations, thinks of theology as "a discovery of our partnership with God as women in the divine act of creating, sustaining and nurturing of life on this planet in both humankind and nature."[100] Astrid Lobo Gajiwala (1957 -), a medical doctor and theologian, is committed to promoting the participation of women in the ministry of the Church, and supports the ordination of women in the Catholic Church. In her writings Lobo "has portrayed the close relationship between bodily experience, woman's life and Eucharist and has also developed innovative liturgies."[101] Evelyn Monteiro, a systematic theologian, contributes significantly to interface feminist theology with ecclesiology, dwelling upon the place of women in the Church, even while she reflects about the mission of the Church in the context of plurality of religions and cultures.

9. Religious Pluralism and Inter-religious Dialogue

Needless to say that plurality of religions is an important factor in the religious experience not merely of India, but the whole of Asia. It has always been a challenge for Christianity to relate with plurality, especially when it comes to their theological position on the universality of Jesus Christ as the redeemer of humanity. Many a catholic theologian in India has grappled with this issue. From his philosophical-theological starting point of understanding reality itself in terms of cosmotheandrism, Raimon Panikkar went on to take reality in terms of its transcendence, history and immanence. These three dimensions of the experience of reality, according to Panikkar, informs all religions, which, for example, can be found in the *karma*, *bhakti* and *jnana margas* of Hinduism or the Trinity of Christianity. While this three dimensional experience informs all religions, the Christian experience, according to Panikkar, reveals this in its 'utmost fullness' in the iconic person of Jesus Christ.

In his later writings, continuing with the theme of experiencing the fullness of the manifestation of reality in Christ, Panikkar spoke of 'Christophany' as a befitting Christological theme for the twenty-first century. As he says, "[C]hristophany stands for a manifestation of Christ to human consciousness and includes both an experience of Christ and a critical reflection on that

[99] Ibid., 328.

[100] Ibid., 348.

[101] Ibid., 350.

experience."[102] It is rooted in the incarnation of Christ, which reveals the Trinity in its entirety. It offers an "image of Christ that all people are capable of believing in...", - all those who nourish an interest in Christ can meaningfully do so. This Christophany, according to him, is open to scientific as well as every religious mind. As Panikkar puts it, "[C]hristophany is constitutively open to a dialogue with the contemporary scientific mind. It is not a discipline enclosed within either temples or academics; its epiphany, on the contrary, is 'like a flash of lightning that comes from the east and manifests itself all the way to the west."[103] It "considers the other religions of the world not as Christians have often interpreted them but as they understand themselves – as, to use scholastic language, *loci theologici*, proper and legitimate places for theological activity..."[104] As Panikkar continues, Christophany is "a question not of converting the whole world to Christianity but of recognizing that the very nature of reality shows the nondualist polarity between the transcendent and the immanent in its every manifestation."[105]

Christophany, then, is not an experience that fulfils or completes other religious traditions, but something that opens the self to a deeper knowledge in the light of the other or a self-critique in the mirror of the other. This Panikkar called as *intra-religious dialogue* in a work published in 1978.[106] Also called by him as 'dialogical dialogue', intra-religious dialogue was that "unfolded within as well as between partners,"[107] which 'stripped each other of their masks' and became a religious event in itself. In this event, as he says, "[W]e question ourselves on the meaning and purpose of life; we venture closer to those experiences at the very heart of the various traditions... [T]he walls of ... our dogmatic attitudes collapse."[108] This dialogue can take place only in a true encounter between religions. A true encounter is something that goes beyond 'sociological' representation or egoism, and opened oneself to "true communion", a mutual fecundation between religions. "The true encounter between religions", in his words, "is in itself a religious encounter, a meeting that transpires in the heart of each participant in search of truth."[109] A dialogue born out of this encounter, according to Panikkar, is the need of the hour

---

[102] Raimon Panikkar, *The Fullness of Man – A Christophany* (NY: Orbis; New Delhi: ISPCK, 2006), 10.

[103] Ibid., 12.

[104] Ibid., 13.

[105] Ibid., 15.

[106] Cf. R. Panikkar, *The Intra-Religious Dialogue* (Bangalore: Asian Trading Corporation, 1978 [1984 – Indian print]).

[107] Ibid., 9.

[108] Ibid.

[109] Ibid., 11.

today, when religions are becoming aware of others as well as themselves in a deeper and intense way.

It needs be mentioned that Francis D'Sa, Varghese Manimala, Dominic Veliath, Clemens Mendoca, Antony Savari Raj, and others continue to explore the insights given by Raimon Panikkar on the cosmotheandric understanding of reality, encounter of religions and religious dialogue, and their relationship to our contemporary problems including the ecological ones.

A well articulated theology of religious pluralism emerges from the writings of Ignatius Puthiadam. After doing an analytical perusal of the existing Christian approaches to non-Christian religions, such as 'exclusivism', 'fulfilment theory', 'anonymous Christians', 'normative Christian revelation', etc., Puthiadam presents a Christian theology of pluralism. He treats it not as a crisis wrought by human wrong-doing, but a God-given reality. In his words: "Both the history of religions, the present pluralism of religions and the tenacity with which individuals and groups cling to their religions seem to indicate that God wants religious pluralism. The same God who wants individuals to be different, groups and nations to grow in their own separateness, seems to want also religious-pluralism."[110] Pluralism, for Puthiadam, is neither accidental differences not unmeaning fragmentations. As he reflects, "Pluralism stamps reality; not brute plurality but the harmonious union of infinite riches."[111] They "remain finite and interrelated by their otherness; they are partly similar, partly complementary, and partly antagonistic to one another."[112] Puthiadam rightly takes note of the absolutist language present in every religion. He says: "Each one brings an absolute point of view; absolute because it is unsurpassable; a point of view because no revelation can express the totality in human language, since man is never totality and never of a piece."[113] Absolutist assertions by different religions, even in opposition to one another, are the ways in which the assertions become meaningful. So, what is necessary amidst pluralism is cultivating the ability to dialogue acknowledging the equal right of every religion to present their absolutes. In his words: "Unless we can cultivate the courage to take the other as the other, the Scriptures of other religions as they are ... we cannot create a theology."[114] Puthiadam is confident that Christian revelation gives us the ground "to understand the possibility of accepting the other as the other."[115] Finally, practical issues connected with pluralism have

[110] Ignatius Puthiadam, "Diversity of Religions in the Context of Pluralism and Indian Christian Life and Reflection," in *Theologizing in India*, eds. M. Amaladoss, T. K. John and G. Gispert-Sauch (Bangalore: TPI, 1981), 426.

[111] Ibid., 427.

[112] Ibid., 430.

[113] Ibid.

[114] Ibid., 429.

[115] Ibid., 430.

to be met in actual contexts of life, wherein "[W]e should without combative apologetics, or giving up our convictions let ourselves be known to them."[116] Thus, Puthiadam gives us a sound theology of religious pluralism, which is very meaningful to our contemporary context.

Yet another catholic theologian who held clear views on religious pluralism was Jacque Dupuis, who taught at Vidyajoti Theological College in Delhi. He accepted the "constitutive uniqueness and universality of Jesus Christ"[117] and he said:

> This uniqueness, however, is not exclusive, but relational, that is, related to all other divine manifestations to humankind in the one history of salvation. Religious pluralism exists as part of God's plan. Religions have their origin in God's self-manifestation to humankind and religious plurality has as its cause 'the superabundant richness and diversity of God's self-manifestations to humankind. Hence elements of truth and grace are found in these religions and they mediate for their followers the mystery of salvation in Jesus Christ... Interactions between Christianity and other religions bring about mutual enrichment... As the reign of God will reach its fullness at the eschaton, so too the convergence between the religions will reach its goal at the eschaton.[118]

There are many other theologians who reflected upon the theology of religious pluralism. Arulsamy Pushparajan (1944 -), who served as the Head of the Department of Inter-religious Relations in Madurai Kamaraj University, gave the insight that "all religions are in search of Truth and thus *satyocentric* (truthcentric) in their pilgrimage... [A]s a pilgrim towards the full actualisation of Truth, the Church further wishes to dialogue with other seekers of Truth so that all may realise the richness of their patrimony, be mutually reassured by the variety of the Word's expressions and enriched by the outpouring of the Spirit."[119] Jyoti Sahi (1944 -), a renowned artist and theologian, endeavouring to relate 'creative imagination to incarnational spirituality, insisted "on the role of symbols and images in theological reflection and the need for a 'visual theology' which goes beyond the verbal, discursive, rational and propositional statements about faith."[120] In this effort of integrating the symbolic dimension in theology, Sahi was open to receive inspirations from symbolic systems of other

---

[116] Ibid.

[117] John C. England, et.al. *Asian Christian Theologies – A Research Guide to Authors, Movements, Sources*, vol. I [Asia Region, South Asian, Austral Asia] (New Delhi: ISPICK, 2002), 268.

[118] Ibid.

[119] Ibid., 332-33.

[120] Ibid., 333-34.

religions as well. Christian faith, for him, is a journey, rooted in Christianity but goes out towards other religions.

Kuncheria Pathil, specialised in ecumenical theology, spoke of the Church as the 'communion of churches', whose role in the contemporary world is to create a 'community of communities' during the contemporary era. Jose Kuttianimattathil (1955 -) proposed a theology of religion in relation to the role of the Holy Spirit. In his words, "As long as we do not pay sufficient attention to the person and mission of the Holy Spirit we will be left without the 'hinge' that can help us turn towards other religions."[121] Xavier Irudayaraj has written on themes of the Guru in the Indian tradition, inculturation, discipleship, inter-faith dialogue, etc. He proposed a 'soil theology', according to which it is the people of the soil, the poor who give meaning to dialogue and inculturation.

It is in place to note that there were theologians who explored the avenue of mysticism too for Hindu-Christian dialogue. Justin Panakal, who taught at the Pontifical Institute of Philosophy and Theology, Alwaye, was a proponent of Hindu and Christian mysticism as their meeting point. According to him, "there is only an accidental difference between Christian and Hindu mysticism."[122]

There are other theologians like Thomas Manickam, Ignatius Irudayam, T. K. John, Subhash Anand, George Gispert-Sauch, Antony Kalliath, Francis Vineeth, and others who have given us open-ended and dynamic theological reflections on the reality of religious pluralism.

10. Moral Theology

Moral theology has been an important area of reflection by catholic theologians. Based on the Social Teachings of the Catholic Church (brought out summarily in the *Compendium of the Social Teachings of the Catholic Church*), moral theology has flourished in its various dimensions. At the regional level, persons like X. D. Selvaraj have taught moral theology, and have involved in struggles of the people for social justice. They have nurtured moral theology not merely intellectually, but also in terms of praxis. At the national level, George V. Lobo (1923-1993), stands out through his published works like, *Current Problems in Medical Ethics, Christian Living according to Vatican II: Moral Theology Today, Human Rights in the Indian Context, Church and Social Justice,* which have contributed much to a contextual understanding of Christian moral theology in India in the light of the Second Vatican Council. He taught and wrote on theological understanding of human rights, bio-medical ethical issues, social justice, etc. Concern for social transformation was an integral part of his moral

---

[121] Ibid., 349.

[122] Ibid., 299.

theology. Similarly Felix Podimattam (1934 -) has contributed significantly to moral theology. There are others as well.

11. Worship and Theology

Paul Puthanangady was a pioneer in post-Vatican II liturgical renewal in the Catholic Church in India. He envisioned a dialectical relationship between liturgy and theology so as to evolve an Indian liturgy as well as theology. "Jesus presents His message through images and symbols. For Him the kingdom of God is a celebration, a feast. He calls His Gospel a mystery, that is, the knowledge that is received through personal communication and not through human speculation and research."[123] And, "Christian faith is not so much an adherence to a doctrinal system, but the celebration of a sacramental presence."[124] The sacramental celebration, according to Puthanangady, is the place for the epiphany of the risen Lord, whose memory the Church is called upon to remember and celebrate. So, according to Puthanangady, liturgy is the fount of faith, and should become the *locus theologicus* for Christian theology. A theology based on liturgical experience will lead us to understand faith not so much as intellectual assent as an awareness of the divine; express faith more symbolically and descriptively rather than propositionally and conceptually; guide the community along greater sensitivity to the presence of the Spirit.[125]

12. Sociology of Religion with Theological Implications

Sociology of Religion has been one of the important approaches integrated by Indian catholic theologians in their theologising. Paul Parathazham, one of the notable Catholic sociologists of religion in India, observes that sociology of religion can shed light upon: one, the *social determinants*, and the other, the *social consequences* / outcomes of religion. The study even of the social determinants, according to him, is an "essential step in theological self-awareness."[126] Because, it can "liberate the theologian from what Berger has termed 'tyranny of the past', and sensitise her / him to be engaged in the "ongoing reconceptualization of theology;"[127] it can also save theology from 'possible ideological distortions'. Similarly, the study of the social consequences of religion, can bring to the awareness of the theologian the manifest as well as

---

[123] Paul Puthanangady, "Liturgy and Theology – The Dialectical Relationship between Liturgy and Theology with a view to a Theology for India," in *Theologizing in India*, eds. M. Amaladoss, T.K. John and Gispert (Bangalore: TPI, 1981), 140.

[124] Ibid.

[125] Ibid., 153-54.

[126] Paul Parathazham, "Sociological Approaches to the Study of Religion: Implications for Theology," in *Religious Pluralism – An Indian Christian Perspective*, ed. Kuncheria Pathil (Delhi: ISPCK, 1991), 18.

[127] Ibid.

the latent functions of religion. While the awareness of the manifest functions can give certain validity to theology and the need for theologizing, the awareness of the latent functions, which go beyond the awareness of the theologian, can, once again, help theologian to discern the meaningful way of theologizing and help her / him to realise the possibilities of theological pluralism as operative in different social contexts.

We find several studies being made from this perspective of sociology of religion with its implication for theology. Rowena Robinson, Professor of Sociology, IIT, has done a good number of studies on the sociology of Christianity in India. Her well-known publications include *Margins of Faith – Dalit and Tribal Christianity in India*, *Religious Conversion in India*, and *Christians in India*. The studies of Walter Fernandes are significant in this regard. His sociological exploration of the emergence of Dalit identity discourse is an insightful one to count. S. M. Michael too has published significant studies within this framework. The well-known works of Stephen Fuchs like *The Rebellious Prophets* is a good contribution for theologising. They are all substantial contributions not merely to sociology of religion but to Christian theology as well. A good number of researchers[128] undertaken at the Department of Christian Studies, at the University of Madras, or at similar secular higher educational settings in India, have thrown much light upon the manifest and latent functions of religion, especially Christianity, in varying social contexts related to the subaltern people of India. They have been a valuable contribution to the process of theologising in India.

Similarly the contributions of social activists in terms of social analysis and involvement have their unique place in theology. Thomas Kocheri, Sr. Alice, and others' work among the fisherfolk, Jesu Marian's work among the Christians of Dalit origin, involvement of others for restoring the tribal rights of the people for their livelihood, involvement of catholic lawyers for creating legal awareness among the poor and marginalised, etc., are great ingredients for theologising in India. A 'Christian Left', a Christian activism, born out of an attempt to bring together Christian faith and a Marxist social analysis, has also been prevalent in the Indian soil, inspiring involvement in social actions and peoples' struggles.

13. More Voices on the Horizon

Joseph Neuner taught theology at Jnana-Deepa Vidyapeeth. He participated in the Second Vatican Council, and had been active in ecumenical and inter-faith

[128] Researchers done by Vincent B. Wilson, P.T. Mathew, Jose Maliekal, G. Patrick, Kochurani Abraham, Francis Gonsalves, Shalini Mulackal, and James Ponniah at the Department of Christian Studies, University of Madras, are good examples. Similarly, sociological critiques of Christianity made by Ms. Bama, and the anthropological descriptive analysis of popular Catholicism made by Francis Jeyapathy too are good contributions to Christian theology in India.

encounters. He contributed much to comparative theology by his openness to accepting God's presence in other religions too. "In his view, Christians must stop isolating Jesus, for in Him, 'God with us', all our human realities, including struggles, agonies and death, are included in God's creative love, to be fulfilled in eternal life."[129]

K. T. Sebastian is a lay theologian, who reflects about the participation of the laity in the mission of the Church. He argued that "[T]he Church can become a catalyst and a corrective force in society only when there is a genuine, committed laity, existing and working along with the hierarchy. The formation of the laity should become an urgent pastoral priority."[130]

Thomas Manickam reflected upon inculturation and eco-theology. Indian theology to be meaningful to Indian people should inculturate itself in the idiom, thoughts and symbolic structure of India, and should take into account the ecological interconnectedness of life-systems with the whole creation.[131]

D. Alphonse brings in a new dimension to Indian Christian theology from psycho-social perspective. Concerned with making theology relevant to the Indian context, he began relating the doctrine of Avatar to Jesus Christ, and now, is engaged in exploring the psycho-social perspective to understanding the personality of Jesus Christ as well as Christian spirituality. He has reflected much on liberatively interpreting for our times the Catholic faith and devotion to Mary.

Kurian Kunnumpuram has contributed significantly on the vision of Second Vatican Council on Church and its mission. He has done yeoman service to theology by authoring relevant books relating to Church and mission, and edited a good number of books on spirituality, Eucharist, priestly formation, religion and violence, etc.

Indian Christian theology is being enriched with other contributors like Errol D'Lima, Jacob Parapally, Ishanand Vempeny, Mathew Vekathanam, Joseph Mattam, Antony Kalliath, and many others.

14. Public Theology

Public theology is emerging to be one of the areas of interest among Catholic theologians of India. It is a theology, relating itself to the public sphere and public life. Politics as the process of decision-making for the public life becomes the arena for doing this public theology. Consequently, achieving substantive democracy, an egalitarian participatory decision-making process, becomes the salient goal of public theology. This is not a bourgeois democracy that provides

---

[129] John C. England, et.al. *Asian Christian Theologies – A Research Guide to Authors, Movements, Sources*, vol. I [Asia Region, South Asian, Austral Asia] (New Delhi: ISPICK, 2002), 246.

[130] Ibid., 277.

[131] Cf. Ibid., 312.

the ambience for neo-liberal free market, but a democracy which intends to achieve economic parity, social justice, inter-religious peace and harmony.

Writing about it way back in 1997, Michael Amaladoss points out to the need of religions relating themselves to the concerns of public life by way of being involved in 'conversations' for common human and spiritual values.[132] These conversations, he avers, will bring to the public the spiritual and religious resources of different religions and help humanity to support their common goals. These conversations will bring up convergences as well as divergences; while being strengthened by the convergences, we should also develop our democratic sense to agree to disagree with differences. But, what is more important about these conversations, according to Michael Amaladoss, is that they result in common commitments or programmes of action for the common good.

Felix Wilfred has published much on the theme of public theology. Two volumes with collected essays, namely, *Asian Public Theology – Critical Concerns in Changing Times* and *Theology to Go Public*, bear the name of public theology, and they explore the methodology and content of public theology. Relating religious studies, especially Christian studies, with social realities in view of contributing to social transformation has been one of the bottom lines of Felix's scholarship. He has argued much for inter-disciplinary approaches to doing theology, and this stance takes him spontaneously to relating theology to public sphere and public life in our contemporary era of 'public religion'. As done in the global scenario, Wilfred distinguishes between 'public theology' and 'theology of public life': while the former is theology relating to the state and the public sphere, the latter presents theological views on issues of public life.

15. Catholic Formation Houses as Theological Centres

The formation houses for catholic clergy in India have been centres of doing theology. *Jnana-Deepa Vidyapeeth* in Pune, *Vidyajoti* in Delhi, *St. Peter's Seminary* in Bangalore, *The Pontifical Institute* in Alwaye, and the *Dharmaram Vidya Ksehtram* in Bangalore are well-known formation houses at the national level, and, *St. Paul's Seminary* in Trichy, *Sacred Heart Seminary* in Chennai, *St. John's Seminary* in Hyderabad, *St. Albert Seminary* in Ranchi, *St.* in Nagpur, *Morning Star Seminary* in Kolkota, *Mary Matha Seminary* in Trichur, *Suvidya* in Bangalore, *Don Bosco Theological College and Oriens* in Shillong and the RTCs (Regional Theological Centres) of the Jesuits are some of the well-known regional formation houses which have been serving as an interface between reflective and pastoral theologies. These institutions have, even while coming out with good theological publications, given a visible meaning to the concept

[132] Cf. Michael Amaladoss, S.J., *Life in Freedom – Liberation Theologies from Asia* (Gujarat: Gujarat Sahitya prakash, 1997), 201.

of 'doing theology' by entering into the field to theologize upon the struggles and aspirations of the people at the grassroots levels.

16. Associations

Indian Theological Association has been a vanguard theological association in the Catholic Church in India. Right from its inception in the year 1976, this association has reflected theologically on such relevant issues as Indian ecclesiology, Indian liberation theology, theology of religions and religious pluralism, communalism in India, Significance of Jesus Christ for India, Ecological crisis, and so on. Doing contextual theology has been its forte.

Conclusion

While looking at the nature of theological reflections from the catholic fold, what comes to mind is the observation made by M. M. Thomas in his forward to Robin Boyd's *Introduction to Indian Christian Theology*. Taking cognizance of the possible criticism that Indian Christian Theology had not produced any system of theology or systematization of theology, as the West had done, Thomas thought of the Indian context as producing "living theology" which was "often fragmentary and partial in character", and expressed his doubt whether, "the Church in future" would "give the same weight to theological systematization as it did in the past."[133] Thomas' observation is becoming truer, especially in the case of Indian Catholic theology, which, in spite of coming up with both qualitatively and quantitatively substantive reflection, remains 'fragmentary and partial', attuned more to its response to the grassroots reality than to speculative coherence and systematization.

[133] M. M. Thomas, "Forward" in Robin Boyd, *Introduction to Indian Christian Theology* (New Delhi: ISPCK, 1994 [1969]), vi.

8

Civic Communitarianism and the Catholic Social Teaching (CST) An Indian Appreciation

Introduction

The many ways by which individuals, groups, associations, NGOs including religious organisations, and other voluntary agencies helped Indians to face up to the COVID 19 pandemic were no less impressive. Starting with material needs, health care, communication links, and psychological solidarity, they also offered spiritual and religious support to those affected. Their contributions enabled a nation of 1.4 billion people to emerge out of the catastrophe with relative confidence.

This is not, however, to claim that the care provided by the voluntary agencies was sufficient to the enormity of the needs of the numerically high number of victims in India. The pain and sufferings, especially of the marginal sections of people, have been heart-rending and inconsolable. The poor, daily-wage labourers, road-side vendors, migrants, pavement-dwellers, slum-dwellers, and transgender persons have borne the brunt of the pandemic with immeasurable pathos, amidst their abysmal poverty, misery and abandonment.

Though the initiatives of the voluntary agencies were spontaneous and timely, they were ad-hoc, sporadic, and fragmented. They probably lacked a concerted co-ordination. Given the kind of "deep fissures" which inflict the Indian society in terms of caste, religion, ethnicity, religion, languages, and so on, they tended to be restrictive and ghettoised. Furthermore, due to the partisan sentiments of "religious communalism" that has entered the veins of the civil society in recent years, the care tended to be even more fragmented.

Can the Indian nation come up with a more rationalised civic care system or a "structure of care" (as in the words of Pope Francis[1]), integrating the remedial measures of the state and the initiatives of civil society, to be more reliable, coordinated and effective is a pertinent question now. Emergence of such a care system would depend unmistakably on the prevalence of a substantive civic community – a space that represents initiatives for common goals, synergies, and mutual responsibilities; it is a "*place where it is possible to rebuild a public ethic based on solidarity, concrete cooperation and fraternal dialogue.*"[2]

According to Pope Benedict XVI, "[B]uilding a just social and civil order, wherein each person receives what is his or her due is an essential task which every generation must take up anew"[3] and, it is the task of our generation too. From this concern, the present essay explores whether the Catholic social teaching, with its vision of human person, "understood as an autonomous, relational being who is open to the Transcendent,"[4] can contribute to the emergence of a substantive civil society working for common good, with a preferential option to the vulnerable, in the Indian context. Starting with a brief discussion on the political philosophical framework of civic communitarianism emerging globally today in a way congenial to a participatory civil society, the essay goes on to look at the history, teachings, and modalities of the Catholic engagement with civil society, and ends with reflections on their possible relevance to the Indian context.

The Civic Communitarian Framework

Today the dominant political theories in relation to the common good and civil society witness a crucial debate between the proponents of liberalism and communitarianism. The liberal tradition, as we know, begins with arguing for the freedom of the individual, endowed with inviolable rights so as to pursue independent initiatives for self-fulfillment and social development; it values individual autonomy, and deters any interference from outside, to the extent even of having an unfettered freedom to accumulate unmeaning levels of wealth. The communitarians, on the other hand, privilege the common good to be constructed with 'visions of moral good' emerging from communitarian

---

[1] Pope Francis, *Life after the Pandemic* (Citta del Vaticano: Libreria Editrice Vaticana, 2020).

[2] Pope John Paul II, *Compendium of the Social Doctrine of the Church* (hereafter cited as *CSDC*), §418, https://www.vatican.va/roman_curia/pontifical_councils/justpeace/documents/rc_pc_justpeace_doc_20060526_compendio-dott-soc_en.html.

[3] Pope Benedict XVI, *Deus Caritas Est*, (hereafter cited as *DCE*), §27, a; https://www.vatican.va/content/benedict-xvi/en/encyclicals/documents/hf_ben-xvi_enc_20051225_deus-caritas-est.html.

[4] *CSDC*, §417.

traditions, including those of religio-cultural traditions;[5] they value the "constitutive communitarian"[6] dimensions of individual personalities and collective visions of common good; they also value pluralism[7] and take care to reflect upon the challenges involved in bringing together 'incommensurable' comprehensive moral doctrines.

Amidst the many context-specific adaptations of liberalism or communitarianism, one is able to perceive some major trends emergent in different regions. The western hemisphere, for example, witnesses to moderate to extreme forms of liberalism, while the east from fair levels of integration of constitutional liberalism with communitarian ethos to certain congeries of communitarianism; and the middle regions, toying with monarchies and dictatorships. A country-specific focus would bring up more of their instances with particular challenges and prospects.

In India, a constitutional liberal democracy has endeavored during the past 75 years, not without a level of success, to integrate itself with the Indian "communitarian ethos." Today, however, we are faced with the challenge of majoritarian politics that sails on the wings of particular "authoritarian communitarian" sentiments. Agendas of religio-cultural nationalism and dynamics of sectarian ethnic identities are distorting the liberal values of individual freedom, equality, and dignity. Constitutional democratic governance, rule of law, and structures of civic participation are yet to develop significantly. We are lacking the civic participation of citizens to an appreciable level so as to constitute a mature democratic polity. Instead, we are confronting a historical scuttling of the democratic process due to the salience of majoritarian forces. In addition, the majoritarian politics is inducing a discourse on religious homogeneity, and thereby making diversities and differences unpalatable to the "common sense" of the people. Minority traditions or communities are made to live as "aliens" or "dependents" in their own land. As a consequence, the process of building up a civic community of fraternity and solidarity at the grassroots to participate in collective projects for common good is weakened or even reversed. As William Johnson Everett, a scholar on religion and federalism, observes, "[T]he public order of constitutionalism is reabsorbed into the private world of kin and caste"[8] due to the religious nationalism in India today.

In this context, as David Hollenbach, a leading contemporary public theologian to interpret the Catholic social teaching, surmises, there can be

---

[5] Michael Sandel, *Liberalism and the Limits of Justice* (Cambridge: Cambridge University Press, 1998 – 2nd Edition).

[6] Ibid.

[7] They speak of 'value pluralism' to argue for radical pluralism. Amitai Etzioni, *From Empire to Community – A New Approach to International Relations* (New York: Palgrave Macmillan, 2004).

[8] William Johnson Everett, *Religion, Federalism and the Struggle for Public Life – Cases from Germany, India and America* (Oxford: Oxford University Press, 1997), 83.

no meaningful vision of the common good and civil society today without attempting to face the challenges of bringing together the liberal and communitarian visions of common good.[9] One finds in a proposal like 'communal liberalism' by Brian Stiltner an attempt to bring about such a synthesis[10] and there are other attempts as well. Amitai Etzioni, for example, exudes confidence to claim that the present global world is moving towards a fruitful synthesis of the liberal ethos of the West and the communitarian worldview of the East.[11] He helps us see how the two regions of the globe have nurtured their respective worldviews for centuries, but that today, in the globalised context, they interact with one another by way of mutually correcting, enriching, and shaping up new context-specific syntheses.[12]

At this juncture, the Catholic social teachings obtain their value. They endeavor to creatively bring together the liberal and the communitarian values, with a faith-based transcendental orientation. They situate the common good within the communitarian tradition of the Christian faith in a transcendent Trinitarian Godhead. They value the radical plurality of traditions (religious, moral, ideological, cultural, political, etc) characterizing the present-day global world. They endeavour to bring together the different traditions (including non-religious ideological traditions) to work towards achieving the common good of social harmony, political amity, integral ecology, solidarity with the poor, the migrants, and the refugees. At the same time, they endeavour to take the best out of the liberal theory as well and attempt to cultivate the values of human rights, dignity, freedom, justice, and, equality. These liberal values can be best cultivated, according to the CST, when the values themselves have a transcendental orientation, and when the methods of cultivating them are

---

[9] In his own words, "achieving a synthesis of the idea of human rights" which stands for liberalism "with concern for the common good is a crucial condition for any viable moral-political theory in our time." David Hollenbach, "A Communitarian Reconstruction of Human Rights: Contributions from Catholic Tradition," in *Catholicism and Liberalism – Contribution to American Public Philosophy,* eds. R. Bruce Douglass and David Hollenbach (Cambridge: Cambridge University Press, 1994), 133; In fact, the Catholic social teachings, right from its encyclical named *Quadragessimo Anno* (1931) had endeavoured to bring together the value of social justice (equivalent to common good at that time) and the human rights. However, the contemporary turn to communitarian political theory has its own newer context.

[10] Cf. Brian Stiltner, *Religion and Common Good – Catholic Contributions to Building Community in a Liberal Society* (Lanham: Rowan & Littlefield Publishers, Inc. 1999).

[11] Amitai Etzioni, *From Empire to Community.*

[12] With a "critical confidence" he argues that the western *libertarianism* which stands for even unfettered freedom of the individual from the state and the Eastern "authoritarian communitarianism" which have conditioned the social, cultural and the political landscapes of the East, are being mutually challenged today. But, at the same time, positive aspects of both the worldviews (individual freedom, human dignity, democracy, non-discrimination, equality, and rule of law from the west, and respect for authority, value for traditions, and communitarian bond from the east), are coming together.

faith-based; and those who endeavor to achieve these values are committed to a communitarian practice of faith.

Today, Pope Francis's oeuvre orients us towards a meaningful synthesis by way of integrating the liberal values with a communitarian framework. Taking a cue from him, this essay argues that a synthesis of liberal values with a 'civic' communitarian framework is relevant and necessary for the Indian context today. Civic communitarinism, verging on the vision of the "neo republican democracy,"[13] seeks to nurture the virtues of citizenship, participation, non-domination, and freedom from arbitrary powers; it considers the civil society as the base for cultivating these virtues; and, it integrates, among others, the religious resources on common good through public forums.

The Indian Catholic Church, or the Indian Christianity in general, though a miniscule minority community, would do well to participate in public "conversations"[14] and initiatives of civil society so as to come up with a civic 'structure of care' not merely to respond more effectively to pandemics like the COVID 19, but also to care for the "vulnerable of the earth" – the poor, the marginalized, the migrants, the women, and the earth. To this end, it would do well to remind itself of the rich heritage of the interaction of the Catholic Church with civil society in terms of history, content and modalities.

Catholic Social Teaching and Civil Society: A Historical Overview

In the course of its history, the Catholic Church has progressively opened itself up to full participation in civil society. During the time of Pope Pius IX, the predecessor to Pope Leo XIII, against the background of the cataclysmic event of the "temporal" political powers taking over the then existing "papal states", the Catholic Church had developed an antagonistic attitude to civil institutions. *The Syllabus of Errors* (1864) indicted the civil powers, which were perceived to be restricting the ecclesial powers of the Church and the latter's "sole" prerogative to instruct and guide the people in faith and morals.

But, even while indicting the civil powers, the Catholic Church, bereft now of the royal power of the State, was gradually realising that it had to

---

[13] Hannah Arendt, Charles Taylor, Michael Sandel, Philip Petit, Iseult Hanon, Cecile Laborde, and others.

[14] Public conversations are dialogues undertaken in forums of public spheres, like those of civil societies, to foster cooperation between different others for pursuing common goals. To understand what is specific about this type of conversation, we can consider the description by Jeffrey Stout. Such a rich dialogue, he suggests, entails "an exchange of views in which the respective parties express their premises in as much detail as they see fit and in whatever idiom they wish, try to make sense of each other's perspectives, and expose their own commitments to the possibility of criticism." Jeffrey Stout, *Democracy and Traditions* (Princeton: Princeton University Press, 2004), 10–11. Stout discusses the appropriateness of the word "conversation" for religious reasoning in public forums in the context of Richard Rorty's famous criticism of religion as a "conversation-stopper."

play a different role as a moral instructor as well as a teacher of faith in the wider society, primarily the civil society. The 'social question' of the Catholic Church was born in this context, and as Pope John Paul II would observe later, they secured a "citizenship status"[15] to the Catholic Church in public life. The Church went full swing with its comments, observations, critiques, moral instructions, religious teachings and other interventions to engage the civil sphere on public policies.[16]

In his encyclical, *On the Christian Constitution of States* (*Immortale Dei, 1885),* Leo XIII laid out the Christian principles of engaging civil, public and political powers. 'Whether Catholics could take part in the conduct of public affairs?' was a topical question answered affirmatively by the pope in a context wherein the Catholic preoccupation still was to rescind from secular public spheres, lest the latter "profaned" the former. "Common good" began, and continues even to this day, to be the norm that validated the Catholic participation in secular public life.[17]

In *Divini Redemptoris* (1937), Pius XI said, "God has ... destined man (*sic*) for civil society according to the dictates of his very nature,"[18] and observed that human beings could not exempt themselves from the "divinely-imposed obligations toward civil society."[19] On the fortieth anniversary of *Rerum Novarum*, in his *Ouadrogesimo Anno*, he introduced the concept of 'subsidiarity', aimed also at securing freedom for the civil society from the interference of the State. He reiterated the value of founding workers' associations with Christian wisdom and virtue. Cautioning the workers of the danger of the liberalist approach of the 'religion-less' secular associations, the pope defended

[15] Pope John Paul II, *Centesimus Annus*, §5, https://www.vatican.va/content/john-paul-ii/en/encyclicals/documents/hf_jp-ii_enc_01051991_centesimus-annus.html.

[16] It is in place to note here the fact that the civil sphere was taken for a long time, as per many documents of the CST, as the secular State or the civil government as distinguished from ecclesial government or power. It was only during the middle of the twentieth century from the Second Vatican Council that the concept gradually opened up to include the civil society consisting of grassroots people, including their voluntary initiatives and institutions.

[17] Leo XIII's reflection on this is instructive: "...it may in some places be true that, for most urgent and just reasons, it is by no means expedient for Catholics to engage in public affairs or to take an active part in politics. Nevertheless ... to take no share in public matters would be as wrong as to have no concern for, or to bestow no labour upon, the common good..." (no. 44). He continues: "It follows clearly, therefore, that Catholics have just reasons for taking part in the conduct of public affairs. For in so doing they ... use their best endeavours ... to infuse, as it were, into all the veins of the State the healthy sap and blood of Christian wisdom and virtue" (no. 45). We see here that Leo XIII envisioned a Church which, through the veins of the civil institutions, could disseminate the "sap and blood of Christian wisdom and virtue" for the common good of humanity.

[18] Pius XI, *Divini Redemptoris,* (hereafter cited as *DR*), §29 https://www.vatican.va/content/pius-xi/en/encyclicals/documents/hf_p-xi_enc_19370319_divini-redemptoris.html.

[19] *DR*, §30.

the Christian associations by saying, "when the regulations of associations are founded upon religion,[20] the way is easy toward establishing the mutual relations of the members, so that peaceful living together and prosperity will result."[21] Thus, religion was duly integrated by the Catholic Church with the associations of workers in civil society.[22]

Pope John XXIII, in the context of the threats of nuclear war, issued the encyclical *Peace on Earth* (*Pacem in Terris*) wherein the concept of common good, giving due importance to human dignity and freedom, was expounded very prominently. It was he who, through his encyclicals *Mater et Magistra* and *Pacem in Terris*, intoned the thinking on common good in terms of wider social conditions necessary for human fulfillment. This thinking on common good eventually got 'defined' in the *Gaudium et Spes* of the Vat II as "the sum total of those conditions of the social life whereby men (*sic*), families and associations more adequately and readily may attain their own perfection."[23] Here the "conditions of the social life" included institutions and structures of civil sphere, which facilitated individuals and groups to pursue their goals of fulfillment / perfection ordained by God. As John Sniegocki, a scholar on the CST, observes, "[U]ndergirding all of Pope John's political reflections is a fundamental emphasis placed upon active citizen participation in public life[24] and upon respect for human rights."[25]

The Second Vatican Council dwelt upon the virtues of civil society in a few of its documents. In *Dignitatis Humanae,* it spoke of the religious freedom to be ensured in civil society: "[R]eligious freedom, in turn, which men demand as necessary to fulfill their duty to worship God, has to do with immunity from coercion in civil society."[26] The document spoke of religious freedom as a civil right: "the right to religious freedom has its foundation in the very dignity of the human person, as this dignity is known through the revealed Word of God

---

[20] Here 'religion' stood for the Christian religion, which alone was considered true by the Church.

[21] Pius XI, *Quadrogesimo Anno*, §32 https://www.vatican.va/content/pius-xi/en/encyclicals/documents/hf_p-xi_enc_19310515_quadragesimo-anno.html.

[22] The promotion of such workers' association earlier by Leo XIII had led to the formation of similar associations for those in other walks of life and had, as per the assessment of pope Pius XI, enriched the life, culture and the polity of the society (European) in a significant way (§37).

[23] *Gaudium et Spes* (hereafter cited as *GS*), §74 https://www.vatican.va/archive/hist_councils/ii_vatican_council/documents/vat-ii_const_19651207_gaudium-et-spes_en.html.

[24] John XXIII, *Pacem in Terris*, §§75- 76 https://www.vatican.va/content/john-xxiii/en/encyclicals/documents/hf_j-xxiii_enc_11041963_pacem.html.

[25] John Sniegocki, *Catholic Social Teaching and Economic Globalization – The Quest for Alternatives* (Wisconsin: Marquette University, 2009), 120.

[26] Paul VI, *Dignitatis Humanae* (hereafter cited as *DH*) §1 https://www.vatican.va/archive/hist_councils/ii_vatican_council/documents/vat-ii_decl_19651207_dignitatis-humanae_en.html.

and by reason itself. This right of the human person to religious freedom is to be recognized in the constitutional law whereby society is governed. Thus it is to become a civil right."[27] John Paul II, in *Christifideles Laici*, spoke of the civil right of religious freedom as the 'measure of all other fundamental rights': "The civil and social right to religious freedom, inasmuch as it touches the most intimate sphere of the spirit, is a point of reference for the other fundamental rights and in some way becomes a measure of them."[28]

Pope Paul VI, encouraging the involvement of lay people in developmental activities, instructed them to "infuse a Christian spirit into people's mental outlook and daily behavior, into the laws and structures of the civil community."[29] The synodal document on *Justice in the World* (1971) lamented the lack of social participation which kept people away from attaining their human and civil rights.[30] And, in a self-reflexive manner, it encouraged greater participation of the lay people within the Church to ensure greater responsibility and participation for women, freedom of expression and the due process of the Church law.[31]

Pope John Paul II was the first to integrate in his documents the present-day understanding of civil society. The *Compendium of the Social Doctrine of the Church* (2004), published during his later years, reflects clearly the present-day understanding of civil society as the "third sector" between the State and the market. It says: "*[C]ivil society is the sum of relationships and resources, cultural and associative, that are relatively independent from the political sphere and the economic sector,*"[32] and speaks of its role as providing space for the expression of the planning capacity of human beings to work, individually or through associations, for the common good by "fostering a freer and more just social life."[33] It also cautions about the risk of this space being dominated over by the 'stronger who prevail over the weaker.'[34] The *Compendium* serves as a good guide not merely on the very understanding of civil society, but also on the kind of relationships that needs to exist between the Church and civil society based on the principles of solidarity and cooperation for common good on the one hand, and between the civil society and the political society (State) based

---

[27] *DH,* §2.

[28] Pope John Paul II, *Christifideles Laici,*§39, https://www.vatican.va/content/john-paul-ii/en/apost_exhortations/documents/hf_jp-ii_exh_30121988_christifideles-laici.html.

[29] Pope Paul VI, *Populorum Progressio*, (hereafter cited as *PP*) §81, https://www.vatican.va/content/paul-vi/en/encyclicals/documents/hf_p-vi_enc_26031967_populorum.html.

[30] *Justice in the World* (hereafter to be cited as *JW*), §9.

[31] *JW*, §40-46.

[32] *CSDC*, §417.

[33] *CSDC*, §417.

[34] *CSDC*, §418.

on the principle of subsidiarity, on the other.[35] It makes a strong case that it is the responsibility of the State to ensure the freedom of religion, which is one of the sublime freedoms to be exercised in civil society.[36]

Pope Benedict XVI, as mentioned above, articulated the Christian responsibility to build up the civil sphere: "Building a just social and civil order, wherein each person receives what is his or her due, is an essential task which every generation must take up anew."[37] In the context of speaking about applying the principles of distributive justice to the economic domain, he advised the developed countries to grant economic aid to underdeveloped countries. Herein he took care to mention that in the distribution of aid, the receiving governments should also involve the "bearers of cultures within civil society, including *local Churches* (italics mine)."[38]

Today, Pope Francis open-mindedly embraces the role of civil society in his vision for the participatory Church – the synodal Church. He relates its role to resolve some of our pressing common concerns like that of the ecological crisis, issue of migrants and refugees, and, misery of the poor. He attributes the present day eco-crises and tragedies suffered by the poor to lack of cultivation in civil society of human responsibility and solidarity to one another and to the nature.[39] He speaks similarly about the condition of migrants: "At present ... migration is affected by the loss of that sense of responsibility for our brothers and sisters on which every civil society is based."[40] He desires the civil society institutions to cultivate these "foundations", even while working for common good beyond the pursuit of economic profit and efficient systems: "What we need in fact are states and civil institutions that are present and active, that look beyond the free and efficient working of certain economic, political or ideological systems, and are primarily concerned with individuals and the common good."[41] Going further, he wants the virtues of citizenship to be cultivated in civil society.[42] He envisions a substantive role to be played by

---

[35] *CSDC*, §§417-420.

[36] *CSDC*, §§421-423.

[37] *DCE*, §28.

[38] Pope Benedict XVI, *Caritas in Veritate* (hereafter cited as *CV*), §58, https://www.vatican.va/content/benedict-xvi/en/encyclicals/documents/hf_ben-xvi_enc_20090629_caritas-in-veritate.html.

[39] He says, "[O]ur lack of response to these tragedies involving our brothers and sisters points to the loss of that sense of responsibility for our fellow men and women upon which all civil society is founded" (LS, §25).

[40] Pope Francis, *Fratelli Tutti* (hereafter to be cited as *FT*), §40, https://www.vatican.va/content/francesco/en/encyclicals/documents/papa-francesco_20201003_enciclica-fratelli-tutti.html.

[41] *FT*, §108.

[42] *FT*, §131.

institutions or organizations of civil society under the principle of subsidiarity in any given political system.[43] And, true to the Catholic spirit, he wants a public role for religion, in a spirit of solidarity, to shape up the institutions of civil society.[44]

Pope Francis's passionate plea as found in his documents to participate in institutions of civil society for the common good, and his efforts at meeting with different political leaders to mediate peace, contribute significantly to a Catholic culture of engaging the civil society. As Rafael Luciani states, "Francis assumes these efforts by supporting social and civil movements, because these movements collaborate to build a more inclusive and just society. His Papacy, inspired by a Latin American ecclesial and theological identity, is a testimony of how secular society and religious institutions can join forces for the common good of all people, based on an ethics of democratic citizenship, ecclesial synodality and social participation."[45]

Thus, we see that the Catholic Church has progressively opened itself up to civil society. From being "the one" which either "antagonized", "imposed itself upon" or "patronized", the Catholic Church has come to participate in civil society with greater mutuality with different others. While doing so, it has come to emphasize the core constituent values of civil society like human dignity, freedom, religious freedom, subsidiarity, solidarity, and common good.

CST and the Core Values of Civil Society

From the beginning of the modern CST, certain fundamentals of civil society have been at its heart. Human dignity and freedom, inspired by the Christian doctrine of *imago dei*, have been consistently promoted as the basis for human rights, equality, solidarity and non-discrimination between human beings; along with them, honesty, truthfulness, transparency and due respect for legitimate authority have been taught as cherished values of public life; and, again, from the beginning, a special care for the poor and the vulnerable has been an integral part of the CST. Similarly, common good, with a transcendental orientation which distinguishes it from secular liberal conceptions of common good, has been promoted to be the very basis for civil society.

From the time of Leo XIII when a revival of the philosophical theology of Thomas Aquinas took place in the Catholic Church, ideas of the external natural order of the universe, the internal conscience and inner order based on moral reasoning, the civil and political order at the societal level, and ultimately the divine order which undergirds all of these came to undergird the Catholic social thought. This thinking in terms of "orders" or "structures" came to inform

---

[43] *FT*, §175.

[44] *EG*, §183.

[45] Rafael Luciani, "Pope Francis and the Theology of the People", in Justin Beaumont, ed. *The Routledge Handbook of Postsecularity* (New York: Routledge, 2019), 221.

the doctrine of common good analogous to a civil structural reality. As seen earlier, through *Mater et Magistra* and *Pacem in Terris* of Pope John XXIII, the idea of the common good evolved to be definitively stated in *Gaudium et Spes* of the Vat II as: "the sum of those conditions of social life which allow social groups and their individual members relatively thorough and ready access to their own fulfillment."[46] This "definition" has been interpreted further in the *Catechism of the Catholic Church*, which speaks of the common good at three levels: 1) God, the ultimate good, standing for the dimension of "fulfillment"; 2) human dignity and freedom for the individual; and, 3) the conditions of social life which include the civil, political and the organs of the State.[47] Thus we see a holistic and substantive understanding of common good, integrating the role of civil society, emergent within the CST.

As Bradley V. Lewis, a political philosopher, observes, the "idea of the common good has played a central normative role in the history of western political thought and occupied a signature place in the modern social teaching of the Roman Catholic Church."[48] While the western political thought secularized this idea in terms of civil government and common wealth supported with theories of 'social contract', the Catholic social thought continued with its religious attributes.

It is interesting to see that a parallel between the Catholic and the secular engagements with common good and civil society lives on. Today, both Pope Francis and the supporters of civic communitarianism speak of the potentials of participation for common good. As Iseult Honohan, one of the leading proponents of civic republicanism, avers, participation brings different others together to be engaged in deliberations for their common future; it enables an individual to be articulate through the mode of 'public reasoning' and join in the process of decision-making for common good; it opens oneself up to dialoguing with different others and consider alien viewpoints, even when they are antagonistic; it instils a sense of ownership with the project being deliberated; and it cultivates the ability to deal with plurality.[49] Pope Francis integrates these dynamics of participation in the synodal project in a significant way, and promotes full participatory momentum both within the Church and in civil society for common good.

---

[46] *GS*, §26.

[47] Pope John Paul II, *Catechism of the Catholic Church*, https://www.vatican.va/archive/ENG0015/_INDEX.HTM.

[48] V. Bradley Lewis, "Catholic Social Teaching on the Common Good," in *Catholic Social Teaching – A Volume of Scholarly Essays,* eds. Gerard V Bradely and E. Christian Brugger (Cambridge: Cambridge University Press, 2019), 247.

[49] Cf. Iseult Honohan, *Civic Republicanism* (UK: Routledge), 216-236.

A Civilization of Love and Civil Friendship

The Catholic social teachings, especially in the *Compendium* and the encyclical *Fratelli Tutti*, speak about creating a "civilization of love." The *Compendium* says: "[S]ocial life becomes more human the more it is characterized by efforts to bring about a more mature awareness of the ideal towards which it should be oriented, which is the "civilization of love."[50] The *Compendium* further observes: "[A] community has solid foundations when it tends toward the integral promotion of the person and of the common good."[51] Creating a civilization of love is an invitation to build a civic community based on the liberal values of freedom and rights on the one hand and on the communitarian values of common good, solidarity and fraternity on the other.

As the CST has dwelt upon it on several occasions, and as Jacque Maritain, the famous philosopher-theologian, has proposed it in his writings,[52] a person is more than an individual: while an individual is understood in a modern framework in terms of an aggregation of traits and merits, endowed with freedom and rights, a human person is a wholesome self that integrates the material dimensions with spiritual dimensions which nurture the transcendental openness of the human. A person is a gift to be encountered in a context of social life with love than to be treated in a calculative measure.

Similarly, a community is a relational space for encounter of persons rather than an aggregate of individuals. Such a community matures when it engages in relationality, interactions, dialogues, networks, and structures that foster common good. Collective goals, pursued in egalitarian participation of human persons, as individuals and groups, nourish the bonds of "civil friendship." By "civil friendship" the *Compendium* means the "the most genuine actualization of the principle of fraternity, which is inseparable from that of freedom and equality."[53] Civic friendship ties together liberal values of freedom and equality with the communitarian virtue of fraternity – a virtue that Pope Francis yearns for in our times.[54] As he laments, "today … we lost the taste of fraternity,"[55] in spite of "gorging" ourselves into networking; [W]e have become "[P]risoners of a virtual reality," but, "lost the taste and flavour of the truly real."[56] To overcome these systemic forms of isolation, fraternity and common good are the signposts to navigate.

---

[50] CSDC, §391.

[51] *CSDC*, §391.

[52] Jacque Maritain, *The Person and the Common Good* (Notre Dame: University of Notre Dame Press, 1972 [originally published in 1946]).

[53] *CSDC*, §390.

[54] *FT*, §8.

[55] *FT*, §33.

[56] *FT*, §33.

As Michael Coulter, a professor of political science, observes, "[C]ivil friendship is an activity that must be learned and practiced, and the Church can play a great role in teaching these duties and helping its faithful acquire the habits of civil friendship."[57] Indian Catholic Church would do well to commit itself to developing this *civic friendship* in the wider Indian society through civic forums and public institutions. The major obstacle to civil friendship in India is the presence of unmeaning hierarchies and discrimination based on caste, and the consequent brokenness of social life. It needs a concerted and sustained intervention to weaken such obstacles of inequality and discriminatory practices. As elsewhere, the Indian Catholic Church is a major player in the sphere of education, and the opportunity can be meaningfully lived out. With its resources in the public domain, it can embark upon a new era of forging civic friendship with the "civic modes" of dialogues.

"Culture of Encounter" and Dialogues / Conversations: The Civic Modes

Pope Francis identifies and promotes a culture of encounter in the present-day globalized context of thick plurality and high interdependence in cultural, economic, political, and social relationships. It is a "culture which privileges dialogue as a form of encounter."[58] He speaks about three major areas of dialogues – "dialogue with states, dialogue with society – including dialogue with cultures and the sciences – and dialogue with other believers who are not part of the Catholic Church."[59] They include one's encounter with God, with one's own self, and with different others, especially with the poor and the marginalized; and they imply dialogues between different cultures, religions, disciplinary sciences, moral goods, ideologies, and political systems. All are perpetually involved in encounters through multiple forms of dialogue.[60] He states that, "a culture of encounter means that we, as a people, should be passionate about meeting others, seeking points of contact, building bridges, planning a project that includes everyone."[61]

An image that the pope uses to capture the nature of the dialogical encounter is *polyhedron*. It stands for an encounter that brings together different others with their own unique features and radical differences. Compared to a

---

[57] Michael L. Coulter, "Serving the Person through the Political Community Reflections on Compendium Chapter 8," *Catholic Social Thought American Reflections on the Compendium*, eds. D. Paul Sullins and Anthony J. Blasi (Lexington Books, 2009), 105.

[58] *EG*, §239.

[59] *EG*, §238.

[60] That entire sections in *Laudato Si'* (chapter 5), *Evangelii Gaudium* (section IV of chapter 4) and *Fratelli Tutti* (chapter 6) are dedicated to examining multiple kinds and levels of dialogues evidence the priority accorded by Pope Francis to dialogue as a primary way for existing in a world of plurality and culture of encounter.

[61] *FT*, §216.

sphere, where different points gain their value in terms of their relationship to a perceived center, in a polyhedron, every point obtains value in terms of its unique potential, resources, and contexts. The pope explains:

> The image of a polyhedron can represent a society where differences coexist, complementing, enriching and reciprocally illuminating one another, even amid disagreements and reservations. Each of us can learn something from others. No one is useless and no one is expendable. This also means finding ways to include those on the peripheries of life. For they have another way of looking at things; they see aspects of reality that are invisible to the centres of power where weighty decisions are made.[62]

In this polyhedral vision, differences are not obstacles but creative elements for progress. In his words: "differences are creative; they create tension and in the resolution of tension lies humanity's progress."[63]

In encouraging dialogue, Pope Francis, as we know, is not beginning a new tradition. Dialogue has been promoted in the Catholic Church for several decades after the Second Vatican Council. For example, the short Vatican II document, *Nostra Aetate*, speaks about "dialogues and collaboration" with people of other religions; [64] *Gaudium et Spes* advocates "brotherly dialogue" to cultivate interpersonal relationships in the context of increasing individualism;[65] and Paul VI's *Populorum Progressio* views "sincere dialogue" to create "brotherly love" as the mark of progress and development; [66] John Paul II discusses the dialogue between faith and reason; [67] and Benedict XVI speaks of truth (logos) that creates dia-logos (dialogue) for communication and communion.[68]

However, there are elements that distinguish Pope Francis from the previous teachings on dialogue. First of all, he widens the horizons of dialogue from the usual religious or cultural realms to social, political, economic, ecological, and educational arenas. The impressive list of levels and fields he brings into the ambit of dialogue marks him out. In *Laudato Si'*, he discusses dialogues to be undertaken at international, national, and local levels to bring together the fields of politics, economics, religion, and the sciences.[69] These

---

[62] *FT*, §215.

[63] *FT*, §203.

[64] *NA*, §2.

[65] *GS*, §23.

[66] *PP*, §73 and §66.

[67] John Paul II, *Fides et Ratio,* (hereafter cited as *FR*), §48. https://www.vatican.va/content/john-paul-ii/en/encyclicals/documents/hf_jp-ii_enc_14091998_fides-et-ratio.htmlJohn Paul II says: "The *parrhesia* of faith must be matched by the boldness of reason."

.[68] *CV*, §4.

[69] *LS*, §163–201.

diverse fields and levels of encounter tell us how every moment of our life is dialogical. They illuminate the richness, spiritual depth, creative potential, and religious visions of a life of dialogue.

Secondly, he differentiates himself in proposing dialogues that are more dynamic, contemporaneous, and open-ended, as distinct from those proposed by the philosopher Pope John Paul II and the theologian Pope Benedict XVI. Pope John Paul II, while proposing dialogue between faith and reason, sees philosophic thought as "often the only ground for understanding and dialogue with those who do not share our faith."[70] Benedict XVI, reflecting on "love in truth" (*Caritas in Veritate*), dwells upon the theme of "truth enlightening love" wherein truth, the logos—analogous to Jesus Christ, the revealed logos, creates dia-logos, "hence communication and communion."[71] While the former focuses on the philosophic thought, the latter sees the truth—the logos—as the basic framework for dialogue. Pope Francis understands dialogue in terms of the ongoing reality of encounter. For him, truth is dynamic, emerging through experiences of dialogue, mutual relationships, and creative initiatives. "Together, we can seek the truth in dialogue," says the pope.[72]

Thirdly, Pope Francis brings in more passionately the poor, the marginalized, and the victims of exploitation, including the earth, to be partners in dialogues. For him, dialogue obtains its primary significance if done with the poor and the marginalized. His words are instructive:

> If we wish to dialogue, we should do this in the first place with the poor. They are not just another party to be won over, or merely another individual seated at a table of equals. They are our principal dialogue partners, those from whom we have the most to learn, to whom we need to listen out of a duty of justice, and from whom we must ask permission before presenting our proposals. Their words, their hopes and their fears should be the most authoritative voice at any table of dialogue..."[73]

Brining the poor to the centre of our dialogical life is very pertinent to our pandemic-vulnerable world. Making the poor, their hopes and fears, the validating concerns of dialogues take us on the path of cultivating responsibility and care for the vulnerable. It is not that the poor become objects of sympathy, but a source of our hope and resilience.

---

[70] *FR*, §104.

[71] *CV*, §4.

[72] *FT*, §50.

[73] Pope Francis, *Querida Amazonia*, §26, https://www.vatican.va/content/francesco/en/apost_exhortations/documents/papa-francesco_esortazione-ap_20200202_querida-amazonia.html.

Indian Context

Indian Christianity, especially the Catholic Christianity, has been involved for over five centuries in different forms of "dialogues" known as "adaptation", "inculturation", "indigenization", "Indianisation", and so on to contextualize the Christian message in the Indian soil. These initiatives are also attempts at inspiring others to appreciate the truth of Christianity. As *Ecclesia in Asia* points out Asia is the cradle of the major religions of the world, including Christianity, and that there are, among the people, an abiding "spiritual quest" and a deep-seated "yearning" to search after the truth. Dialogues, not as "instruments" but as the very way of life, enable Christians to engage with these quest and yearning, even while bearing witness to its own truth. The "social teachings of CBCI" (Catholic Bishops Conference of India), even by 2004, had articulated four major areas of dialogue as 1) with cultures, 2) with religions, 3) with ideologies, and 4) with the poor and the marginalized, and encouraged its faithful to implement them.[74]

These initiatives and attempts have indeed born fruits, however small may be their visibility amidst a sea of humanity with their innumerable faith-traditions. The many dialogue centres, personalities and journals dedicated to this cause continue to nourish abilities for mutual learning. However, today they have, unwittingly though, stirred a new challenge in the context of the Hindutva radicalization: A "suspicion" has been cast upon the Christian involvements in "dialogue"! Initiatives under this banner are seen as invidious attempts at converting the other into the Christian fold! The suspicion keeps spawning antagonism towards the very practice of dialogue itself.

In this context, the broad-basing of dialogues, integrating even economic and political aspects of life and reorienting them in polyhedral modes, opens up civic avenues for interactions with others for the sake of common good. The encyclical *Ecclesia in Asia*, even while appreciating the religious creativity of Asian people and even recognizing the "soteriological" character of their traditions, speaks of the need of bringing to birth a civilization of love by cultivating the values of human freedom, dignity and rights, along with solidarity and common good. The Indian Catholic Church has been living out its social concerns by undertaking huge projects of poverty-alleviation, disaster management, establishing units of health care, literacy campaigns, developmental initiatives and national integration programmes. It is time now that the Church entered the civic space, by improving upon "conversational" abilities and resources, to work in solidarity with others for common good.

The dialogical method of cultivating fraternity, solidarity and common good, emphasized very much by the more recent Catholic social teachings,

---

[74] John Desrochers, *The Social Teaching of the Church in India* (Bangalore: NBCLC/CSA, 2006), 65-78.

especially those of Pope Francis, inspires newer visions of "dialogues" in an Indian context of civil society. The way the Pope widens the arenas of dialogue from religion and culture to social, political, economic and educational realms, and that too in a polyhedral model, not merely captures a wider reality of life, but also gives a "civic orientation" to dialogue.

The Catholic social teachings, as seen above, have come today to give importance to community, fraternity, solidarity and common good. This goes with the long-standing emphasis on human dignity, freedom, autonomy and rights. Indeed, both these sets of values are being integrated in a civilization of love ultimately springing from our deep faith in a transcendent creator God. This fundamental import or vision of the CST, premised upon the philosophical-theology of natural law, has potentials to "converse" with similar visions like the religio-ethical vision of dharma in the Indian context. Dharma is being propagated today as the overarching vision to support public policies, political power, governance, and even individual and family lives in the Indian context. Dharma, an ancient concept of Indian traditions, initially stood for a universal cosmic and moral order. But, unfortunately, it was distorted to build up a *varna* dharma that has been discriminatory, divisive, authoritarian, and oppressive. The *varna* dharma became an lopsided ethical and religious ground to trample upon the human dignity and rights of people treated as "low castes" and "depressed classes" for many centuries. In the present-day revival of the concept, one finds also the presence of "concerted ambiguities", which make the concept Janus-faced. In this context, it would do well that the vision of CST dialogues with dharma so as to redeem the latter's positive potentials to build up a civic community based on the universal values of human rights and duties. Similarly, it would do well that the CST strengthens its bearings on the communitarian dimension by its dialogue with the vision of dharma. A fruitful public conversation between CST and dharma would be in the right direction today.[75]

Entering the civil spheres by developing the conversational skills and involving in public conversations with other axiomatic moral visions like dharma can go a long way to create a civilization of love based on multiple forms of civic friendship. Such a civilization of love will also create a civic system of care that will see humanity through thick and thin in more confident and dignified ways.

---

[75] For a more detailed discussion on dharma and a dialogue with it from the Christian perspective, see my articles: Gnana Patrick, "Pope Francis, Culture of Encounter, the Common Good, and Dharma: Public Theological Conversations Today," *Theological Studies,* Vol. 84(2), 2023, 212-228. DOI 10.1177/00405639231171730; Gnana Patrick, "A Public Theology of Dharma." *Vidyajoti Journal of Theological Reflections* 81 (2017), September, 644-662. ISSN 0970-1079. Reg. No. 45761/86.

Conclusion

Among the many vulnerabilities exposed by the pandemic COVID 19, the lack of a "civic structure of care" makes India yet more vulnerable. It bodes ill for facing up to future catastrophes of similar nature. While thinking of constructing a "civic structure of care", one finds meaningful the present-day endeavours of forging syntheses between the liberal and the communitarian political principles of human dignity and common good. They seek to nurture the bonds of civil society upon the indices of human rights, citizenship, equality, liberty, fraternity, solidarity, participation and common good on a communitarian-liberal framework. In this regard, the Catholic social teaching stands out as a potent corpus that can be resourced to cultivate the values of this synthesis. The corpus has been engaging with civil society in a progressively open-minded manner, and it has come today to envisage the civil society as the main arena for addressing the major common concerns today. It seeks to develop a civilization of love constituted by civic friendship, wherein human freedom and dignity, premised on the transcendental orientation of humanity, are integrated with virtues of solidarity, fraternity and common good, resourced from the Christian faith-community. As a method of developing these virtues, the corpus has come to dwell elaborately today upon the dialogical modes of a culture of encounter. The Catholic Church in India would do well to converse in public with other Indian visions of moral common good to strengthen the bonds of civil society and come up with a "civic structure of care."

9

Pope Francis, Culture of Encounter, the Common Good, and Dharma Public Theological Conversations Today

Introduction

Today, resonances of Francis's pontificate reach across regions and sociopolitical landscapes. An apt testimony to this is given by Nageswari Annamalai, a person with a Hindu background and author of *Pope Francis—New Manifestation of Hope*.[1] She observes that she wrote the book because of her appreciation for Pope Francis's character and activities—in particular, his non-judgmental attitude to other religionists; his readiness to dialogue with different religious and political leaders; his concern for ecological well-being, the poor, migrants, and refugees; and his readiness to play a role in settling political disputes. Annamalai believes that everyone, regardless of religion or region of the world, can benefit from the pope's values and contributions.[2]

In this essay, I want to take a cue from her writing and explore aspects of public theology in Pope Francis's writings.[3] His reflections on the culture of encounter and the common good can join in a public theological conversation

---

[1] Nageswari Annamalai, *Pope Francis—Nambikkaiyin Puthiya Parimanam* [Tamil; trans. Pope Francis—New Manifestation of Hope] (Trichy: Adaiyalam Publications, 2017).

[2] She took up the challenge of getting to know the person and activities of Pope Francis by extended research, evident in the content and quality of the book.

[3] For a concise understanding of public theology, see Sebastian C. H. Kim, *Theology in the Public Sphere: Public Theology as a Catalyst for Open Debate* (London: SCM Press, 2011); Sebastian Kim and Katie Day, eds., *A Companion to Public Theology* (Leiden: Brill, 2017).

with dharma,[4] a core religioethical teaching found in the many forms of Hinduism, Buddhism, Jainism, and even in the oral literature of popular religious traditions in South Asia. I will explore the possibilities of this conversation in four steps. In the first step, I will highlight certain aspects of Francis's public theology. I will then present his reflections on the culture of encounter and the common good. In the third section, I will give an account of the concept of dharma. Finally, I discuss a few areas of public theological conversation that are possible between Francis's reflections and dharma.

Public Theology and the Theology of Public Life

Coursing through current writings on public theology, we find two streams: public theology *as such*" and theology of public life.[5] Doing public theology, in the first sense, would, as envisioned by David Tracy, mean reflecting on the very "publicness" of theology.[6] Such a reflection would defend the possibility that faith in a transcendent God is valid and meaningful to life and that theology has a place in the public sphere like other sciences. The theology of public life is different: it reflects ethically and theologically on common concerns of public life and does it from within a particular faith-tradition. This position is the methodological corollary of the contemporary linguistic realization that we are all, in a fundamental sense, located within our own particular traditions and must duly acknowledge their role in our lives. A theologian practicing the theology of public life is one who is located within a particular religious tradition and yet strives to speak in ways accessible to both the religious and the non-religious in a public forum about concerns common to all.[7]

---

[4] Public theological conversations are dialogues on religious insights undertaken in forums of public spheres, like those of civil societies, to foster cooperation between different others for pursuing common goals. To understand what is specific about this type of conversation, we can consider the description by Jeffrey Stout. Such a rich dialogue, he suggests, entails "an exchange of views in which the respective parties express their premises in as much detail as they see fit and in whatever idiom they wish, try to make sense of each other's perspectives, and expose their own commitments to the possibility of criticism." Jeffrey Stout, *Democracy and Traditions* (Princeton: Princeton University Press, 2004), 10–11. Stout discusses the appropriateness of the word "conversation" for religious reasoning in public forums in the context of Richard Rorty's famous criticism of religion as a "conversation-stopper."

[5] For a discussion on this distinction see Felix Wilfred, *Asian Public Theologies: Critical Concerns in our Challenging Times* (New Delhi: ISPCK, 2010).

[6] David Tracy, *The Analogical Imagination: Christian Theology and the Culture of Pluralism* (London: SCM Press, 1981).

[7] Charles T. Mathewes, *Theology of Public Life* (Cambridge: Cambridge University Press, 2007).

Aspects of Public Theology in Pope Francis

In light of the foregoing discussion, Pope Francis can be seen as embodying some important aspects of public theology. For example, we see him arguing in public forums with those of different traditions about the need to reawaken the faith in a transcendent God today. Of course, the Catholic Church has always spoken about the need for faith in a transcendent God; it is the mainstay of the Catholic faith. What is new in Pope Francis is his call for a "reawakening of faith" in the present-day context of deeply entrenching materialistic ethos, along with unbridled greed and the associated ecological problems that it has ensued. For example, in the "Document on Human Fraternity for World Peace and Living Together," jointly issued with the Grand Imam of Al-Azhar Ahmad Al-Tayyeb, Francis argues for reawakening "religious awareness among young people so that future generations may be protected from the realm of materialistic thinking and from dangerous policies of unbridled greed and indifference."[8] The need for "awakening religious consciousness" is necessary, the document argues, in order to "confront tendencies that are individualistic, selfish, [and] conflicting."[9] Similarly, *Fratelli Tutti* calls the church to "'reawaken the spiritual energy' that can contribute to the betterment of society,"[10] and *Predicate Evangelium* suggests that the primary service of the church to human well-being is "to awaken in all peoples the hearing of faith" and bring the "supernatural gift of faith ... 'as a light for our way, guiding our journey through time.'"[11]

In addition, the pope, along with his predecessors, challenges those who privatize religion: "no one can demand that religion should be relegated to the inner sanctum of personal life, without influence on societal and national life, without concern for the soundness of civil institutions, without a right to offer an opinion on events affecting society."[12]

---

[8] Francis and the Grand Imam of Al-Azhar Ahamad al-Tayyib, "A Document on Human Fraternity for World Peace and Living Together" to the United Arab Emirates (February 4, 2019), https://www.vatican.va/content/francesco/en/travels/2019/outside/documents/papa-francesco_20190204_documento-fratellanza-umana.html.

[9] Francis, "Human Fraternity."

[10] Francis, *Fratelli Tutti*, Encyclical Letter on Fraternity and Social Friendship, October 3, 2020, §270, https://www.vatican.va/content/francesco/en/encyclicals/documents/papa-francesco_20201003_enciclica-fratelli-tutti.html (hereafter cited as *FT*).

[11] Francis, *Praedicate Evangelium*," Apostolic Constitution on the Roman Curia and Its Service to the Church in the World, March 19, 2022, §1–2, https://www.vatican.va/content/francesco/en/apost_constitutions/documents/20220319-costituzione-ap-praedicate-evangelium.html.

[12] Francis, *Evangelii Gaudium* (24 November 2013), §150, https://www.vatican.va/content/francesco/en/apost_exhortations/documents/papa-francesco_esortazione-ap_20131124_evangelii-gaudium.html.

What characterizes Francis's stance is a "founding rupture" with Christian theology's inhibition towards the public sphere, one that originated in the Enlightenment era. This is the argument made in a recent article by a group of three public theologians: Alfredo Teixeira, Alex Villas Boas, and Jefferson Zeferino.[13] They argue that Pope Francis's writings point to a new theological "going forth" that can be taken as an instance of the founding rupture. In their own words: "the current Catholic pontificate may be understood as a movement of instaurational rupture in favor of a public theology dynamic."[14] Thus we see the pope defending a public theological role for the papacy and, by implication, for every Christian.

Aspects of the Theology of Public Life in Pope Francis

As discussed above, a theology of public life reflects upon common concerns of humanity from within one's own tradition but in a public sphere wherein multiple traditions are present. Such reflections offer an open invitation to others either to be inspired by this particular tradition or to theologize similarly from within their own particular traditions about the common good. *Lautado Si'* offers a good example: the pope takes up "the care of the earth"—a concern throughout the world—as the subject of a theological reflection. The encyclical seeks to "bring the whole human family together to seek a sustainable and integral development" as a remedy for our present-day crisis.[15] The theological reflection arises out of the Christian, if not specifically Catholic, tradition. This particular grounding is evident in how it takes its inspiration from Saint Francis of Assisi (a Catholic saint), integrates a biblical theology of creation, analyzes the root causes of the problem with the help of sciences, proposes dialogue at both the international and national level for "integral ecology," and ends with spiritual exhortations calling for the sacramental practice of Eucharist, faith in Trinity, and devotion to Mary. It is, thus, a moral theological document on a public concern that firmly emerges from the Catholic tradition, even as the intended audience extends beyond that tradition—that is, other religionists, along with non-believers and those indifferent to religion.

The pope observes that "we need to realize that the solutions will not emerge from just one way of interpreting and transforming reality" and therefore encourages wider participation of people from different ideological

---

[13] Alfredo Teixeira, Alex Villas Boas, and Jefferson Zeferino, "Public Theology in the Context of the Religious Dualization Phenomenon in Multiple Modernities," *International Journal of Public Theology* 16, no. 2 (June 2022): 216–37, https://doi.org/10.1163/15697320-20220041.

[14] Teixeira, Boas, and Zeferino, "Public Theology," 235.

[15] Pope Francis, *Laudato Si'*, Encyclical Letter on the Care for Our Common Home (May 14, 2015), §13, https://www.vatican.va/content/francesco/en/encyclicals/documents/papa-francesco_20150524_enciclica-laudato-si.html (hereafter cited as *LS*).

persuasions in order to solve a common problem.[16] Such participation, in the form of dialogues or conversations at various levels, should seek to integrate the "various cultural riches … their art and poetry, their interior life and spirituality" in response to the problems facing us.[17] If humanity is earnest in finding a remedy for the ecological crisis, then "no branch of the sciences and no form of wisdom can be left out," the pope observes, "and that includes religion and the language particular to it."[18] He encourages all to embrace an "'ecological citizenship' that can be understood as the foundation of new civic forms of relationships between humans and other living beings."[19]

This is a good example of a theology of public life found in Pope Francis's writings. Though concern for the environment is present in Catholic social teaching starting with Pope Paul VI's encyclical *Octogesima Adveniens*,[20] Pope Francis's treatment of the subject is more elaborate, gripping, and dialogical: he devotes an entire encyclical to this common concern and invites everyone to join in public conversations for cultivating the virtue of integral ecology. The culture of encounter that he advocates very pertinently facilitates such conversations.

A Culture of Encounter and the Common Good

Pope Francis identifies, as well as promotes, a culture of encounter in the present-day globalized context of thick plurality and high interdependence in cultural, economic, political, and social relationships. These relationships deeply impact us, even amidst conflicts, confrontations, and fragmentations. Quoting Vinicius de Moraes, a Brazilian poet, the pope states that "life, for all its confrontations, is the art of encounter."[21] And the space created by this encounter is, for the pope, the "luminous space opened up by God's love for all his creatures."[22] It is indeed an opening of new horizons and hope in our lives.

The pope points to several requirements on our part for experiencing the culture of encounter. It requires that we be available to the other more openly. He states, "a culture of encounter means that we, as a people, should be passionate

[16] *LS*, §63.

[17] *LS*, §63.

[18] *LS*, §63.

[19] *LS*, §211 and Jelson Roberto de Oliveira and Clovis Ultramari, "The Eutopian City: The Challenge of Urban Conviviality in the *Laudato Si'* and *Fratelli Tutti* Encyclicals," *International Journal of Public Theology* 16, no. 2 (2022): 168, https://doi.org/10.1163/15697320-20220038.

[20] Paul VI, *Octogesima Adveniens*, Apostolic Letter (May 14, 1971), §21, https://www.vatican.va/content/paul-vi/en/apost_letters/documents/hf_p-vi_apl_19710514_octogesima-adveniens.html.

[21] *FT*, §215.

[22] Francis, *Veritatis Gaudium*, Apostolic Constitution on Ecclesiastical Universities and Facilities (January 29, 2018), §4.a.

about meeting others, seeking points of contact, building bridges, planning a project that includes everyone."[23] It is a "culture which privileges dialogue as a form of encounter."[24] This dialogue is not just a method of achieving consensus for Pope Francis but a way of life. It includes one's encounter with God, with one's own self, and with different others, especially with the poor and the marginalized in social relationships, as well as dialogues between different cultures, religions, disciplinary sciences, moral goods, ideologies, and political systems. All are perpetually involved in abiding encounters through multiple forms of dialogue.[25]

An image that the pope uses to capture the dialogical encounter is the polyhedron, which reflects his appreciation of the reality of plurality today. It stands for a type of encounter that brings together different others with their own unique features and radical differences. With a sphere, different points gain their value in terms of their relationship to a perceived normative center. In contrast, with the polyhedron, every point obtains value in terms of its unique potential, resources, and contexts. He explains:

> The image of a polyhedron can represent a society where differences coexist, complementing, enriching and reciprocally illuminating one another, even amid disagreements and reservations. Each of us can learn something from others. No one is useless and no one is expendable. This also means finding ways to include those on the peripheries of life. For they have another way of looking at things; they see aspects of reality that are invisible to the centres of power where weighty decisions are made.[26]

In this polyhedral vision, differences are not obstacles but creative elements for progress. He says: "differences are creative; they create tension and in the resolution of tension lies humanity's progress."[27]

In encouraging dialogue, Pope Francis is not beginning a new tradition. Dialogue has been promoted in the Catholic Church for a long time. For example, the short Vatican II document, *Nostra Aetate*, speaks about "dialogues and collaboration" with people of other religions; [28] *Gaudium et Spes* advocates

---

[23] *FT*, §216.

[24] *EG*, §239.

[25] That entire sections in *Laudato Si'* (chapter 5), *Evangelii Gaudium* (section IV of chapter 4) and *Fratelli Tutti* (chapter 6) are dedicated to examining multiple kinds and levels of dialogues evidence the priority accorded by Pope Francis to dialogue as a primary way for existing in a world of plurality and culture of encounter.

[26] *FT*, §215.

[27] *FT*, §203.

[28] Paul VI, *Nostra Aetate*, The Relation of the Church to Non-Christian Religions (October 28, 1965), §2 https://www.vatican.va/archive/hist_councils/ii_vatican_council/documents/vat-ii_decl_19651028_nostra-aetate_en.html.

"brotherly dialogue" to cultivate interpersonal relationships in the context of increasing individualism;[29] and Paul VI's *Populorum Progressio* views "sincere dialogue" to create "brotherly love" as the mark of progress and development; [30] John Paul II discusses the dialogue between faith and reason;[31] and Benedict XVI speaks of truth (logos) that creates dia-logos (dialogue) for communication and communion.[32]

However, there are elements that distinguish Pope Francis from the previous teachings on, and engagement with, dialogue. First of all, the impressive list of levels and fields he brings into the ambit of dialogue marks him out. In *Laudato Si'*, he discusses dialogues at the international, national, and local level that bring together the fields of politics, economics, religion, and the sciences.[33] These diverse fields and levels of encounter underscore how every moment of our life is dialogical. They illuminate the richness, spiritual depth, creative potential, and religious visions of a life of dialogue.

Secondly, he distinguishes himself in proposing dialogues that are more dynamic, contemporaneous, and open-ended, as distinct from those proposed by the philosopher Pope John Paul II and the theologian Pope Benedict XVI. Pope John Paul II, while proposing dialogue between faith and reason, sees philosophic thought as "often the only ground for understanding and dialogue with those who do not share our faith."[34] Benedict XVI, reflecting on "love in truth" (*Caritas in Veritate*), dwells upon the theme of "truth enlightening love" wherein truth, the logos—analogous to Jesus Christ, the revealed logos, who said, "I am the truth" (Jn 10:6)—creates dia-logos, "hence communication and communion."[35] While the former focuses on philosophic thought, the latter sees the truth—the logos—as the basic framework for dialogue. Pope Francis understands dialogue in terms of the ongoing reality of encounter. For him, truth is dynamic, emerging through experiences of dialogue, mutual

[29] Paul VI, *Gaudium et Spes,* Pastoral Constitution on the Church in the Modern World (December 7, 1965), §23, https://www.vatican.va/archive/hist_councils/ii_vatican_council/documents/vat-ii_const_19651207_gaudium-et-spes_en.html.

[30] Paul VI, *Populorum Progressio*, Encyclical on the Development of Peoples (March 26, 1967), §73 and §66, https://www.vatican.va/content/paul-vi/en/encyclicals/documents/hf_p-vi_enc_26031967_populorum.html.

[31] John Paul II, *Fides et Ratio,* Encyclical Letter to the Bishops on the Relationship between Faith and Reason (September 14, 1998), §48. John Paul II says: "The *parrhesia* of faith must be matched by the boldness of reason," https://www.vatican.va/content/john-paul-ii/en/encyclicals/documents/hf_jp-ii_enc_14091998_fides-et-ratio.html.

[32] Benedict XVI, *Caritas in Veritate,* Encyclical Letter on Integral Human Development in Charity and Truth (June 29, 2009), §4, https://www.vatican.va/content/benedict-xvi/en/encyclicals/documents/hf_ben-xvi_enc_20090629_caritas-in-veritate.html.

[33] *LS,* §163–201.

[34] John Paul II, *Fides et Ratio*, §104.

[35] Benedict XVI, *Caritas in Veritate,* §4.

relationships, and creative initiatives. "Together, we can seek the truth in dialogue," says the pope.[36] His observation in *Evangelii Gaudium* regarding the proclamation of the Gospel is instructive:

> It should not impose the truth but appeal to freedom; it should be marked by joy, encouragement, liveliness and a harmonious balance which will not reduce preaching to a few doctrines which are at times more philosophical than evangelical. All this demands on the part of the evangelizer certain attitudes which foster openness to the message: approachability, readiness for dialogue, patience, a warmth and welcome which is non-judgmental.[37]

This dynamic opening to others through a process of dialogical encounters comes rather spontaneously to the pope. This may be due to his Jesuit background. David Hollenbach, a leading contemporary public theologian on Catholic social teaching and the common good, observes that the Jesuits have a history of bold missionary encounters with different civilizations.[38] This opening to others adds to Francis's credibility as a public theologian in a characteristically pluralist and multi-polar world, which, nevertheless, endeavors to live by the ideals of common good.

Pope Francis on the Common Good

Pope Francis's articulation of the common good is shaped by the rich history of Catholic social teaching on the subject. Pointing to the role of faith in the Catholic vision of the common good, he says, "faith is truly a good, a common good."[39] Underscoring the value of the dignity and rights of the human person, he states: "underlying the principle of the common good is respect for the human person as such, endowed with basic and inalienable rights ordered to his or her integral development."[40] In regard to family life, the pope observes that respecting the individuality of marriage partners is an important aspect of the common good.[41] In his writing on the environment, he says, "climate is a

---

[36] *FT*, §50.

[37] *EG*, §227.

[38] David Hollenbach, *The Common Good and Christian Ethics* (Cambridge: Cambridge University Press, 2004).

[39] Francis, *Lumen Fidei*, Encyclical Letter on Faith (June 29, 2013), §51, https://www.vatican.va/content/francesco/en/encyclicals/documents/papa-francesco_20130629_enciclica-lumen-fidei.html.

[40] *LS*, §157.

[41] Francis, *Amoris Laetitia,* Post-synodal Exhortation on Love in the Family (March 19, 2016), §139, https://www.vatican.va/content/francesco/en/apost_exhortations/documents/papa-francesco_esortazione-ap_20160319_amoris-laetitia.html.

common good."[42] Advocating distributive justice for marginal communities, he says, "the common good calls for social peace, the stability and security provided by a certain order which cannot be achieved without particular concern for distributive justice."[43] Emphasizing the smooth functioning of civil institutions and nations, he speaks for their independence and autonomous development as part of the common good.[44] Envisioning a global community of fraternity, the pope states: "The development of a global community of fraternity based on the practice of social friendship on the part of peoples and nations calls for a better kind of politics, one truly at the service of the common good."[45] Treating our solidarity with future generations as part of the common good, he says: "the global economic crises have made painfully obvious the detrimental effects of disregarding our common destiny, which cannot exclude those who come after us. We can no longer speak of sustainable development apart from intergenerational solidarity."[46] Thus we see that Pope Francis's articulation of the common good is well situated within Catholic social teaching.

However, we see that Francis treats the subject more as an open-ended process and a project in which everyone should be involved in ways that build on their distinctive potentials and empower their gifts. In *Rerum Novarum,* Leo XIII stated that all citizens were called to contribute to the common good, even while the responsibility for ensuring the right conditions for the common good had largely been thought to be the responsibility of civil / public authorities or the state.[47] In *Mater et Magistra*, John XXIII described the common good as the "social conditions which favour the full development of human personality" but believed that the responsibility of providing these conditions rested with public authorities.[48] The common good was more definitively articulated in structural terms by Paul VI in *Gaudium et Spes* as "the sum of those conditions of the social life whereby men, families and associations more adequately and readily may attain their own perfection."[49] This tradition of understanding the

---

[42] *LS*, §23.

[43] *LS*, §157.

[44] *FT*, §108, §143.

[45] *FT*, §154.

[46] *LS*, §159.

[47] Leo XIII, *Rerum Novarum*, Encyclical on Capital and Labor (May 15, 1891), §34, https://www.vatican.va/content/leo-xiii/en/encyclicals/documents/hf_l-xiii_enc_15051891_rerum-novarum.html.

[48] John XXIII, *Mater et Magistra*, Encyclical on Christianity and Social Progress (May 15, 1961), §65, https://www.vatican.va/content/john-xxiii/en/encyclicals/documents/hf_j-xxiii_enc_15051961_mater.html.

[49] Paul VI, *Gaudium et Spes,* §74.

common good in terms of the conditions of social living continues, and Pope Francis integrates this aspect in *Laudato Si.'*[50]

However, in several instances in his writings, the pope presents the common good more as a *process* in which everyone is involved and that its content and methods emerges through the loving participation of all in the process. For example, in the context of speaking about the role of communication in the contemporary world, the pope says, "we need constantly to ensure that present-day forms of communication are in fact guiding us to generous encounters with others, to honest pursuit of the whole truth, to service, closeness to the underprivileged and to the promotion of the common good."[51] Again, speaking about social peace, he says "it is an open-ended endeavour, a never-ending task that demands the commitment of everyone ... [and] this task summons us to persevere in the struggles to promote a culture of encounter."[52] At the center of this task is human dignity and the common good. Furthermore, he teaches that "we believers need to find occasions to speak with one another and to act together for the common good and the promotion of the poor."[53] These few selected statements give us a sense that working for the common good is a constant commitment of all by joining in a continuing open-ended process.

Pope Francis's understanding of the common good as an ongoing process grounds his focus on the concerns of the present day. Prominent among these is care for our earth in the face of the epochal environmental crisis, social friendship or fraternity in the face of alarmingly increasing social conflicts, and care for the vulnerable in the globalized context wherein the poor, migrants, and refugees are victimized. Though these concerns have been treated by previous popes, especially by his two immediate predecessors, I believe the elaborate and passionate way in which they are treated as indispensable concerns of the common good is distinct to Pope Francis.

For example, the pope integrates the well-being and dignity of the vulnerable, the poor, refugees, migrants, and the marginalized into his articulation of the common good. The pope articulates it aptly in *Laudato Si'*:

> In the present condition of global society, where injustices abound and growing numbers of people are deprived of basic human rights and considered expendable, the principle of the common good immediately becomes, logically and inevitably, a summons to solidarity and a preferential option for the poorest of our brothers and sisters. This option entails recognizing the implications of the universal destination of the world's goods, but, as I mentioned in

---

[50] *LS*, §156.

[51] *FT*, §205.

[52] *FT*, §232.

[53] *FT*, §282.

> the Apostolic Exhortation *Evangelii Gaudium*, it demands before all else an appreciation of the immense dignity of the poor in the light of our deepest convictions as believers. We need only look around us to see that, today, this option is in fact an ethical imperative essential for effectively attaining the common good.[54]

This import of the common good, which is a transcendental yet a temporal good, constituted by a concern for individual dignity, along with an emphasis on the rights of the poor, sustained by civil institutions, and continually nurtured through a culture of encounter, can well be an inspiring partner with others in public theological conversations.

Dharma

Dharma, a religioethical doctrine of universal well-being prevalent in South Asia, can become a potential partner in a public theological conversation. It is treated in a number of texts: in the Sanskritic scriptural texts of the Vedas, Upanishads, harmasutras, dharmashastras, *Puranas,* and *Bhagavad Gita*; in the texts of Buddhism and Jainism; in the texts of Saivism and Vaishnavism; and in the oral literatures of many grassroots popular religious traditions. As Indologist Patrick Olivelle observes, "dharma is ... central not only in the Brahmanical / Hindu traditions, but also in the Buddhist and Jain."[55]

Etymologically, the term dharma comes from the Sanskrit root *dhr*, which means to hold or support.[56] The term, in its verb form *dharman*, occurs in *Rig Veda*—the first of the four Vedic texts—and speaks of the cosmic actions of gods;[57] for example, "holding the sky and earth apart,"[58] "taking care of the smooth transitioning of seasons," and "protecting the creatures."[59] The actions of the gods were believed to be self-abnegating, carried out to maintain the cosmic order. Subsequently, these actions of the gods were mirrored in priests

---

[54] *LS*, §158.

[55] Patrick Olivelle, trans. and ed., *Dharmasutras: The Law of Codes of Apastamba, Gautama, Baudhayana, and Vasistha* (Oxford: Oxford University Press, 1999), xxxvii.

[56] For a detailed understanding of the etymological origin of this word see Patrick Olivelle, ed., *Dharma: Studies in its Semantic, Religious and Cultural History* (New Delhi: Motilal Banarsidas Publishers, 2009); Adam Bowles, *Dharma, Disorder and the Political in Ancient India: The Apaddharmaparvan of the Mahabharatha* (Leiden: Brill, 2007), 84; Paul Horsch, "From Creation Myth to World Law: The Early History of *Dharma*," trans. Jarrod L. Whatker, in Olivelle, *Dharma,* 2; Joel P. Brereton, "*Dharman* in the *Rgveda,*" in Olivelle, *Dharma*, 28.

[57] Bowles, *Dharma, Disorder and the Political*, 85; Brereton, "*Dharman* in the *Rgveda*," 27-67.

[58] Holding the sky and earth apart was considered the sublime activity of gods as per the Vedic cosmogony. Bowles, *Dharma, Disorder and the Political*, 85.

[59] Horsch, "From Creation Myth," 2.

who, through their ritual actions, were believed to be imitating the gods.[60] As Joel P. Brereton opines, these ritual actions were considered indispensable to the stability, regularity, and permanence of the cosmic order.[61]

During the age of Upanishads (ca. 700–500 BCE), which followed the Vedic age, the ritual and cosmic senses of dharma came to represent predominantly actions to maintain the social order. A group of Indian philosophers came to perceive dharma as a major transition from *rta* (the order in nature, the macrocosmic order) to *satya* (the inner microcosmic order, the moral law).[62] Human actions to maintain this order were prescribed in the dharmasutras and the dharmashastras, important Sanskritic texts that emerged towards the end of the Vedic age.[63] Here we begin to see two contrasting concepts of dharma. The Vedas deemed the fulfillment of the ritual actions as dharma, while the dharmasutras and dharmashastras defined dharma as fulfilling one's duty in social relationships. The latter prescribed duties as per one's *varna*, which was the primordial fourfold social division. Dharma (duty) as per the *manu-smriti (Laws of Manu, ca. 100 CE)* became *ashrama* dharma according to one's *varna* and therefore was known as *varnashrama* dharma.[64] As Indologist Paul Hacker notes, "*dharma* is by definition *varnashrama dharma*, that is the *dharma* of castes and life-stages."[65] Thus we see that the original meaning of dharma as action in relation to the outer cosmic order and the inner moral order was restricted to duties related to *varna*-based social order. This *varnashrama dharma* has held sway over the social relationship in the South Asian region for many centuries.

---

[60] Horsch, "From Creation Myth," 6.

[61] Brereton, "*Dharman* in the *Rgveda*," 29.

[62] Horsch, "From Creation Myth," 1–26.

[63] Adam Bowles places the emergence of dharmasutras between 600 and 400 BCE. Bowles, *Dharma, Disorder and the Political*, 37ff.; Patrick Olivelle notes P.V. Kane's dating of early documents of dharmasutras: "Kane (1962–75, i) has given some tentative upper and lower limits: Gautama 600–400, Apastamba 450–350, Baudhayana 500–200, and Vasistha 300–100, all BCE," Olivelle, *Dharmasutras: The Law Codes*, xxxi. Some of these periods coincide with those of Upanishads (700–500 BCE) which came at the end of Vedas. However, Olivelle himself places the period for the emergence of the earlier documents of dharmasutras between early third to the middle of second century BCE (Olivelle, *Dharmasutras,* xxxiv). If one goes by Olivelle, the period could be even after the period of the Upanishads. Since the focus of my article is not on the time-period, I request the readers to consult the experts on the subject.

[64] *Ashrama* stands for a stage in life and the anglicized plural *ashramas* refers to the four stages in life as prescribed in the *manu-smriti*, https://www.britannica.com/topic/Manu-smriti; Bowles, "*Dharma, Disorder and the Political*," 37; Neeraj Arjun Gupta, ed., *Views on Hindu Dharma by M.K. Gandhi* (London: Routledge, 2018), 82. Mahatma Gandhi claims to derive the concept of *varnashrama* dharma from *Bhagavad Gita.*

[65] Hacker, "Dharma in Hinduism," in Olivelle, ed. *Dharma*, 478.

However, today spiritual leaders and philosophers seek to revive the original meaning in terms of a universal order—cosmic and moral. For example, in *Hindu Dharma: The Universal Way of Life*, Chandrasekharendra Saraswathi, a well-known teacher of Vedantic Hinduism, makes a case for the universality of Hindu dharma.[66] He believes that this dharma, rooted in the Vedic religion, is the universal law that is present in the physical world and from which human beings derive their moral law (dharma). As nature experiences harmony when the physical laws are in order, so will human beings experience order when they submit themselves to this age-old dharma.[67] According to Saraswati, we should return to this dharma so that we can live in harmony, truthfulness, and justice.[68] It is apt to note here that Mahatma Gandhi, the face of the struggle for Indian political independence, also exhorts Indians to "restore the *varna dharma* to its purity," which, according to him, is a calling for a particular occupation as per one's birth and has nothing to do with the caste discrimination.[69]

There were also other versions of dharma prevalent in the South Asian region from very ancient times. For example, Buddhism spoke of *dhamma* (the rendering of dharma in the Pali language) as a core moral good cultivated through the four "immeasurables" (four jewels): *metta* (loving kindness), *karuna* (compassion), *mudita* (empathetic / sympathetic joy), and *upekkha* (equanimity). All four immeasurables are altruistic virtues oriented towards the well-being of all. As Annabella Pitkin observes, these virtues evoke "the foundational Buddhist values of love and compassion extended equally toward all living beings without bias or restriction."[70]

Furthermore, the many internal variations within the two major Hindu theistic traditions—Saivism and Vaisnavism—offer alternate interpretations of dharma. For example, a major popular narrative in Vaisnavism is about the ten avatars who were born at different epochs to establish dharma, the righteous moral and social order, whenever adharma, the opposite of dharma, surged ahead.[71] Another set of narratives, emergent during the modern era, especially

[66] Chandrasekharendra Saraswati, *Hindu Dharma: The Universal Way of Life* (Chennai: Bharathiya Vidya Bhavan, 1995), 70.

[67] Saraswati, *Hindu Dharma*, 31.

[68] Social reformers in India have invariably denounced this *varnasrama* dharma as the root cause of the caste system which legitimizes social discrimination and oppression. However, Saraswati defends it by saying: "according to our reformers all our ills are due to the caste system. But it is this land with this unique system—varnasrama—that has excelled all other nations in metaphysics, in the arts, in social values and in wisdom" Saraswati, *Hindu Dharma*, 99.

[69] Gupta, *Views on Hindu Dharma*, 84.

[70] Annabella Pitkin, "Love of Neighbour in Buddhism," in vol. 2, *Encyclopedia of Love in World Religions*, ed. Yudit Kornberg Greenberg (Santa Barbara: ABC-CLIO, 2008), 379.

[71] Ten avatars are generally believed to have manifested or appeared at different epochs. For a detailed study see Robert Antoine, Richard de Smet and Josef Neuner, eds., *Religious Hinduism: A Presentation and Appraisal* (Allahabad: St. Paul Publications, 1964).

in the socioreligious movements of the subaltern or marginalized sections of society, are significant reinterpretations of the very concept of dharma itself. Many of them are informed by their sociocultural contexts and highlight the emancipatory aspirations of marginalized and oppressed people for dignity and equality.[72] A good example of this is a socioreligious movement known as *Ayya Vazhi*, a heterodox Hindu tradition premised on emancipatory theological propositions.[73]

In a different vein, Chaturvedi Badrinath, a Sahitya Academy Awardee,[74] argues that dharma is a civilizational concept. "The true identity of Indian civilization has been *dharmic*...the one concern from which everything in Indian thought flowed, and on which every movement of life ultimately depended, is dharma, order."[75] Dharma, he believes, should be nurtured as a civilizational concept.

Thus, we see multiple meanings of dharma depending on their specific traditions. At the risk of simplification, the following can be taken as its core: what emerges from the major traditions is a recognition of a universal sphere, identified as cosmic, moral, and social order; what are given in the Buddhist traditions are courses of ethical actions oriented towards the well-being of others; and, what emerges from socioreligious movements are reinterpretations that are focused on achieving freedom, equality, and dignity for marginalized and oppressed people. As an overall concept, dharma can be taken to mean a universal cosmic, moral, and social order, embodying virtues of righteousness, equanimity, dignity, equality, and the well-being of all in the global family.

Whether these traditions can meaningfully converse with Pope Francis's vision of the common good in the ambience of a polyhedral culture of encounter is the question for us here. I would like to address this question in an elaborate and in-depth manner. However, within the confines of this article, I will limit myself to suggesting some possible areas of public theological conversations.

---

[72] Stephen Fuchs, *Rebellious Prophets: A Study of Messianic Movements in Indian Religions* (Bombay: Asia Publishing House, 1965).

[73] G. Patrick, *Religion as Subaltern Agency: Ayya Vazhi, a Subaltern Religious Phenomenon in South Tiruvitankur* (Chennai: Department of Christian Studies, University of Madras, 2002). Similar socioreligious movements have been studied by Stephen Fuchs in *Rebellious Prophets – A Study of Messianic Movements in Indian Religions* (Mumbai: Asia Publishing House, 1965) and Kenneth W. Jones, *Socio-Religious Reform Movements in British India* (Cambridge: Cambridge University Press, 1990).

[74] The Sahitya Academy is an Indian governmental body that annually awards best literary creations in the Indian context.

[75] Chaturvedi Badrinath, *Dharma, India and World Order: Twenty-one Essays* (Edinburgh: Saint Andrews Press, 1993), 11 and 32.

Possible Areas of Conversation

I want to suggest some possible areas in terms of some convergences and divergences between the common good and dharma.

An important area of convergence is the theology of natural law. This supports the Catholic doctrine of the common good on the one hand and the belief in dharma as the universal cosmic and moral order on the other. Both believe in a given order of reality that is moral, transcendental, universal, and eternal. This order ensures harmony in nature (the macrocosmos) and in humans (the microcosmos) when recognized and adhered to through right conduct. It also binds humanity to the environment with a deeper sense of affinity. As T. N. Koshoo reflects, "there is a deep interconnectedness between dharma, ecology and environment that surround all forms of life all the time."[76] The concept of *vasudhaiva kutumbakam* ("the earth, is thus, a family") is a kindred theme of dharma and further augments the affinity and convergence with the vision of integral ecology as elaborated by Pope Francis.[77] It also resonates well with the ecological spirituality that the pope advocates in *Laudato Si.'*[78]

Yet another area of convergence is found in the care for the vulnerable, the poor, the oppressed, refugees, migrants, and the marginalized—those who are victims of an unjust social order. Pope Francis integrates this care with great empathy in his vision of the common good. Spurred on by the Argentinian theology of the people, the pope makes a passionate plea not merely to care for the vulnerable but to establish justice for victims in a malfunctioning social order. He combines the "cry of the poor" with the "cry of the earth" and finds the technocratic paradigm to be at the root of the suffering of both. What emerges in Francis's teachings on the common good is an unmistakable appeal to a distributive justice that contributes to both social and environmental harmony.

In the case of dharma, the theme of avatar embodies the religious vision for the preferential care of the victims of unjust social order. As mentioned above, Vaisnavism, a major theistic Hindu tradition, speaks elaborately about the belief in the birth of gods (avatars) to establish righteousness (dharma) whenever unrighteousness (adharma) takes over. It is a faith in divine interventions to set right the moral order so as to do justice for the powerless, the lowly, and the oppressed.[79] Many socioreligious movements within this

---

[76] T. N. Khoshoo, "The Dharma of Ecology," *Current Science* 77, no. 9 (10 November 1999): 1147, https://www.jstor.org/stable/24103696.

[77] *Maha Upanishad*, trans. Dr. A. G. Krishna Warrier, http://www.advaita.it/library/mahaupanishad.htm, §71–73,

[78] *LS*, §217ff.

[79] This might remind us of the Christian doctrine of incarnation, but is not the same as an avatar. Nonetheless, a public conversation about the doctrines of incarnation and avatars may well be apt for our world.

tradition reinterpret the doctrine of dharma as action for the uplift of the lowly and the oppressed. Teachings like these can be potent for addressing our contemporary public concerns. For example, in the case of India, the constitutional provision for reservation (affirmative action) to the depressed classes of people can be effectively implemented when these teachings inform the conscience of the people. Pope Francis's care for the vulnerable and the idea of divine interventions that establish dharma for the powerless can converse fruitfully in the public domain.

Perhaps a good opportunity to learn from each other lies in the radical divergence in their cosmogonies. While the Catholic vision of the common good roots itself to a creator God who is the author of the natural law, the doctrine of dharma is, for the most part, understood as an impersonal ultimate reality: eternal, without a beginning or a creator.[80] Likewise, the Buddhist vision of *dhamma* does not support the idea of a creator God. This radical difference is a challenge for both sides, but it also presents an opportunity to encounter the other by engaging in conversations across incommensurable and comprehensive doctrines. Francis's insight on the polyhedron helps us enter the conversation with confidence.

Another area of a productive but challenging conversation can be the theological anthropology of the individual and the community. Pope Francis, in line with Catholic social teaching, has emphasized the dignity and the inalienable rights of the individual, as each person was created in the image and likeness of God. This becomes the cornerstone of the Catholic vision of human communities, which are organically constituted by rights-bearing dignified individuals. This theological anthropology can well be an issue for the dharma-based vision of the individual, who is primarily a duty-performing agent deeply embedded in kinship-based ascriptive communities. Individuals are expected to perform the duties prescribed to the community into which they are born. This is a good place to recall that in the 1990s, the prime ministers of Malaysia and Singapore countered the validity of the UN-sponsored human rights discourse on the ground that "Asian values," which are kinship-based community bonds, differed from that discourse.

The danger of such ascriptive kinship-based community bonds can also lead to the dominance of communities over individuals, with the unintended salience of oppressive control over the freedom of individuals. Thus, today we are faced with majoritarian and nationalistic politics that sail on the wings of particular communitarian identities. Agendas of religiocultural nationalism and sectarian, ethnic identities are distorting the liberal values of individual freedom, equality, and dignity. The ideals associated with liberal democracy—

[80] It is to be noted that in some theistic Hindu traditions, dharma was treated as the will of a personal deity. For example, in *Bhagavad Gita*, the deity Krishna instructs the warrior Arjuna on his dharma.

constitutional democratic governance, the rule of law, and the structures of civic participation—are, to say the least, at a weak stage of development in South Asia. The democracies of the region are fledgling political systems in spite of lofty claims. What is lacking in these countries is perhaps at the very heart of democracy: the civic participation of citizens at an appreciable level so as to constitute a reasonably good democratic polity. Instead, we are confronting a historical scuttling of the democratic process due to the salience of majoritarian forces feeding on kinship-based ascriptive communitarian bonds.

It would do well that the dharmic vision is challenged, interrogated, and nourished by the teachings on the dignity and rights of individuals. A public conversation in this regard will contribute significantly to the process of maturation of democratic principles in South Asia. However, Western culture also has much to learn. For example, it has given birth to extreme forms of liberal individualism, which is incapable of questioning the abysmal rich-poor divide, inducing an unjust economic order. It has also contributed to an ambience of in difference to common concerns. Such situations can be creatively countered by the positive dimensions of the communitarian visions of the common good.

It is understandable, then, that Western political philosophers are gripped by this concern over the place of the individual, leading to a crucial debate on the common good between the proponents of liberalism and communitarianism. As David Hollenbach states, there can be no meaningful vision of the common good today without attempting to face the challenges of bringing together the liberal and communitarian perspectives.[81] Among the attempts to bring about a synthesis of the two is the proposal for communal liberalism by Catholic ethicist Brian Stiltner.[82]

At this juncture, the reflections of Pope Francis on the common good find their relevance. True to the Catholic tradition, he situates the communitarian vision within the framework of the Christian faith in the transcendent God. However, he also values the radical plurality of communitarian traditions (religious, moral, ideological, cultural, political, etc.) emerging in the present-day process of globalization and endeavors to bring together these traditions (including atheistic ideological traditions) into public theological conversations through a culture of encounter. A conversation between Pope Francis's vision of the common good and the positivity of dharma as a universal, cosmic, moral order, which embodies equanimity, equality, and the well-being of all, especially of the vulnerable, is in the right direction.

---

[81] David Hollenbach, *The Common Good*, 133.

[82] Brian Stiltner, *Religion and Common Good: Catholic Contributions to Building Community in a Liberal Society* (Lanham, MD: Rowan & Littlefield, 1999).

Conclusion

The resonances of Francis's pontificate reach distant shores today. People across cultures, religions, regions, and sociopolitical systems appreciate his personality, values, and efforts as a spiritual leader of public significance. As a public theologian, he speaks out for the public role of faith in God as mediated by different religions. As a theologian of public life, he speaks on contemporary common concerns. Based on the global public impact the pope is making today, it would do well if we bring his reflections into public conversations with similar teachings across the globe. As an example, this essay has indicated the possibility of a conversation in an ambience of the culture of encounter between Francis's articulation of the common good and the theme of dharma from South Asia, and I have highlighted some possible areas of public theological conversations in terms of certain convergences and divergences. Case studies on particular aspects, which have not been done here due to lack of space, would further promote public theological conversations for the cause of the common good in our pluralistic global world today.

10.

Pope Francis and Political Engagement A Public Theological Model

Pope Francis's Vision of Politics

Pope Francis discusses the relevance and value of political commitment in such terminologies as 'lofty vocation', 'political charity', 'noble politics', etc. In *Fratelli Tutti,* he calls for a "renewed appreciation of politics as a 'lofty vocation' and (as) one of the highest forms of charity."[1] This encyclical openly speaks of the necessity of the political participation of the Churches when it says: "… the Church, while respecting the autonomy of political life, does not restrict her mission to the private sphere. On the contrary, 'she cannot and must not remain on the sidelines' in the building of a better world, or fail to 'reawaken the spiritual energy' that can contribute to the betterment of society."[2] And the next number reiterates the political commitment by clarifying the role of church ministers and the laity where it says: "It is true that religious ministers must not engage in the party politics that are the proper domain of the laity, but neither can they renounce the political dimension of life itself, which involves a constant attention to the common good and a concern for integral human development.[3] The Church "has a public role over and above her charitable and educational activities."[4] Thus we see the dimensions of a public theologian coming out in the documents issued by the Pope.

---

[1] *FT,* §180.

[2] *FT*, §266.

[3] *FT*, §267.

[4] *FT,* §267.

He speaks of the primary duty of every individual who value freedom to "take politics seriously" at local, regional, national and global levels[5] and instructs everyone to have the virtue of charity at the heart of one's political activity so as to remain anchored in 'justice, equality, mutual respect, sincerity, honesty and fidelity.'[6]

In *Laudato Si'*, he speaks of "the special virtue of 'political charity' as a form of love 'overflowing with small gestures of mutual care'[7] and spreads as 'social love' through the veins of society to create a "culture of care which permeates all of society."[8] It breaks open the individualist mind-set, "expressed in a spirit of openness to everyone"[9] and takes in deep awareness of the society and expresses itself in actions for the common good.[10] In his message to the 52 World Day of Peace in 2018, the Pope titled his address as 'good politics is at the service of peace' and went on to say that "[P]olitics is an essential means of building human community and institutions"[11] and "[I]f exercised with basic respect for the life, freedom and dignity of persons, political life can indeed become an outstanding form of charity."[12]

The Pope is aware that politics these days is not respected well because of several "vices" like corruption, dishonesty, infidelity, etc., but he takes care to assert that we cannot exist without the great contributions of politics. "Can our world function without politics? Can there be an effective process of growth towards universal fraternity and social peace without a sound political life? – are his pointed questions.[13] It is interesting to see how the Pope relished quoting a Vietnamese Cardinal who spoke of the 'Beatitudes of a Politician' in the following way:

> Blessed be the politician with a lofty sense and deep understanding of his role.
> Blessed be the politician who personally exemplifies credibility.
> Blessed be the politician who works for the common good and not his or her own interest. Blessed be the politician who remains consistent.
> Blessed be the politician who works for unity.

[5] Francis, "Human Fraternity for World Peace and Living Together", 2.

[6] Francis, "Human Fraternity for World Peace and Living Together", 3.

[7] *LS*, §231.

[8] *LS*, §231.

[9] *FT*, §190.

[10] Cf. *FT*, §§182, 252.

[11] Francis, "Good Politics is at the Service of Peace", 2, LII World Day of Peace 2019 - Good politics is at the service of peace | Francis (vatican.va).

[12] Ibid.

[13] *FT*, §176.

> Blessed be the politician who works to accomplish radical change.
> Blessed be the politician who is capable of listening.
> Blessed be the politician who is without fear.[14]

So the Pope's 'feel for politics' as a public good is positive and energetic; it propels the recipients of the message into political commitments for the greater cause of common good. Furthermore, his invitation for active and responsible citizenship adds to his character as a theologian of public life. He reminds us: "Let us not forget that "responsible citizenship is a virtue, and participation in political life is a moral obligation."[15] He further explicates on the concept as: "The concept of citizenship is based on the equality of rights and duties, under which all enjoy justice. It is therefore crucial to establish in our societies the concept of full citizenship..."[16]

The apostolic exhortation *Laudate Deum* speaks of a political practice from below, incorporating the role of civil society groups, to work towards achieving the ecological goals of minimizing the carbon footprints. It calls it a "new multilateralism from below" anchoring on the dialogical abilities of people and their civil organizations rather than on the power of the elites.[17] The pope is critical of the institutional authorities and their elitist bias, but hopeful of power of the grassroots people and their civil society organizations. Such a confidence on the civil sphere makes him share the confidence of public theologians to dialogue and bring forth the power of the people.

An imagery the Pope uses to bring forth the democratic potentials of the people is, as mentioned in earlier chapters, polyhedron. *Evangeli Gaudium*, under the section on the common good, envisages a sphere of dialogue not as a hierarchised structure but as a polyhedron; whereas the former functions with parts positioned at an equidistance from the centre and therefore 'determined' to a great extent, the polyhedron works as a converging point of distinctive parts. After a brief explanation of the difference between the 'sphere' and 'polyhedron', the document goes on to add that "Pastoral and political activity alike seek to gather in this polyhedron the best of each."[18] Along with the pastoral, the political is valued to play an important role in the bringing forth of the best in everyone to be gathered in the polyhedron. It would imply that the political has a valued role to 'initiate new processes' in the journey of life, endeavoring to become a people.[19]

---

[14] Francis, "Good Politics is at the Service of Peace", 3, LII World Day of Peace 2019 - Good politics is at the service of peace | Francis (vatican.va).

[15] Evangelium Gaudium, §220.

[16] Francis, "Human Fraternity for World Peace and Living Together", 5.

[17] Laudate Deum, §38.

[18] Evangeli Gaudium, §236.

[19] Evangeli Gaudium, §230.

His prayer for politicians capable of effective dialogue is instructive:

> I ask God to give us more politicians capable of sincere and effective dialogue aimed at healing the deepest roots – and not simply the appearances – of the evils in our world! Politics, though often denigrated, remains a lofty vocation and one of the highest forms of charity, inasmuch as it seeks the common good. … I am firmly convinced that openness to the transcendent can bring about a new political and economic mindset which would help to break down the wall of separation between the economy and the common good of society.[20]

The Pope's Political Interventions

The Ecumenical Pilgrimage of Peace the Pope undertook in January 2023 along with the Archbishop of Canterbury and the Moderator of the General Assembly of the Church of Scotland to the Democratic Republic of Congo and the Republic of South Sudan is a good example of the public intervention the Pope was making to end violence. His meeting with authorities, civil society and diplomatic corps took him to the public sphere of these countries.

His apostolic journey to the kingdom of Bahrain in Nov. 2022, to attend the "Bahrain Forum for Dialogue: East and West for Human Co-existence," his meeting with the members of the Muslim Council of Elders and his participation in the ecumenical meeting and prayer for peace is yet another public intervention of the Pope.

Similarly, his apostolic journey to Iraq in March 2021, meeting with the president, authorities, civil society and diplomatic corps is yet another instance of his public sphere interventions. Many more of such journeys of the Pope could be enlisted. His call to provide shelters to migrants and to treat them kindly is a topical intervention of the Pope Francis's pontificate.

Pope Francis's Synthesis of the Liberal and Communitarian Visions of Common Good

Today the dominant political theories witness a crucial debate between the proponents of liberalism and communitarianism. The liberal tradition, as we know, begins with arguing for the freedom of the individual, endowed with inviolable rights so as to pursue independent initiatives for self-fulfillment and social development; it values individual autonomy, and deters any interference from outside, to the extent even of having an unfettered freedom to accumulate unmeaning levels of wealth. The communitarians, on the other hand, privilege the common good to be constructed with 'visions of moral good' emerging from

[20] Evangeli Gaudium, §205.

communitarian traditions, including those of religio-cultural traditions;[21] they value the "constitutive communitarian"[22] dimensions of individual personalities and collective visions of common good; they also value pluralism[23] and take care to reflect upon the challenges involved in bringing together 'incommensurable' comprehensive moral doctrines.

Amidst the many context-specific adaptations of liberalism or communitarianism, one is able to perceive some major trends emergent in different regions. The western hemisphere, for example, witnesses to moderate to extreme forms of liberalism, while the east from fair levels of integration of constitutional liberalism with communitarian ethos to certain congeries of communitarianism; and the middle regions, toying with monarchies and dictatorships. A country-specific focus would bring up more of their instances with particular challenges and prospects.

In India, a constitutional liberal democracy has endeavored during the past 75 years, not without a level of success, to integrate itself with the Indian "communitarian ethos." Today, however, we are faced with the challenge of majoritarian politics that sails on the wings of particular "authoritarian communitarian" sentiments. Agendas of religio-cultural nationalism and dynamics of sectarian ethnic identities are distorting the liberal values of individual freedom, equality, and dignity. Constitutional democratic governance, rule of law, and structures of civic participation are yet to develop significantly. We are lacking the civic participation of citizens to an appreciable level so as to constitute a mature democratic polity. Instead, we are confronting a historical scuttling of the democratic process due to the salience of majoritarian forces. In addition, the majoritarian politics is inducing a discourse on religious homogeneity, and thereby making diversities and differences unpalatable to the "common sense" of the people. Minority traditions or communities are made to live as "aliens" or "dependents" in their own land. As a consequence, the process of building up a civic community of fraternity and solidarity at the grassroots to participate in collective projects for common good is weakened or even reversed.

At this juncture, the Catholic social teachings (CST) obtain their value. They endeavor to creatively bring together the liberal and the communitarian values, with a faith-based transcendental orientation. They situate the common good within the communitarian tradition of the Christian faith in a transcendent Trinitarian Godhead. They value the radical plurality of traditions (religious,

---

[21] Michael Sandel, *Liberalism and the Limits of Justice* (Cambridge: Cambridge University Press, 1998 – 2nd Edition).

[22] Sandel, *Liberalism.*

[23] They speak of 'value pluralism' to argue for radical pluralism. Amitai Etzioni, *From Empire to Community – A New Approach to International Relations* (New York: Palgrave Macmillan, 2004).

moral, ideological, cultural, political, etc) characterizing the present-day global world. They endeavour to bring together the different traditions (including non-religious ideological traditions) to work towards achieving the common good of social harmony, political amity, integral ecology, solidarity with the poor, the migrants, and the refugees. At the same time, they endeavour to take the best out of the liberal theory as well and attempt to cultivate the values of human rights, dignity, freedom, justice, and, equality. These liberal values can be best cultivated, according to the CST, when the values themselves have a transcendental orientation, and when the methods of cultivating them are faith-based; and those who endeavor to achieve these values are committed to a communitarian practice of faith.

Today, Pope Francis's ovure orients us towards a meaningful synthesis by way of integrating the liberal values with a communitarian framework.

Ecclesiastical Leadership in India

Active Engagement in Public Sphere

There is a certain tendency among some sections of Indian ecclesiastical leadership to withdraw or shy away from the public sphere. It is not so much a result of personal preferences as a "habitude" induced by various historical factors, including some of our spiritual beliefs and outdated theological orientations. Among the many, that Indian Christians had been depending on the western missionaries for their resources, spiritual, financial, etc., for a very long time could be a major factor that isolated Indian ecclesiastical leadership from the Indian public sphere; or that the Indian Christians came to be counted among the minorities in the independent India could be yet another socio-political factor that inhibits public interventions; or even the spiritual beliefs that our kingdom is not so much of "this world" as the eternal one could also have cast its shadow on our public propensities and produced a certain "modesty" in not venturing into the political public sphere. In the Catholic Church, a clerical domination could have inhibited the laity from engaging the public sphere.

Whatever be the historical reasons, we need active engagements in public sphere today. Our leaders, after the model of Pope Francis, have to be public theologians as well as theologians of public life. We need to make it clear to ourselves that being a religious voice in the public does not hurt a secular constitutional nation.

Deepening the Knowledge of Indian History, Culture, and Religious Traditions

Much has been lost by the historical indifference to other cultures and religious traditions, an indifference perhaps caused by the dictum 'extra ecclesia nulla salus'. We need to actively learn and understand Indian traditions, including their histories. A sound knowledge of these traditions not merely situates us deeply in our soil, but also helps to freely converse with different others in the public.

Forming inter-denominational Forums for Public Interventions

What is very relevant today is an inter-denominational Christian forum for addressing public issues and concerns. Given the historical background of independent developments of different denominational churches, it is indeed a challenge to bring them together on a common platform for public interventions. But, taking up this challenge and forming a forum will go a long way in shaping up the Christian response in today's socio-political context.

A Truth and Reconciliation Effort Needed

That our forerunners have decried other religions as satanic or demonalatry is a public knowledge now. Documents are in the public domain. It would do well to make a public statement by way of setting things right. Following the lead given by the Vat II council, we need to highlight the "true and holy" in different religious traditions. This is not an initiative born out of certain contingencies, but a manner of opening ourselves up to the ever-revealing divine in whom we strongly believe.

11

The Synodal Church Engaging Civil Society Journeying together, towards Frontiers...

Preliminary Considerations

Synodality, an ecclesial event initiated in the Catholic Church today, stands for 'journeying or walking together' - a process of 'participation of all' in the life and mission of the Church. It seeks to strengthen the structures and facilities for participation, and bring about a community of faithful who are more and more involved in the life and mission of the Church; it seeks to mobilise the participatory potentials of the Catholic faithful to take up more responsibilities and share the ecclesial power; it seeks also to revitalise the principles of collegiality, subsidiarity, solidarity, and prepare the Catholic Church to play an active role for common good in the present-day global world.

As narrated in the document *Synodality in the Life and Mission of the Church* brought out in 2018 by the International Theology Commission of Vatican, synodality has been present in the life and mission of the Church all along its history, starting with the archetypal participatory event of the 'Jerusalem council' (Acts 15). Subsequently, it was manifest in the proceedings of the ecumenical councils, and survived through the challenges of the Middle Ages. It differentiated itself from conciliarism which arose during the fourteenth-fifteenth centuries to claim the decision making powers of the council independent of the pope.[1]

---

[1] It was in the context of the existence of three popes at the same time and therefore the dilemma of identifying a centre of papal power led to the assertion of the power of the council to decide independently. Once the issue of the multiple popes was settled, the demand for conciliarism died out.

During the modern era, synodality took different forms of participation in various denominational Churches, and the Catholic Church proceeded on a path within the framework of 'hierarchical communion'. The post-Vat II phase of the Catholic Church witnessed to the emergence of the spirit of episcopal collegiality, giving further push to the synodal path. Pope Paul VI, in his *motu proprium* named *Apostolica Sollicitudo*, issued by the end of the Second Vatican Council, instituted the "synod of bishops", a representative body of the universal catholic episcopate, as a "perpetual" institution to provide "information and advice", and even to exercise certain "powers of decision making" when such were conferred upon it by the pope for a time or for a purpose. This was a response to the "signs of the times" the Catholic Church was experiencing as it was opening itself up to the modern democratic world.

Pope Francis is calling us today for an event of 'walking together' to introduce a momentum or a new phase in ecclesial participation of all, which he thinks, is going to be the signature trait of the Catholic Church hereafter. 'Participation of all' would imply, for Pope Francis, a special emphasis on the participation of 'the people', the grassroots of the church, especially the poor and the marginalized in the governance of the Church. An Argentinian Jesuit, Pope Francis brings with him the resonances of the 'theology of the people', otherwise known as the 'Latin American Theology' popularly present in Argentina from the middle of the twentieth century. This theology took the category of 'people' as the locus of theology and emphasised the religio-cultural resources of the poor and marginalised for their own liberation.[2] Prominent Argentinian theologians like Lucian Gera, Rafael Tello, and Victor Manuel Fernandez proposed this theology through their writings and initiatives. Inspired by this theology, the pope is more spontaneously drawn to activities which trust in the power and resources 'of the people', the grassroots of the Church and the society. The pastoral theological vision embedded in his documents, his activities and personal attitudes bear witness to his earnestness to ensure an emphatic ecclesial participation of the people, especially the poor, the indigenous, the migrants, the refugees, and not the least, the earth (through human mediation) as the victim of the mindless technocratic paradigm.

In this context, this chapter attempts to explore how the synodal church engages or may engage the civil society with its dynamics of participation. Civil society is being understood today as a relatively autonomous space between family, state, and market forces wherein individuals or groups can creatively express themselves in the multiple public forums of a democratic polity for the sake of common good. It is a space of relative freedom – freedom that believes in the active agency of human beings against structural determinisms. It is a freedom for religious practices, cultural expressions, socio-political interventions

[2] It was different from the liberation theology which had integrated the Marxian vision of class struggle and socialist society.

through associations and initiatives. It is a freedom from the control of the State, dominance of the market, and ascriptive hierarchical ties of ethnic communities. Whether this freedom is actually available in any given situation, wherein multiple dominant forces like patriarchal, capitalist, consumerist, and sectarian communalist forces are operative, is a point of criticism being raised against the concept of civil society. That it can be an instrument of the bourgeois liberal freedom or unbridled liberty of technocratic market forces is the main point of this criticism. However, there is indeed a general optimism among the wider population and the activists that civil society is a relevant concept to stand for a creative freedom available as well to signify an ideal to be actualised.

It is in place here to note that secular theorising on civil society is increasingly being situated today within the communitarian political philosophy of civic republicanism which seeks to overcome the extremes of liberal individualism on the one hand, and the pre-modern ethnic 'communalism' on the other. It is pertinent here to see that some core themes and dynamics of civic republicanism converge with those of synodality: both of them privilege the concept of participation and consider it indispensable. As Iseult Honohan, one of the leading proponents of civic republicanism, explains: participation brings different others together to be engaged in deliberations for their common future; it enables an individual to be articulate through the mode of 'public reasoning' and join in the process of decision-making for common good; it opens oneself up to dialoguing with different others and consider alien viewpoints, even when they are antagonistic; it instils a sense of ownership with the project being deliberated; and it cultivates the ability to deal with plurality.[3] Very interestingly Pope Francis takes in all these dynamics of participation in the synodal project, and situates it within an overarching model of 'polyhedral' dialogical encounters. As different from a sphere wherein every point shares the sameness in an aggregative whole (Evangelii Gaudium, 236), polyhedron represents "a society where differences coexist, complementing, enriching and reciprocally illuminating one another, even amid disagreements and reservations" (Fratelli Tutti, 215). In addition, both synodality and civic republicanism speak of citizenship,[4] freedom from domination, individual rights and duties, and common good; both of them give importance to the communitarian origin of individual selves; and, both believe democracy to be the best political framework for human flourishing and common good.

With these preliminary considerations, it is time to enter the exploration of the question of how the synodal church engages the civil society. The exploration begins by taking an overview, through the Catholic Social Teachings, of the way the Catholic Church has sought in its modern history to engage the

[3] Cf. Iseult Honohan, *Civic Republicanism* (UK: Routledge, 2006), 216-236.

[4] Pope Francis speaks about ecological citizenship.

civil society; it then goes into the way Pope Francis envisions the engagement, bringing it to the "frontiers"; and, ends with some practical suggestions.

1. Engaging Civil Society: Sifting through the Catholic Social Teachings

The theological document *Synodality in the Life and Mission of the Church* provides a starting point, though by an indirect reference, to an understanding of the Catholic vision of engaging the civil society. After dealing with the event of synodality through the entire document, in terms of its history, theology and practical implementation, the document, towards its very end, speaks about the "social diakonia" of the Church. It observes that "social diakonia" stands for the "promotion of a social, economical and political life of all peoples under the banner of justice, solidarity and peace" (§119). It further observes that, "[T]he practice of dialogue and the search for effective joint solutions by which we commit ourselves to peace and justice are an absolute priority in a situation where there is a structural crisis in the procedures of democratic participation and a loss of confidence in its principles and inspirational values, with the threat of authoritarian and technocratic aberrations" (§119). The document thus identifies a "crisis of democratic participation" due to the salience of authoritarian political systems and the technocratic "aberration" found in the present-day market economy. While the former endangers human freedom, autonomy, rights of individuals and collectives, the latter exploitatively homogenises human needs, priorities, and values, thereby paralysing the basic freedom of choice. At the same time, the document accords "absolute priority" to dialogically work together with different others for peace and justice, "the universal destination of goods, the primacy of solidarity and care for our common home" (§119).

We find in this reference to "social diakonia" an aspiration for a healthy democratic participation and an indirect invitation to engage the civil society, which is the bulwark of any democratic polity. By dialogically working with different others for peace and justice, with an option for the poor and the vulnerable, we engage or bring to birth a civil society, which in turn will sustain a participatory democracy. Though this is only a brief reference, when situated within the gamut of the Catholic social teachings, engaging civil society becomes a concerted pursuit of the Catholic Church.

The CST, starting from the *Rerum Novarum* of Leo XIII, have more directly related themselves to institutions of 'civil authority', 'public authority', 'the State', 'civil government', 'civil power', and 'civil society'. During the time of Pius IX, the predecessor to Leo XIII, against the background of the cataclysmic event of the "temporal" political powers taking over the then existing "papal states", the Catholic Church had developed an antagonistic approach to these institutions. *The Syllabus of Errors* (1864) indicted the civil powers, which were perceived to be restricting the ecclesial powers of the Church and its unilateral prerogative to instruct and guide the people in faith and morals.

Even while condemning the temporal power, the Catholic Church, bereft now of the royal power of the State, was gradually realising that it had to play a different role as a moral instructor as well as a teacher of faith in the wider society, including the civil society. The 'social questions' of the Catholic Church was born in this context, and as pope Benedict XVI observed later, they secured a "citizenship" status for the Catholic Church in the wider society. The Church went full swing with its generous comments, observations, critiques, moral instructions, religious teachings and other interventions to engage the civil sphere. It is in place to note here the fact that the civil sphere was taken for a long time, as per many documents of the CST, as the sphere of the secular State or the civil government as distinguished from ecclesial government or power. It was only during the middle of the twentieth century from the Second Vatican Council that the concept gradually opened up to include the voluntary initiatives and institutions of the grassroots people.

In *Rerum Novarum*, we have several social questions addressed: the workers' situation, just wages, dignity of work, dignity of the human, relation of state to capital, right to private property, common good, rights of workers for association,[5] collective negotiations, etc. Addressing these questions certainly involved the engagement of the civil sphere. In his encyclical, *On the Christian Constitution of States* (*Immortale Dei, 1885),* Leo XIII laid out the Christian principles of engaging civil, public and political powers. 'Whether Catholics could take part in the conduct of public affairs?' was a topical question answered affirmatively by the pope in a context wherein the Catholic orientation still was to rescind from secular public spheres of activities, lest they "profaned" them. "Common good" began, and continues even to this day, to be the norm that validated the Catholic participation in secular public affairs. Leo XIII's reflection on this is instructive: "...it may in some places be true that, for most urgent and just reasons, it is by no means expedient for Catholics to engage in public affairs or to take an active part in politics. Nevertheless ... to take no share in public matters would be as wrong as to have no concern for, or to bestow no labour upon, the common good..." (no. 44). He continues: "It follows clearly, therefore, that Catholics have just reasons for taking part in the conduct of public affairs. For in so doing they ... use their best endeavours ... to infuse, as it were, into all the veins of the State the healthy sap and blood of Christian wisdom and virtue" (no. 45). We see here that Leo XIII envisioned a Church which, through the veins of the civil institutions, disseminated the "sap and blood of Christian wisdom and virtue" for the common good of humanity.

In *Divini Redemptoris* (1937), Pius XI said, "God has ... destined man for civil society according to the dictates of his very nature" (DR, 29), and he

[5] *Octogesimo Anno*, 30.

continued to observe that human beings could not exempt themselves from the "divinely-imposed obligations toward civil society" (DR, 30). On the fortieth anniversary of *Rerum Novarum*, in his *Octogesimo Anno*, he introduced the concept of 'subsidiarity', aimed also at securing freedom for the civil society from the interference of the State. We see here an early instance of distinguishing civil society from the State. He reiterated the value of founding workers' associations with Christian wisdom and virtue. Cautioning the Christian workers of the danger of the liberal stance of the 'religion-less' secular associations of workers, the pope defended the Christian associations by saying, "when the regulations of associations are founded upon religion,[6] the way is easy toward establishing the mutual relations of the members, so that peaceful living together and prosperity will result" (no. 32). Religion was consistently integrated by the Catholic Church with the associations of workers. The pope observed: "[T]hus associations of this kind have molded truly Christian workers who, in combining harmoniously the diligent practice of their occupation with the salutary precepts of religion, protect effectively and resolutely their own temporal interests and rights, keeping a due respect for justice and a genuine desire to work together with other classes of society for the Christian renewal of all social life" (no. 33). The promotion of such workers' association earlier by Leo XIII had led to the formation of similar associations for those in other walks of life and had, as per the assessment of pope Pius XI, enriched the life, culture and the polity of the society (European) in a significant way (no. 37). Pius XII (1939-58), heading the Church during the hey-days of the 'development' discourse in the West, is known for his support for liberal democracy and development, and for his call to the developed countries to share their riches with poorer ones.[7]

Pope John XXIII, in the context of threats of nuclear wars, spoke of *Peace on Earth* (*Pacem in Terris*) wherein the concept of common good, giving due importance to human dignity and freedom, was expounded very prominently. It was he who, through his encyclicals *Mater et Magistra* and *Pacem in Terris*, intoned the thinking on common good in terms of social conditions necessary for human fulfillment. Such a thinking on common good later got 'defined' in the *Gaudium et Spes* of the Vat II as "the sum total of those conditions of the social life whereby men (*sic*), families and associations more adequately and readily may attain their own perfection" (GS, 74). Here the "conditions of the social life" include institutions and structures of civil sphere, which facilitate individuals and groups to pursue their goals of fulfillment / perfection ordained by God. Thus we see that Pope John XIII engaged the civil society from the

---

[6] Here 'religion' stood for the Christian religion, which alone was considered true by the Church.

[7] John Sniegocki, *Catholic Social Teaching and Economic Globalization – The Quest for Alternatives* (Wisconsin: Marquette University Press, 2009), 114.

concern for common good. As John Snigocki observed, "[U]ndergirding all of Pope John's political reflections is a fundamental emphasis placed upon active citizen participation in public life (PT 75-76) and upon respect for human rights."[8]

The Second Vatican Council, in a few of its documents, dwelt upon the virtues of civil society. In *Gaudium et Spes*, it spoke of the freedom of everyone to participate in the process of establishing the "constitutional bases" of political communities, referring to civil society. It said: "It is in full accord with human nature that juridical political structures should, with ever better success and without any discrimination, afford all their citizens the chance to participate freely and actively in establishing the constitutional bases of a political community, governing the state, determining the scope and purpose of various institutions, and choosing leaders (GS, 75). In a similar vein, it spoke of the religious freedom to be ensured in civil society: "Religious freedom, in turn, which men demand as necessary to fulfill their duty to worship God, has to do with immunity from coercion in civil society" (*Dignitatis Humanae*, no. 1). The document *Dignitatis Humanae*, basing religious freedom upon human dignity, realized through divine revelation and human reason, spoke of it as a civil right: "the right to religious freedom has its foundation in the very dignity of the human person, as this dignity is known through the revealed Word of God and by reason itself. This right of the human person to religious freedom is to be recognized in the constitutional law whereby society is governed. Thus it is to become a civil right" (Religious Freedom, 2). In fact, John Paul II, in *Christifideles Laici (CL)*, spoke of religious freedom as the 'measure of all other fundamental rights': "The civil and social right to religious freedom, inasmuch as it touches the most intimate sphere of the spirit, is a point of reference for the other fundamental rights and in some way becomes a measure of them" (*CL*, 39).

Paul VI, encouraging the involvement of lay people in the process of development, instructs them to "infuse a Christian spirit into people's mental outlook and daily behavior, into the laws and structures of the civil community" (*Populorum Progressio*, 81), and exhorts them that "civil progress and economic development are the only road to peace" (PP, 83). The synodal document on *Justice in the World* (1971) lamented the lack of social participation which kept people away from attaining their human and civil rights (JW, 9). And it encouraged greater participation by the lay people in the Church to ensure greater responsibility and participation for women, freedom of expression and the due process of the Church law (JW, 40-46).

John Paul II was perhaps the first to integrate the present-day understanding of civil society in his reflections. Benedict XVI said: "My predecessor John Paul II drew attention to this question in *Centesimus Annus*, when he spoke

[8] Sniegocki, *Catholic Social Teaching*, 120.

of the need for a system with three subjects: the market, the State and civil society" (*Caritas in Veritate*, 38). The *Compendium of the Social Doctrine of the Church* (2004), published during the time of John Paul II, reflects clearly the present-day understanding of civil society as the "third sector" between the State and the market. It says: "the civil society is *the sum of relationships and resources, cultural and associative, that are relatively independent from the political sphere and the economic sector*" (417), and speaks of its role as providing space for expression of planning capacity of human beings to work, individually or through associations, for the common good by "fostering a freer and more just social life" (417). It also pays attention to the risk of this space being dominated over by the 'stronger who prevail over the weaker' (418). The *Compendium* serves as a good guide not merely on the very understanding of civil society, but also on the kind of relationships that needs to exist between the Church and civil society based on the principles of solidarity and cooperation for common good, and between the civil society and the political society (State) based on the principle of subsidiarity (417-420). It makes a strong argument that it is the responsibility of the State to ensure the freedom of religion, which is one of the sublime freedoms to be exercised in civil society (421-423).

John Paul II appreciated the role of civil society for its service to the weak and defenseless: "how many initiatives of help and support for people who are weak and defenseless have sprung up and continue to spring up in the Christian community and in civil society, at the local, national and international level, through the efforts of individuals, groups, movements and organizations of various kinds!" (*Evangelium Vitae*, 26). Encouraging the people to celebrate a "Day of Life", as part of his pro-life policy, he enlisted the role of civil society to uphold the meaning and value of human life at every stage. Observing that respect for life was a fundamental virtue of civil society, he linked it with Church's duty to defend a "human state" which ensured the fundamental rights of human persons, especially of the weakest (EV, 101).

He had recognized civil society as the natural setting for "gratuitous economic activity and fraternity." By associating economy with civil society, the pope envisioned the possibility of an economy to be based on human fraternity, gratutiousness and solidarity. He elaborately reflected on this, by underlining the role of institutions and persons of civil society to mediate economic equality, mutual aid between countries, solidarity with workers from underdeveloped countries, etc. He envisaged that this role would also be a moral guide for economic undertakings.[9]

---

[9] It would do well to remember that during the nineteenth century, civil society was taken to be the space for the economic initiatives, undertaken freely without the interference of the State, and subsequently, when it came to represent the unbridled freedom of the neo-capitalists, civil society movement distanced itself from the sphere of economy to represent a space independent from economy, State and family. However, today, in the post-liberal era, there is criticism raised

Pope Benedict XVI, in his *Deus Caritas Est*, articulated the Christian responsibility to build up the civil sphere when he said:

> [B]uilding a just social and civil order, wherein each person receives what is his or her due, is an essential task which every generation must take up anew. As a political task, this cannot be the Church's immediate responsibility. Yet, since it is also a most important human responsibility, the Church is duty-bound to offer, through the purification of reason and through ethical formation, her own specific contribution towards understanding the requirements of justice and achieving them politically (*Deus Caritas Est*, 28).

Pointing out to the limitation of powers of States taking place due to the dominance of international trade and finance, and consequently the restricted roles of political authorities, Benedict XVI foresaw "new forms of political participation" (*Caritas et Veritate*, 24) emerging from civil society organizations, embodying the citizen's interest in participating in the *res publica* (24). In addition, the pope, in the context of speaking about applying the principles of distributive justice to business, advised the developed countries to grant economic aid to underdeveloped countries, and took care to say that in the distribution of this aid, the receiving governments should also involve the "bearers of cultures within civil society, including local Churches" (CV, 58). Again, speaking about labour unions, which, according to the pope, the Church had always encouraged and supported, he pointed out to "civil society as the proper setting for their necessary activity of defending and promoting labour, especially on behalf of exploited and unrepresented workers, whose woeful condition is (was) often ignored by the distracted eye of society". (64).

These then are some of the instances from the Catholic Social teachings (until the pontificate of Pope Francis) to attest to the "synodal" virtues of the Catholic Church to participate in and walk with the civil society. From a very remote past when not merely the civil but the entire society was under the spiritual, moral and the "royal" power of the Church, passing through phases of antagonism and conflict, it has come a long way today. In *Rerum Novarum*, it claimed a unilateral right to be the moral instructor and religious teacher, with an emphatic claim to be the "true religion" of the world... In his *On the Christian Constitution of States,* Leo XIII spoke in terms of endeavouring "to bring back all civil society to the pattern and form of Christianity" (no. 46). When such a unilateral project of the Catholic Church could not be palatable to the increasing liberal and pluralist ethos of civil society, as Anna

against this stance of independence, which claims neutrality or equi-distance from all ideological or actual forces. In this newer context, it is meaningful to bring economic activity too under the sphere of civil society, integrating it with moral goals and transcendental orientations.

Roper Rowlands observes,[10] Catholic Church founded its own civil society or a parallel civil society in terms of building educational institutions, charitable organizations, medical aid facilities, and so on.[11] What John Paul II tells us in *Sapientia Christiana* clearly confirms this: "when civil authorities, to promote the common good, began and developed their own universities, the Church, loyal to her very nature, did not desist from founding and favoring such kinds of centers of learning and institutions of instruction. This is shown by the considerable number of Catholic universities established in recent times in nearly all parts of the world" (II, *Sapientia Christiana*, JP II).

However, as the times kept changing, its approach gradually became more accommodative, open, mutual and inter-subjective in relation with different others. Today the Catholic Church has come to acknowledge the independence of civil society; participation in civil society is considered a prime value for the Catholic Church.

2. Pope Francis

Today, Pope Francis open-mindedly embraces the role of civil society in his vision for the participatory Church – the synodal Church. He sees it as an arena that fosters the dialogical culture of encounter to work towards the common good of the global community. He relates its role to resolving some of our pressing common concerns like that of the ecological crisis. He appreciates the role played by civil society institutions in bringing to our awareness the extensiveness of the damage done to our eco-system and creating moral qualms in us (LS, 38). He says: "[W]orldwide, the ecological movement has made significant advances, thanks also to the efforts of many organizations of civil society. It is impossible here to mention them all, or to review the history of their contributions. But thanks to their efforts, environmental questions have increasingly found a place on public agendas and encouraged more far-sighted

---

[10] Cf. Anna Roper Rowlands, *Towards a Politics of Communion – Catholic Social Teaching in Dark Times* (T&T Clark, 2021).

[11] "During this same period from the 1840s onwards, largely through the work of religious orders and lay social Catholicism, the Church devoted considerable energy to developing the structures of an alternative Catholic civil society. It did so, not as an outright rival to the state, for it was retreating gradually from such a view. Rather it sought a full expression of a Catholic social world – within a social world in which it found itself often not totally at home – through the foundation of hospitals, universities, schools, welfare services and new intellectual publications. These were tangible signs of not only the fullness of its own life, but also its dislocation in important ways from its own secular contexts. These civic initiatives were each conceived of as means to ensure the formation in faith in a world seen as increasingly hostile to faith, as well as enactments of Christian service within a world consecrated to Christ. This Catholic civic world was not simply a counter cultural rejection of, or separation from, modernity: it created deeply social expressions of a shifting Catholicism in complex dialogue with its context." (Rowlands, 22).

approaches" (LS, 166). Furthermore, he points to the cultivation of human responsibility, solidarity, social capital, relationships of trust, rule of law, dependability (LS, 128), etc. as the foundation for civil society. He attributes the present day eco-crises and tragedies suffered by the poor to lack of cultivation in civil society of human responsibility and solidarity to one another and to the nature. He says, "[O]ur lack of response to these tragedies involving our brothers and sisters points to the loss of that sense of responsibility for our fellow men and women upon which all civil society is founded" (LS, 25). He speaks similarly about the condition of migrants: "At present ... migration is affected by the loss of that sense of responsibility for our brothers and sisters on which every civil society is based" (*Fratelli Tutti*, 40). He desires the civil society institutions to cultivate these "foundations", even while working for common good beyond the pursuit of economic profit and efficient systems: "[W]hat we need in fact are states and civil institutions that are present and active, that look beyond the free and efficient working of certain economic, political or ideological systems, and are primarily concerned with individuals and the common good" (FT, 108). Going further on, he wants the virtues of citizenship to be cultivated among the people in the civil society (FT, 131). He envisions a substantive role to be played by institutions or organizations of civil society under the principle of subsidiarity in any given political system (FT, 175). And, true to the Catholic faith, he wants a public role for religion in shaping up the institutions of civil society. He states: "no one can demand that religion should be relegated to the inner sanctum of personal life, without influence on societal and national life, without concern for the soundness of civil institutions, without a right to offer an opinion on events affecting society. Who would claim to lock up in a church and silence the message of Saint Francis of Assisi or Blessed Teresa of Calcutta?" (*Evangelii Gaudium*, 183).

Pope Francis, without giving up the unique role of the Catholic Church in faith and morals, speaks about encountering radically different others, with their own differences, in the civil sphere. His passionate plea as found in his documents to participate in institutions of civil society for the common good, and his efforts at meeting with different political leaders to mediate peace contribute significantly to a Catholic culture of participating in civil society. As Rafael states, "Francis assumes these efforts by supporting social and civil movements, because these movements collaborate to build a more inclusive and just society. His Papacy, inspired by a Latin American ecclesial and theological identity, is a testimony of how secular society and religious institutions can join forces for the common good of all people, based on an ethics of democratic citizenship, ecclesial synodality and social participation."[12]

---

[12] Rafael Luciani, "Pope Francis and the Theology of the People", in Justin Beaumont, ed. *The Routledge Handbook of Postsecularity* (New York: Routledge, 2019), 221.

2.1. Entering the Frontiers

In the post-Vat II phase of the Catholic Church, we have been hearing more about the value of consultation. The *Apostolica Sollicitudo* (1965) by which was the synod of bishops instituted as a "permanent institution" spoke of the consultative role of the bishops, but also of a deliberative role (Can. 343) if called to perform by the Pope (no. 3, *Episcopalis Communio*, 2018). This new institution of the synod of bishops was to be continuously improved and improvised. John Paul II said: "perhaps this instrument (the synod of bishops) can be further improved. Perhaps the collegial pastoral responsibility can be expressed in the Synod even more fully" (cited in no. 4, *Episcopalis Communio*). Furthering this quest, Pope Francis calls for recognizing and implementing the participatory dimension of the "consultative" role, which contributes significantly to decision-making. His words are instructive:

> ... the fact that the Synod ordinarily has only a consultative role does not diminish its importance. In the Church the purpose of any collegial body, whether consultative or deliberative, is always the search for truth or the good of the Church. When it is therefore a question involving the faith itself, the consensus ecclesiae is not determined by the tallying of votes, but is the outcome of the working of the Spirit, the soul of the one Church of Christ. Therefore the vote of the Synod Fathers, "if morally unanimous, has a qualitative ecclesial weight which surpasses the merely formal aspect of the consultative vote" (no. 7, *Episcopalis Communio*).

Thus we see that the consultative role often is not a mere non-consequential 'consultation', and the deliberative role that is not often spoken about is not factually absent in the life and mission of the Catholic Church. The deliberative role, at appropriate spaces, within the framework of the "hierarchical ecclesial communion" is present and supported by the principle of subsidiarity. That the oriental synods of the Catholic Church enjoy factually deliberative power in selecting bishops for their dioceses is a case in point. Thus we see a possibility of performing both the roles as emergent upon the institution of synod of bishops. Starting with the advocacy of collegiality among bishops, the present pope's all-out promotion of a culture of encounter have dwelt upon the necessity of consultation in every sphere to solve problems, find solutions, etc.

The pope has also gone ahead to speak of initiating creative processes which would bring about "creative tensions" between radical differences in a polyhedral framework of working for common good. Going by the pope's suggestion, it would be in order to create spaces of creative tensions between the now-practised "consultative" procedures of decision-making and the ideals of "deliberative" participation. We could well be on the frontiers between these two paradigms today. That the centrality given to participation in the synodal event resonates vibrantly with the civic republican ideal of deliberative participation adds further strength to the argument that we are in the frontiers today.

Moreover, the pope shows keen interest in giving fresh life to the vision of the Church as the "people of God" as taught in *Lumen Gentium* of the Vat II. As we know, the Council discursively reversed the then existing hierarchical image of the Church by placing the chapter on the people of God before that of the hierarchy. This prominence given to the people, recognised on the basis of the common baptism shared by all, had to be materialised in terms of their participation in various ministries, structures like pastoral and financial councils, and very prominently in the wider society as transforming agents. The latter, dwelt elaborately in documents like *Lumen Gentium*, *Gaudium et Spes* and *Christifideles Laici,* was considered to occupy the prime role to actualise the faith and mission of the Church in the world "outside". Pope Francis is said to be interested in infusing further energy into this ecclesial vision of Vat II.[13] This ecclesial dimension, as distinct from his two immediate predecessors who were known for their philosophical and theological interests, would become typical of the pontificate of Francis. He is interested in shaping up the Catholic Church as a spiritually formed ecclesial communion, walking together as the people of God, engaging in missions through a dialogical culture of perpetual encounters. He is giving out a call to increase the level of participation of all in the life and mission of the Church. Embedded in his call is the possibility of a thick participatory event which could take us to the frontiers of the power of participation, discernment and negotiation wherein the hierarchy too can become more dynamic, participatory and democratic, rather than being self-imposing, paternalistic, top-down and autocratic.

Furthermore, the *Working Document for the Continental Stage* of the synodal process that carries brief reports from different regions evinces a keen interest in participating in ecclesial structures like parish and diocesan pastoral and financial councils *with deliberative roles*. The document says: "Many reports show the need for these bodies to be not only consultative, but places where decisions are made on the basis of processes of communal discernment rather than on the majority principle used in democratic rights" (no. 78). And the *Document* instructs: "The synodal journey has brought out a number of tensions ... We should not be afraid of them, but articulate them in a process of constant communal discernment, so as to harness them as a source of energy ... only in this way will it be possible to continue walking together, rather than each going their own way. This is why the Church also needs to give a synodal form and way of proceeding to its own institutions and structures, particularly with regard to governance" (no. 71).

[13] Rowlands, "Towards the Politics ..."

Catholic Church, the biggest religious organization of the world today, is known for its well-knit operation of power. That it has its unique history, which has brought about such a centralized system, is understandable. However, it cannot remain closed to the voices which are sympathetic and yet critical. While appreciating the effective administration of power, especially when it comes to the organization of care and concern for the poor and the marginalized, these voices feel uncomfortable when it comes to the thickly centralized process of decision-making. Human dignity, liberty, freedom, equality and fraternity have become major democratic values informing civil societies which cut across religions, regions, and socio-political landscapes. The Catholic Church, especially its hierarchy, has to open its doors and create an ambience of democratic culture within itself. Synodality could be a loud knock at our door. Pope Francis helps us hear the sound of the knock. He has walked a distance from one extreme end of the "consultative paradigm" towards the frontiers of the "deliberative paradigm." It is now our responsibility to make synodality happen in our local and regional contexts, respectfully and responsibly entering the realm of deliberative participatory synodality with discernment and solidarity. We need to initiate processes by which deliberative bodies could be set up and negotiate the hierarchical structures in a way fitting for a religious community. As Job Kozhanthadam would put it, "[A] participatory, collaborative, well-informed, interdisciplinary approach in an atmosphere of sincerity, openness, selflessness and prayerfulness with genuine sensitivity, prudent firmness, care and concern is the ideal Francis would like to have in the process of decision-making in the Church of Christ."[14]

3. Practically Speaking...

3.1. Within the Catholic Church

Civic virtues could become more pronounced in the inner life of the Catholic Church, which already has obtained a relative merit in terms of the characteristics of civil society. It could cultivate within its bodies the art of public reasoning, which is one of the benchmarks of civic participation. Civil society is an arena of the culture of encounter, articulated through discursive performances. Skills of listening, presenting a view-point, arguing, debating, discerning, arriving at consensus, respecting differences, etc., need to be cultivated with due care.

Membership in the Church can be discussed in terms of an "ecclesial citizenship." A baptized member, analogous to a citizen of a constitutional polity, need to be treated with rights and duties which derive from the ecclesial communion. The rights to an ecclesial citizen to participate fully in the life and

[14] Job Kozhamthadam, "Pope Francis, the Game-Changer: From the Top-Down Tradition to Down-Up, Communitarian Approach", in Kuruvilla Pandikattu SJ, ed. *Pope Francis – His Impact on and Relevance for the Church and Society* [Commemorating Five Years of His Papacy] (Pune: Jnana-Deepa Vidyapeeth & Christian World Imprints, 2018), 329.

mission of the church must be respected. Hurdles emerging from gender, caste, and rites need to be eradicated.

The embedded presence of ascriptive ties in Catholic Churches, in terms of kinship and caste needs to be eradicated to engage the civil society more effectively and inspiringly. The Indian Catholic Church, unlike the Indian Reformation Churches, is still 'conditioned' by caste and kinship preferences, and they shape up an invisible ambience to practice endogamy to create a niche in the caste-based hierarchical web.

3.2. Outside the Catholic Church

Synodality could also be practiced inter-denominationally. Participatory bodies between denominational churches for spiritual solidarity, economic cooperation, political solidarity, and social harmony could be created at local, regional and national levels. The Indian Catholic Church, being the numerically strong communion among others, has a responsibility to take the lead in this regard. A sphere of solidarity and collaboration beyond theological, liturgical, and spiritual layers is a must for today.

As mentioned earlier in this paper, there was a time when the Catholic Church attempted to constitute itself to be a civil society against the challenges posed by the liberal modern society. It founded several civil society institutions like educational institutions, social service organizations, political forums, etc. to contribute to the common good of humanity. These have come to the present-day Catholics as valuable patrimonies, with which it can be substantively active in the wider civil society today.

Christian presence in the domain of education, an important component of civil society, is facing up to increasing challenges: first of all, the process of "commercialization" of education, a global phenomenon though, is posing a big challenge to the Christian mind. Promoting literacy, higher education and scientific pursuits have always been promoted by the Catholic Church as necessary pathways to develop the potentials as well as the moral character of the human person as ordained by God. But the present-day challenge of commercialization, sailing on the impulses of the technocratic paradigm and profit-making, is tempting us to walk a path of immanentist anti-witness. It creates a typical "tensive" moment for the Church. Deep analysis and discernment among the Christian agents of education is a necessity today.

Moreover, some major shifts in educational polices introduced by the Government do not resonate well with the Christian values. For example, if there is a project of homogenization of cultures written into some educational policies, how can Christians collaborate with it? Right from the beginning of the Catholic Social teachings, homogenization of the civil sphere by the industrial forces has been severely critiqued on the ground that it damages the dignity and freedom of the human person. How can we, therefore, go in support of such projects?

Social service and health ministry, which are also parts of the civil society, too are facing up to challenges. A deep suspicion is cast upon the Christian project of social service under the label of 'conversion'. Starting from the local fanatics, to doctrinaire scholarship, and to sections of prejudiced judiciary, the Christian agency becomes victim of the suspicion. Conversion as a religious experience gets lost in the din of partisan political discourses, and the human right associated with it becomes suspect. "Social service is welcome, but not conversion" is the slogan heard today. Though not in any way instrumentalising social service for conversion, disconnecting the social service from a religious inspiration paralyses the Christian mind, personality and the collective body. How do we face this crucial challenge?

Facing up to these challenges and questions need deeper discernments and participation in wider circles of conversations. As Pope Francis would have it, we need to participate in a dialogical culture of encounter. Polyhedron, as mentioned above, is the image he uses to bring radically different others around the table of dialogue or conversation. This image gives the inner strength to take on these challenges and questions as part of our participation in the culture of encounter.

Conclusion

The Catholic social teachings tell us that the Catholic Church has progressively opened itself up to engage the civil society in a manner of *participation*. Though there were phases of 'dominating over', 'instructing and guiding', 'being antagonistic', 'parallel functioning', and 'instrumentalising', the synodal Church today has come to "participate" in the civil society along with different others. This participation is deliberative in the sense of leading to substantial decision-making on public policies. Promoting the common good, nurturing the dignity of human persons with rights and duties, caring for the poor, the migrants, the refugees and other vulnerable people, cultivating a culture of encounter with different others, and relating all of the above with faith in God, the transcendental source, are the reasons for the Catholic Church to engage the civil society. The now initiated synodal event by Pope Francis introduces a momentum of the participatory dynamic by which the Catholic Church enters the frontiers of deliberative participation both within the Church as well as in the wider civil society. The overall impact of this event will make the Catholic Church more conscious and conscientious to practice civic virtues within the Church and participate pro-actively in public forums of civil society to discuss, debate, discern and decide on public policies.

Part-III

Religions, Public Conversations, and Strivings for Freedom

12

Interfaith Dialogues
New Horizons and Pathways

Conventional Insights and Initiatives for Interfaith Dialogues

Interfaith dialogues are not new to our era. There are those who trace their origin even to the birth of the Axial age (@800 – 200 BCE) when there took place in different parts of the globe a reflexivity over ritual practices leading to "dialogues" of different 'philosophies' or 'theoria.'[1] In the Indian context, interfaith forums had been created by emperors, religious institutions and mystic individuals from very ancient days. We have emperors like Asoka and Akbar, religious institutions like sanghas, ashrams and monastries, and mystics like Kabir, Ramakrishna, and innumerable others who had initiated the prototypes of interfaith dialogues leading to tolerance and communal harmony. Their initiatives were born out of the deeply embedded realisations on the unity as well as diversity of faith traditions in India. The upanishadic aphorism *ekam sat vipra bahudha vadanti,* meaning, 'reality is one, sages call it differently' is one of the deeply embedded insights which highlights the oneness and the differences of faith traditions, and the relationship between them. The famous Jaina wisdom story of 'blind men and the elephant' is adduced to argue that, in addition to the fact of the incomprehensibility of reality, human perception is radically perspectival, and therefore, differences are germane to culture and civilisation. The Jaina doctrine of *anekantavada* (many-sidedness of reality) and its epistemology of *syadvata* (that every judgement is conditional to certain perspective) give a philosophical grounding to the reality of pluralism – whether religious, cultural, or philosophical. These teachings have been existing with us

[1] Cf. Leonard Swidler, "The History of Interreligious Dialogue," in *The Wiley-Blackwell Companion to Interreligous Dialogue*, ed. Catherine Corneille (UK: Wiley-Blackwell, 2013), 3-19.

for long and have nurtured deep senses of plurality as well as networked unity in us. They have indeed flowed down into our veins today. During the more recent times, Vivekananda intoned the need for dialogue by speaking about the 'gospel of the harmony of all religions' at the Parliament of World Religions in 1893.

Today the term 'dialogue', according to Catherine Corneille, a scholar in interreligious studies, has come to stand for "a constructive engagement between religious texts, teachings, and practices oriented toward the possibility of change and growth."[2] It implies a wide spectrum of initiatives, "ranging from peaceful coexistence and friendly exchanges, to active engagement with the teachings and practices of the other, and from cooperation toward social change to common prayer and participation in the ritual life of the other."[3] Jose Kuttianimattathil, yet another scholar in the field of interreligious studies, identifies the different forms of dialogues as: dialogue of life, dialogue of action, dialogue of theological exchange, and dialogue of religious experiences.[4] The 'dialogue of life' takes place in the day-to-day life-world of the people, where they exchange ideas, opinions, insights, etc of their respective religions in the context of actual life; 'dialogue of action' takes place in organised efforts by different religionists for goals of common good; 'dialogue of theological exchange' takes place in 'dialogue centres' or academic circles; and, 'dialogue of religious experience' takes place in centres or religious sites where a facility for sharing of different religious experiences or living together (like an ashram) is in place. Ours has, thus, become an era of multipronged and multi-dimensional interfaith dialogues.

New Horizons

Scholars, commentators and practitioners of religions observe today that there is a resurgence or revitalisation of religion everywhere. This phenomenon goes against the 'secularization thesis' once emphatically prevalent not only among the academic circles and public intellectuals but also among those activists spearheading social movements. Today, a 'post-secular' or a non-secular ethos is on the horizon. Religions are being believed and practised today without the overbearing framework of the 'secular.' Scholars speak of the emergence today of what is called 'public religions', i.e., religion in the public sphere.

Religions are increasingly getting integrated with the construction of social, cultural, civilizational and political identities today. Social relationships are initiated or maintained along religious lines; cultural practices of a given

---

[2] Catherine Corneille, "Conditions for Interreligious Dialogue," in *The Wiley-Blackwell Companion to Interreligous Dialogue,* ed. Catherine Corneille (UK: Wiley-Blackwell, 2013), 20.

[3] Ibid.

[4] Cf. Jose Kuttianimattathil, sdb, *Practice and Theology of Interreligious Dialogue* (Bangalore: Kristu Jyoti Publications, 1995), 588.

community is increasingly being informed by what its religion sanctions or advocates; civilisational zones are being imagined along religious boundaries; and, political behaviour of people are being led by religious preferences or identities. The situation is such that scholars like Samuel Huntington could voice out, though not convincingly, a warning of 'civilization clash' at the core of which is religion. Conflicts or violence, implicating religion overtly or covertly, have proliferated. Open acts of terror and violence, let loose on religious others, have become gruesome scenes. Stereotyping and targeting of religious identities, especially if they are minorities in majoritarian polities, are a growing phenomenon.

Religious plurality is becoming a thick and irreversible experience today. Phenomenologically speaking, plurality of religious beliefs and practices fill the air through media representations, public performances, individual observances, and so on. Being linked to history and identity of people, religious observances have become sites of increasing involvement by communities of people.

In such a context, one cannot remain content with the conventional practices of interfaith dialogues, conducted by professionals within the walls of religious institutions. Interfaith dialogues need to be practiced today in the public spaces.

Dialogues / Conversations in Public Spaces

What are meant by public spaces are those sites wherein the public involves in religious studies, interreligious reflections, conversations, argumentations, interreligious initiatives for common good, etc. Some of these prominent sites are academia, media, intra-religious forums, inter-religious dialogue forums, and networks of civil societies.

Academia

Academia, especially of the higher educational institutions, provides the prominent public spaces wherein interfaith dialogues have to be substantively initiated through inter-religious and inter-disciplinary studies of faith-traditions. It is in place to note that the western academia has a substantive component of religious studies in their curriculum, and it generates deep knowledge and wisdom on the nature, content, and dynamics of religions, which are made available to the wider public through publications, seminars and conferences. Consequently there emerges an informed public that can involve in relatively richer and more harmonious conversations and dialogues on religions. In the Indian context, there are research institutions found in Universities for religious studies. But they are too few and their voice too feeble.

There was a time when the western academia spoke about doing 'comparative religious studies.' Comparativists gathered huge data on religious symbols, rituals, beliefs and practices, and highlighted the similarities and dissimilarities between them. Claims and counterclaims to uniqueness and supremacy proliferated. However, soon enough, the phenomenologists took comparative religion towards identifying commonalities between religions. They went on to identify common sacred experiences lying beneath the manifest forms of religion.

Today comparativists hold a bottom-line position of 'beyond compare', i.e. to hold that religions are beyond comparisons, because of their incommensurability. Each tradition is unique, and it cannot be compared in an evaluatory manner. What can be done, however, is study of religion in an inter-religious or multi-religious or inter-textual manner. Such 'inter-textual' or 'inter-religious' studies have great potentials to moderate the absolutist stances of religions and contribute to communal harmony.

Media

In our age of the boom of Information and Communication Technology, religious media has come to occupy a predominant place in the religious consciousness and observances of our people. Starting with the traditional print media to the contemporary virtual or cyber media, religion has come to wield a predominant presence in them; and they are also serving as public spaces for interfaith dialogues or even disputations in a big way.

It is instructive to note that the sites of social media, supported by internet communication, have become leading players in the area of informal, semi-formal and even formal interfaith dialogues. These sites sponsor different types of forums. In a study, I identified that there are, firstly, websites which use the name 'forum' and are sponsored by particular religious traditions, giving information about particular traditions.[5] They host materials on their particular traditions, include testimonies and apologetics, and are intended for presenting their tradition only. They are *forums* to the extent that they are interactive, in the sense that a visitor can ask question, clarify matters, etc. Such forums are information rich, but lack the dynamics of conversation, characteristic of an interfaith dialogue.

The second type could be forums which are sponsored by particular religious traditions, but, incorporate a space for dialogue, wherein a visitor is allowed to express a different or even opposite point of view. There is a level of dissent allowed. However, the different or opposite views will be arbitrated within the framework of the particular tradition that sponsors the forum.[6]

---

[5] Examples are: http://www.hindudharmaforums.com/HINDUDHARMAFORUMS, http://www.forumforhinduawakening.org/ 'Forum for Hindu Awakening', https://www.gawaher.com/Islamic Forum, https://www.christianforums.com / Christian Forums, https://www.worthychristianforums.com/ Worthy Christian Forum, etc.

[6] Examples could be http://thehinduforum.com/index.php The Hindu Forum, https://www.islamicity.org/forum/ Islamic City Forum, http://www.city-data.com/forum/christianity/ Christianity Forum – City Data Forum, etc.

The third types are forums which openly name themselves as interreligious forums to involve in interfaith discourses and learning. They provide resources for understanding different others, and encourage to learn about one another. They carry 'common' names like 'beliefnet', 'bridge-builders', etc. There is a clear orientation in these sites to study religions comparatively with ongoing mutual learning.[7]

Civil Society Networks

Civil society provides multiple-layered public spaces for voluntary initiatives on interfaith dialogue to take place. Civil sphere, a relatively free space that emerges between a family, a state and an economic system, and a space of independent initiatives in art, culture, and social welfare, oftentimes expressed through formation of NGOs, including faith-based NGOs, is congenial for religious dialogues. Reading clubs, neighbourhood collectives, literary forums, activist forums, forums for professionals, social movements, and the like can serve as the civil sites for interreligious dialogues. It is these conversations which are relatively better adept at arresting the formation of such retrograde forces as religious fanaticism, majoritarianism and fundamentalism.

Intra-Religious Dialogue

Intra-religious dialogues can very powerfully contribute to the practice of healthy inter-religious dialogues. Raymond Panikkar, a well-known scholar of religion, spoke of his individual life as one that journeyed through different faith traditions, gaining deeper realisations ultimately upon his own tradition. He famously said, "I came to India as a Christian, found myself a Hindu, and returned as a Buddhist, without however ceasing to be a Christian." The interfaith journey that he had undertaken, according to him, was one not only of *inter-religious* dialogue, but one that became a deep experience of *intra-religious* dialogue.

Intra-religious dialogue, according to him, is an "inner dialogue within myself (oneself), an encounter in the depth of my (one's) personal religiousness, having met another religious experience on that very intimate level."[8] It is a moment of transformation that takes place in the innermost spaces of one's life. When someone goes through an encounter of religious beliefs within oneself, the intrapersonal dialogue occurs. As he puts it: "The real religious ... task ... begins when two views meet head-on inside oneself, when dialogue prompts genuine religious pondering, and even a religious crisis, at the bottom of a Man's heart; when interpersonal dialogue turns into intrapersonal soliloquy."[9]

---

[7] A good example of this type is: https://www.scarboromissions.ca/interfaith-dialogue/principles-and-guidelines-for-interfaith-dialogue.

[8] R. Panikkar, *The Intra-Religious Dialogue* (Bangalore: ATC Publications, 1978), 78.

[9] Raymond Panikkar, *The Intrareligious Dialogue* (Bangalore: ATC, 1978), 48.

This "[D]ialogue is not bare methodology but an essential part of the religious act par excellence..."[10] It is an experience of loving the other as the other would love herself / himself / itself, and this act would become possible not from one's own vantage point, but when one endeavours to adopt an vantage point between or over the other and oneself, and this vantage point could be named as God, ultimate reality, Divine mystery, Parabaran, etc. "This is an experience in itself, not an experimentation, a "genuine experience undergone within *one's own faith*."[11]

To open oneself up to this experience, Panikkar proposes certain root-metaphors as paradigms or models. He names them as The Geographical Model – Ways to the Mountain Peak, The Physical Model – The Rainbow, The Geometrical Model – The Topological Invariant, and The Anthropological Model – Language.[12] 1. The geographical model poises a seeker / pilgrim towards a summit, either transcendent or immanent, and enables a pilgrimage towards it. The pilgrim begins with a path and progresses upon it keeping herself / himself open to learn from different pathways which may lead to the summit. 2. The physical model of the rainbow envisions that when the divine reality falls upon the prism of the human, it diffracts into a harmony of colours like in a rainbow. There are not just seven colours, but innumerable colours in between, like innumerable faith-traditions which exist between apparently bounded traditions. One may start with the experience of one colour, but can grow in the experience of other colours as well. 3. The geometric model presumes a common ground or topological space which lends itself for multiple geometric transformations. Same can be found in an experience of the sacred space, which lends itself to multiple formations of traditions. 4. The anthropological model of a language conveys the insight that any religion is as complete as a language is and yet "opens to growth and evolution as any language is."[13] No language grows on its own, but always in relation to neighbouring languages. "Similarly with religions: they influence each other and borrow from one another without losing their identity."[14] These models, needless to say, are healthy root-metaphors to open a seeker to embark upon an intra-religious dialogue, leading to deeper inter-religious dialogues and encounters.

Ours is time when such intra-religious dialogues need to take place also within each particular religious tradition. Hinduism, Islam, Christianity, Jainism, Buddhism, Sikhism, and several other faith-traditions would do well

---

[10] Ibid. 48.

[11] Ibid., 50.

[12] Cf. R. Panikkar, *The Intra-Religious Dialogue* (Bangalore: ATC, 1978), 23ff.

[13] Ibid., 33.

[14] Ibid., 33.

to undertake intra-religious dialogues, by learning to get to know of other traditions so as to grow into deeper realisations of one's own particular tradition. Such a manner of learning will certainly contribute to deeper experiences of communal harmony in the society.

Going Beyond Stereotypes

While we reflect upon such healthy pathways of opening oneself to the other in dialogues, we need also to become aware of the inadequacies of some of the stereotypical approaches prevalent in the field of religious dialogues. Exclusivism, inclusivism and pluralism are some of these approaches which have been seriously called into question by scholars as well as practitioners of interfaith dialogues today. An observation on their limitations by Werner G. Jeanrond is worth noting:

> *Exclusivists* know from the outset that they alone own adequate approaches to God and thus are not likely to expect any further revelation or insight through encountering other approaches to the mystery of God. *Pluralists* lack a self-critical hermeneutical awareness of being rooted within a living tradition. Therefore they are likely to miss the significance of this limitation but also of the constructive potential of this predicament for thinking about God. *Inclusivists* may mislead themselves when they suggest that they are able to integrate new insights and approaches to the divine mystery without that deeper struggle that unavoidably affects their own religious self-understanding when confronted with the religious other.[15]

Accepting these inadequacies is necessary for genuine interfaith dialogues. Among the three, the approach of religious pluralism holds certain validity today, but in a different sense. Religious pluralism needs to free itself from creating a culture of passive indifference to religion in general and other religions in particular. An *interactive pluralism* therefore is in place today. It is an approach which seeks to know and understand the other, and live in the presence of the other in a radical sense of dialogical mutuality and encounter in the public space.

Virtues of Dialogues in Public Spaces

Dialogues in public spaces need virtues, which make the experience of dialogue refreshing, creative, and liberative.

---

[15] Werner G. Jeanrond, "Thinking about God Today," in *The Concept of God in Global Dialogue*, eds. Werner G. Jeanrond & Aasulv Lande (Maryknoll: Orbis Books, 2005), 90-91.

Epistemological Humility, Hospitality Towards Others, Commitment, Interconnection, and Empathy

Catherine Corneille, whom we quoted above, identifies 'epistemological humility', 'hospitality towards others', 'commitment', 'interconnection', and 'empathy' as virtues needed for interfaith dialogue.[16] Epistemological humility for a religion would mean becoming aware of the finitude / historical dimension of every religious tradition and being ready to learn from others; hospitality would mean a respect and openness towards others; commitment would mean involvement or commitment to a particular religious tradition which makes the dialogue an 'engaged one'; interconnection would imply recognizing certain commonality between religions which, as a general rule, engage with questions of human existence, its future, etc.; and empathy would mean stretching one's religious imagination beyond one's own tradition to warmly *understand* and not explain away another tradition. These virtues, though very challenging, have been attempted in the practise of interreligious dialogues in actual contexts of life.

Dialogues and not Debates

In the light of the post-metaphysical realisations, it becomes clearer that dialogues are not debates. While debates are argumentative, born out of a desire to prove the truth of one's claim, dialogue works in a different sense of mutuality, wherein the partners share their experiences or opinions without holding on to any claim for superiority to their experiences or opinions. Dialogues work with the assumption that truth is a realisation that occurs in mutuality, which sheds light upon one another, and even challenges one another.

Justice and Freedom

Dialogues need be oriented consciously towards greater justice and freedom. There is a temptation to make the exercises of dialogues as a process of *Modus Vivendi*, trying to join in conflict resolutions, however temporary they may be. Such dialogues become easy prey to the operation of power, swinging towards the wielders of power. On the other hand dialogues committed for greater goals of justice and freedom, even to the very discourse of them, have the power to take the dialogue to deeper realisations and creative experiences.

Empowerment of the Marginalised

Dialogues, especially when they are carried out in public spaces, need be rooted in concerns of emancipation of the marginalised and the subaltern. In our contemporary realisations, the subalterns are not only those sections of humanity who live under multiple forms of subordination, but also the

[16] Catherine Corneille, "Conditions for Interreligious Dialogue," in *The Wiley-Blackwell Companion to Interreligous Dialogue,* ed. Catherine Corneille (UK: Wiley-Blackwell, 2013), 21.

animals, plants and the entire eco-system which are being dominated over by the humans. Freedom for these subalterns must be at the heart of public dialogues. It is this concern that can become a legitimate locus of dialogue in every field. The realisation that occurred to Paul Knitter, a prominent promoter of interreligious dialogue, when he made the concerns of the poor as the ultimate concerns of dialogue, is very meaningful to be recalled here.

Comprehensive Doctrines and Conversations

It is important to note also the emergent realisation that the method or mode of interfaith dialogues is addressed today as 'interfaith conversations'. In our contemporary context wherein the realisations of the narrativity of human experience and the indispensable role played by language in mediation of reality have come to the fore, *conversations* become the appropriate modalities of interactions between faith-traditions, ethical doctrines, etc., which are the comprehensive doctrines that guide the lives of people. These comprehensive doctrines are 'incommensurable', i.e., not to be substituted by others, let alone co-opted by others. These incommensurable comprehensive doctrines need to come together in the context of bringing humanity together on public concerns for common good.

Where can these conversations take place is an important question too. Rajeev Bhargava, one of the leading liberal political philosophers in the Indian context, would characterise democratic polity as having three realms: ends, institutions and policies. The realm of 'ends' deals with the goals of a democratic polity, 'institutions' stand for such structures as parliaments, bureaucracy, etc., and the realm of policies stand for the space of formation of general will wherein viewpoints on public concerns are expressed, debated, and represented. Relating religion or 'establishing' religion at the realm of 'ends', as it happens in theocratic societies, would be antagonistic to religious pluralism and detrimental to liberal democracy; bringing the realms of institutions and religion too would not serve the cause of egalitarian democracy; and, the realm of 'policy making', the civil and public spheres, including the judiciary, are those wherein religion can be related meaningfully with democratic political processes. It is in and through these realms that interfaith conversations can take place and contribute to communal harmony and national integration.

Interfaith Conversations and Social Work

Among the many points of convergence between interfaith conversations and social work, a significant one that comes to my mind is nurturing bonds of healthy sociality, especially at the grassroots of the society. Bonds of healthy sociality are ones which weaken the systems of closures – systems which keep excluding sections of people from growth and development in terms of caste, colour, creed, region, religion, language, etc. They keep opening spaces so as to empower the hitherto excluded and oppressed. By so doing, they create channels of empowering communication and ensue in associational life, which in turn, enhances social capital, the factor of social trust that is necessary for collaboration for development and communal harmony.

Conclusion

Interfaith dialogues, in formal and informal ways, have a long history. They infuse harmony into the lifeworld of the people especially as everyday forms of dialogues of life. The contemporary post-secular era has revitalised peoples' engagement with religion in multiple ways and has opened up public spaces like the academia, media, and civil society networks for intra and interfaith dialogues. These new spaces go with new methodologies, new virtues and new partners of interfaith conversations. When they mature to be public interfaith conversations, they have the potential to nurture communal harmony and national integration from the grassroots. What more a praxis of communal harmony and national integration can look for?

13

Public Theological Conversations on Cities

Introduction

After the emergence of modern cities, which occurred in many Asian countries during the colonial era, bigger and larger cities keep growing all over the Asian continent until today. According to the recent UN-HABITAT figures, "cities in the Asia-Pacific are now home to around half of the world's urban population,"[1] and therefore, the culturalized realities emergent in these regions will characterise the nature of urbanity as a lived-reality for humanity everywhere.

India, as one of the most populous countries of the world, with many modern cities to count, plays a vital role in constituting the Asian experience of cities or urbanities today. Its cities represent recognisable economic vitality and cultural diversity. As Jan Nijman observes, "[T]he most striking quality of big cities in India is their incredible capacity to contain a bewildering range of economic activities, from the preindustrial, muscle-powered to the post-industrial, computer-driven."[2] They contribute the major share of the economic output of the country. "[T]he McKinsey Global Institute (2010) estimates that Indian cities today account for 60% of GDP"[3] of India. Like any other fast developing region, India is building today global smart cities, catering to the need of a burgeoning global community of trade, commerce and industry.

---

[1] Tim Bunnell, Daniel P. S. Goh, Chee-Kien Lai and C. P. Pow, "Introduction: Global Urban Frontiers? Asian Cities in Theory, Practice and Imagination," *Urban Studies*, Vol. 49, No. 13, Special Issue: Global Urban Frontiers? Asian Cities in Theory, Practice and Imagination" (OCTOBER 2012), p. 2785. https://www.jstor.org/stable/10.2307/26144113.

[2] Jan Nijman, "India in the Urban Revolution." *Indian Anthropologist*, July - December 2012, Vol. 42, No. 2 (July - December 2012), p. 12; https://www.jstor.org/stable/41922303.

[3] Ibid., 2.

Modern cities in India, in the specifically *modern* format as they are now, originated, as mentioned above, during the colonial era. Notwithstanding the present-day claims in some quarters that the Indian subcontinent was home to some ancient civilisations wherein cities were built with meticulous planning, where city-life flourished with considerable comfort and civic facilities, etc., it can well be ascertained that it was during the colonial era that cities with mass settlements emerged and grew with liberal civic ethos, to provide habitat for everyone in a non-discriminatory manner. Trade and commerce, being the core-interests that motivated to build cities, especially port-cities in India, generated economic activities, which, by their very logic, tended more and more to include different others in the economic process rather than exclude any section of them. And the civic consciousness emergent upon the modern education should have characterised the cities with relative openness and universality.

While acknowledging this openness of Indian cities, we need also to reckon with the fact that Indian cities keep experiencing certain dynamics of exclusion, some of which do not augur well for the universality, equality, civic virtues, and urban creativity. Dynamics of 'inclusion and exclusion', even though common to many other major cities of the world, seem to function in the Indian context with their typical features and characteristics. The present article is an attempt to take a look at the Indian specific dynamics of inclusion and exclusion occurring in the Indian cities, and reflect upon them with certain normative keys / insights emerging from public theology today.

Dynamics of Inclusion and Exclusion in the Colonial Period

Beneath the apparent vitality of urbanisation, Indian cities, built by the British colonial powers, seem to have lent spaces also for dynamics of segregation in a manner of laying discriminatory boundaries between different sections of the society. Eric Lewis Beverley's exploration of the concept of 'colonial urbanism' in the Indian context helps us in this regard.[4] Reviewing the literature existing until the year 2011 on the dynamics of urban worlds or city making during the colonial regime in the South Asian context, Beverley opines that "[T]hese dynamics suggest that urbanism in colonial South Asia was fundamentally about spatial segregation of populations."[5] The colonisers differentiated the cities between 'white towns' and 'black towns', subdividing the 'white towns' further into 'military cantonments', 'civil settlements' and 'hill stations' having administrative buildings as well as houses for the whites within walled cities in the civil settlement areas. Spatially removed from them, the natives lived in

[4] Eric Lewis Beverley, "Colonial Urbanism and South Asian Cities." *Social History*, November 2011, Vol. 36, No. 4 (November 2011), pp. 482-497; https://www.jstor.org/stable/2307265.

[5] Ibid., 483.

segregated 'black towns', which, however, could be controlled by the British military. As Beverley observes:

> Cities were organized to enable military intervention when necessary and to safeguard the needs and ensure the discipline of soldiers. Permanent military stations - initially walled forts, later sprawling cantonments — were the classic forms of spatial segregation under the Raj. Military areas combined with civil stations for European residences and institutions to form what during the early colonial period was imagined as the inviolable 'white town'. Cantonments were nerve centres for instilling discipline and exercising control. While people and ideas constantly transgressed the sections of the split colonial city, the division of zones was decisive as both ideology and material practice.[6]

One of the main arguments of Beverley, as seen above, is that the British colonial regime, by introducing such segregations, created a regime of social control and domination in the cities. It amounted then to creating city spaces with exclusionary borders, even while including the excluded through a process of enlisting the latter's role in the running of the cities by their 'menial' jobs. As he continues to argue: "[U]rban segregation during the colonial period, ... is a key antecedent for forms of class segregation (often overlapping with religious, ethno-linguistic or caste segregation) that structure postcolonial South Asian cities, their neighbourhoods and suburbs."[7]

Contemporary Neo-Liberal Period

The phase of colonial urbanism passed over. From the predominance of industrial economy, cities passed over to multidimensional economic activities provided by the neoliberal global economic prospects. Neoliberal economies all over the world, premised upon the success of the market-forces, are said to be impacted less by dictates of regions, religions, gender, race, and other ascriptively hierarchical ties, and more by liberal frameworks of merit, universality, equality, and liberty. Asian cities, from Shangai to Hong Kong to Mumbai to Dubai, do work on the logic of neo-liberalism at one level, especially at the level of commerce and consumerism.

However, neo-liberalism has not guaranteed non-discriminatory urban spaces even in most advanced countries like North-America. Grown with liberal values that respected different others, one would expect North-America to be free of discriminatory segregations. Unfortunately, as Laura Tach, through a study, has pointed out, what has emerged there are subtle dynamics of "micro-segregations" based on race, colour, religion, region and the like, even through

---

[6] Ibid., 6.

[7] Ibid., 83.

the medium of civic associations. She gives an account of it, based on her empirical study:

> ... a closer examination of their daily lives and their use of neighborhood organizations and public spaces revealed that proximity and appreciation for diversity did not lead to much cross-race or cross-class contact. Instead, residents developed patterns of microsegregation, or homogenous pockets of interaction and organization within the larger neighborhood. Microsegregation occurred informally—through daily routines, interactions, and use of neighborhood space—and also more formally through neighborhood associations and organizations. In turn, patterns of microsegregation fueled race and class-based perceptions of inclusion and exclusion that belied the simple, idealized characterizations of diversity residents initially espoused.[8]

The most advanced nation seems to suffer acute inequality in terms of economic standard, poverty, unemployment and underemployment, which, overlap with more deeply layered racial discriminations. These segregatory dynamics restrict and reduce access to "high-quality housing, institutions, and services for poor and minority residents, which reproduces and exacerbates racial and economic inequalities."[9]

Post-colonial Indian Cities / Urban Development

As the colonial phase faded away, the Indian independent nation began to follow its developmental path with five-year plans and other policies of urban development. Further growth in industrialisation involved continued growth in urban centres, and modern Indian cities continued to grow in number. Development from villages to towns, and towns to small cities, and to mega cities of metropolitan and cosmopolitan nature gradually unfolded in the Indian history of urban development. Today creating 'smart cities' so as to attract global investments from mega multinational corporate companies has become the avowed goal of the Indian government.

Whether this progressive path of urban development has done away with or reduced considerably the undercurrents of exclusion and inclusion, running across racial, ethnic-linguistic, religious, and caste segregations is a question to be probed into. Jan Nijman reflects about the 'urban revolution' taking place in India, taking Mumbai as an example, and avers that the "most

---

[8] Laura M. Tach, "Diversity, Inequality, and Microsegregation: Dynamics of Inclusion and Exclusion in a Racially and Economically Diverse Community." *Cityscape*, Vol. 16, No. 3, American Neighborhoods: Inclusion and Exclusion (2014), p. 26; https://www.jstor.org/stable/10.2307/26326904.

[9] Ibid., 14.

striking quality of big cities in India is their incredible capacity to contain a bewildering range of economic activities, from the preindustrial, muscle-powered to the postindustrial, computer-driven. The Indian city harbours different modes of production that are historical eras apart in the cities of the western world."[10] That the Indian cities have "bewildering range of economic activities" is something to be appreciated, but, whether everyone is able to participate in every economic activity in a non-discriminatory manner is the concern of the day. The creation of different classes of people as lower-middle-upper categories, with their sub-categories as well, in terms of income, power of consumption, and spaces for housing with necessary amenities has become the problem of Indian city-making. As Nijman himself puts it, "[T]he new middle class is carving out a conspicuous consumptive niche in the urban landscape but it is doing so in competition with about six million slum dwellers for whom a living space is a matter of survival, not a luxury."[11] Slums in Indian cities bespeak of the double-standard of Indian urbanity. Appalling conditions of slum dwellers keep interrogating the validity of comfort and riches available for the middle and upper classes of people in the Indian cities. Slums seem to be the bête-noire of cities in India as they are elsewhere during the present phase of urban development. They generate a basic duality in city-dwelling, generating dual, hierarchised, and discriminated habitats – physical, cultural, and psychological. "Mumbai" for example, as pointed out to by Nijman, "is still two cities, one deemed modern and desirable, and the other the city of the slums, unintended and undesirable. The undesirable city in colonial times was Native Town, outside the colonial enclave; today it is the multitude of slums that dot the urban landscape."[12]

Swapna Banerjee-Guha, another researcher on urban studies, identifies a homogenous process across the country of re-conceptualisation and restructuring of urban spaces that is going on in the field of urban development in India today. To aid this process, a scheme of gentrification is promoted by urban planners and developers. She argues that these programs 'intensify the un-evenness in inter-urban and intra-urban development.'[13] About the character of the emerging urbanity, she says:

> The overall character represents a gradual fragmentation of territories, economic decline and displacement of a large majority, increasing socio-spatial in-equality and a simultaneous emergence

---

[10] Nijman, "India in the Urban Revolution", 10.

[11] Ibid., 11.

[12] Ibid., 11.

[13] Swapna Banerjee-Guha, "Neoliberalising the 'Urban': New Geographies of Power and Injustice in Indian Cities." Economic and Political Weekly , May 30 - Jun. 5, 2009, Vol. 44, No. 22 (May 30 - Jun. 5, 2009), p. 95; https://www.jstor.org/stable/40279062.

> of new/modern activities in specific locales, implying an aggravation of "spaces of difference." In the process of reconstructing space as a part of the above re-conceptualisation of the contemporary "urban", displacement and dispossession of the poor and weaker sections have surfaced as a fundamental aspect, aided by other methods of marginalisation, like closure of small-scale manufacturing and retail units, anti-poor legal order, regulations against informal workers, hawkers, waste pickers, privatisation of basic services like water, sanitation, housing, health and education, and, last but not the least, restricting access to open spaces for making available more arenas for elitist consumption. Ideology, armed with power, is found to bring about patterns of domination and repression in many Indian cities in current times."[14]

Thus we find an urban development programme, with contradictions of inequality, inaccessibility, poverty, etc. taking place in India. The excluded are people living in marginal conditions, excluded from the mainstream of the society due to economic deprivation and other related social ills. It is necessary to note that these excluded people are, from yet another angle, included in the whole process of development and maintenance of Indian cities. Migrant workers, daily-wage labourers, domestic workers, and others involved in service sectors have become an indispensable population of cities, living on the margins of the very cities they build or maintain. In that way, there is a convergence of exclusion and inclusion, which, cruel though, has become the order of urban life in India.

Indian Specificity: The Ritual Dimension of Purity and Impurity

While much of these contradictions are present in many metropolitan or cosmopolitan cities all over the world, what is specific to the Indian context is that these forms of exclusion and inclusion are exacerbated by what is called 'ritual purity and pollution divide', peculiar to a caste-based social system. Few decades ago, Louis Dumount, the famous social anthropologist, argued in his book on *Homo Hierarchicus* that it was ultimately the axis of purity and pollution upon which the discriminatory borders between castes existed. Depending upon the level of ritual purity of one community, as perceived by another, that any community got treated as 'touchable' or 'untouchable' and the social distance was prescribed as per the level of such purity or pollution. Unfortunately, such unmeaning practices of untouchability or social distancing seem to get adapted to the urban conditions of life too. In most of the cities, those who get excluded to live along the margins are also those treated as ritually polluting and socially 'untouchable' in the wider society.

[14] Banerjee-Guha, pp. 96-97.

Experiences of denial of houses for rent in selected spaces of the city to Dalits and other communities on the supposedly lower rungs of social hierarchy are heart-rending. An incident goes as follows:

> The first time, I went with an upper-caste colleague. The landlord said about five times that he wanted 'good people'. I took that to mean I qualified, as I don't drink or party; we are quiet people and I am an academic researcher. But the questions my wife faced from the landlady, when we said we were Buddhist, persisted, and one day my wife said we were from a Scheduled Caste. We were asked to leave. My mother insisted we go and ask the landlady again, who told us clearly that her God doesn't allow her to rent house to a low-caste family. She gave us a month to find another place.[15]

Such instances are not rare in Indian cities, wherein caste-based discrimination has become a 'normal' practice today. As Vidayathil et.al. argue, "[A]s India urbanises, the caste and religious dimensions of exclusion persist and interact with other forms of discrimination in terms of class, gender and region to produce new forms of urban inequality."[16] Among these forms of discrimination, those against the Dalits and Tribals are more violent and widely prevalent, but more veiled and coded than in villages. As Vidayathil et al continue: "[D]iscrimination against urban Dalits is insidious, often violent, and widely acceptable, although sometimes more coded in its expression than the discrimination and violence faced by Dalits in rural India."[17] And as these authors find out, "[R]ecent research in five metropolitan cities in the NCR indicates clear evidence of homeowner prejudices in renting homes to both Muslims and Dalits, with Muslims facing more severe censorship."[18]

Denial of homes correlate with other amenities that a city provides for those included in its prime place. As Pranav Sidhwani observes:

> It also finds a medium to strong negative correlation between the proportion of Scheduled Castes / Tribes in the population and access to in-house drinking water across wards in Chennai and Kolkata, a moderately high negative correlation between the proportion of Scheduled Castes / Tribes in the population and access to in-house latrines in Pune, Bangalore, Chennai, Jaipur, Ahmedabad

[15] An experience narrated by a person named Dr. Nitin in Delhi and published in the *Indian Express*, widely circulated English Daily in India. Tina Vithayathil, et. al. "ONLY 'GOOD PEOPLE', PLEASE: Residential Segregation in Urbanising India." India International Centre Quarterly, WINTER 2016–SPRING 2017, Vol. 43, No. 3/4, The Contemporary Urban Conundrum (WINTER 2016–SPRING 2017), p. 45 https://www.jstor.org/stable/26317313.

[16] Tina Vithayathil, et.al. 46.

[17] Ibid., 46.

[18] Ibid.

> and Mumbai, and moderate to strong negative correlation between the proportion of Scheduled Castes / Tribes in the population and ownership of two-wheelers in Pune, Chennai, Ahmedabad, Delhi and Mumbai.[19]

Cities practise untouchability in invisible manners. The practical aspects of the belief in purity and pollution are manifest in quotidian ways of allowing and avoiding the potential pollutants in the vicinity of livelihood or neighbourhood. Avoiding Dalits or other so-called polluting castes in a neighbourhood by refusing houses on rent to them or villanising them for their dietary habits are ways of practising untouchability in invisible manners.

It is typical of the Indian village to include as many occupational groups of people as possible within the limits or borders of a village, even while keeping them apart within their respective boundaries drawn in terms of the purity-pollution logic of Indian caste system, the erstwhile *varna* system to be specific. At the centre of a typical Indian village, there is the temple; and immediately around the temple are houses of the priestly class; next to them are the mercantile or agricultural classes of people who form the mainstay of a village; and, finally, we have those doing the day-to-day menial jobs of washing clothes, cutting hair, etc. at the periphery of the village. All these segments of the village population together form the village, the habitat much romanticised by persons like M. K. Gandhi. The village includes all occupational and all caste-based groups with their own housing spaces, marked out in terms of their social eminence and the logic of purity and pollution. Accordingly, the most pure priestly class are at the centre of the village, immediately next to the temple; and then the other castes in terms of their perceived honour, and finally the polluting menial workers. A village cannot function without all these people, but it cannot also function by collapsing the borders between them. Everyone needs to be included, but kept at a distance, marked by beliefs and practices.

Public Theology of Indian Cities

A public theology of cities in India or an Indian urban public theology would do well to go by some of its basic insights. As Elaine Graham captures them, one of the fundamental public theological insights is to 'treat the city not merely as a built environment of materiality, but a space which embodies human values and meanings' which give them a transcendental dimension. According to Graham, "[T]he built environment is a tangible sign of a culture's underlying ideals and aspirations, and any process of exposing the deeper values underpinning the tangible substance of our urban contexts represents an

---

[19] Pranav, Sidhwani, "Spatial Inequalities in Big Indian Cities." *Economic and Political Weekly*, Vol. 50, No. 22 (MAY 30, 2015), p. 55; https://www.jstor.org/stable/24482493.

important public theological task."[20] Similarly, the editorial of an earlier issue of the *International Journal of Public Theology* on public theology of urbanity speaks of the "the theological 'aeration' of the city's meanings, structures and possibilities"[21] as the task of public theology of urbanity. As the editorial goes on to reflect: "...in its efforts at knowledge production, urban theology engages with the spaces of the city and relates these to God's roominess or God's taking space in the city."[22] These theological reflections enable us to look deeply at the embedded values, ideals, meanings and structures of cities everywhere, and, in our case, the Indian cities as built environments embodying deeper meanings and structures which need to be affirmed as well as interrogated from the perspective of faith in God, the transcendental divine mystery that is, at every step forward, beckoning us beyond the temporal cities, but only in and through them. Our biblical faith invites us to build cities of which God is "not ashamed."

A pertinent question to begin with is whether Christians themselves create urbanity with transcendental values? Are Indian Christians free from the dictates of purity and pollution, in their relationships with different social others, who may or may not be Christians? An absolute answer for or against may not be possible. Segregations run deep in social relationships – they may be of residential segregations, marital segregations, ritual segregations, and so on. Indian Christians, though freed from some of them, to some extent, are not totally free, for example, to mingle with different caste communities at the level of forging marital relationships. However, at the civic level of social behaviours, they seem to be more open and liberal. Even while they can inspire others to go beyond social segregations at the civic level, how can they themselves be healed from this purity-pollution based discriminatory sinfulness is a concern for us.

We look up to the Bible and the Christian tradition to help us free from such unmeaning social behaviours. Apparently, experiences of purity-pollution have been serious concerns for the Biblical communities. Israelites, for example, had formulated stringent laws to safeguard the people from pollution in individual and group living. As Blidstein, Moshe observes, "[C]oncepts and practices of purity and defilement shaped the understanding of human nature, sin, history, and ritual in early Christian communities. Purity and defilement were instrumental for articulating difference, hierarchy, and change in these communities."[23] However, the early Christians endeavoured to overcome it through their own purificatory rites like baptism and other spiritual observances.

[20] Elaine Graham, "What Makes a Good City? - Reflections on Urban Life and Faith." *International Journal of Public Theology*, 2 (2008), 15.

[21] Ibid., 1.

[22] Ibid., 2.

[23] Ibid., 3.

Christian faith in the incarnate God, and the wellsprings of theologies flowing around this fountain of faith, provide the best resource for a Christian public theology to interrogate and cure the purity-pollution divide operative in social relations, including in city-spaces, and in the social psyche of communities in India. Faith in incarnation is a deep and transformative theological interfacing of materiality and spirituality, immanence and transcendence, history and eternity, physics and metaphysics, and life here and hereafter. It inspires the human to experience holiness / sacredness in the embodied life here on earth, even while beckoning to rise above the conditionings of the 'flesh'; it motivates the human to forge a relationship with different others, including the ecological other surrounding the human, in a non-exploitative, non-dominating, but inter-subjectively harmonious manner.

The biblical accounts of Jesus going forth to 'touch' the people with leprosy (thought to be a polluting disease in an earlier stage of history), befriending those labelled as 'sinners' and sharing table-fellowship with them, and undergoing the crucifixion with deep sense of a purpose beyond the cross signify aspects of divine incarnation in potent ways. The early Christians, centring their faith-based living, round the Eucharistic worship embodying the remembrance of the death and resurrection of Jesus, go to witness to the abiding sense of the power of incarnation present in their living. Paul, for his part, endeavoured to open the world of faith and grace to the Jews whose religious sensibilities were closed upon or conditioned by ritualistic thinking and acting. He told them, "there is neither Jew or Greek,... for you are all one in Christ Jesus (Gal. 3:28)", which meant a radical manner of overcoming the conditionings of the 'flesh' as in his words.

From yet another dimension, Christianity is enabled to overcome some of the perceived pollutants in the Indian contexts. Indian religious literatures speak of five pollutants: birth, death, menstruation, spittle and caste contact. Christian faith and its theology treat them as not only non-pollutants, but as the very point of divine entry or contact with the human. Therefore, Christianity celebrates the birth of the Jesus Christ as the point of divine incarnation and the death of Jesus Christ as the redemptive act for human salvation; menstruating woman is healed by touching the cloak of Jesus and Jesus opens the eyes of a blind person by smearing with his spittle. Only the 'pollutant of the caste contact' is not interrogated by Christianity as it developed in the European context, and is left to Indian Christianity to develop it.

Over the centuries, the Christian culture that developed in the European context, was nurtured with relative openness though was challenged by feudal aristocracies. When it came to India in a big way during the sixteenth century, Indian Christian missionaries had ambivalent approaches to the question of caste premised upon the purity-pollution divide. Some Catholic missionaries opposed it openly and called for a conversion not only to Christian faith but to its culture as well; but others argued for separating the culture from faith, thus providing concession to the practice of caste within Christianity. It happened in Catholic and Protestant circles in India.

In the history of Christianity's encounter with the Indian caste system, in terms of resisting its purity-pollution indoctrination, the present-day Pentecostalism seemed to gain more vitality to overcome it. The oft-repeated evangelical statement of Pentecostals that "if you are in Christ, you are saved" help them to look beyond caste identities to converge in the identity of being saved in Christ. However, the proverbial python sticks its head out in the mushrooming of Pentecostal Churches, organised around different caste groupings.

In this context, what Michael Northcott tells us sounds relevant: "... urban Christians and urban theologians need to be alive to the action of the Spirit which 'blows where it wills' and to the spiritual yearnings present in the inherent creativity of the cultures, languages, stories and struggles of those who are on the margins of the society."[24] As a public theological effort to 'be alive to the action of the Spirit', and being motivated by this faith to explore and converse with the emancipatory aspirations of people living on the margins of the society, Christianity would do well to publicly converse with religious traditions of India which interrogate or teach to overcome the purity-pollution schema of the Indian Psyche. For example, the teachings of Virasaivism or the Lingayats, who originated during the twelfth century South India in the then Canara region, offer a good conversational partner on this count. This religious tradition seems to have a particular focus on opposing the teachings and practices related to purity and pollution in relation to the observance of caste. It "aimed at the elimination of pollution as a pre-condition for the abolition of caste itself."[25]

The Lingayats worship the *linga* – a form of artistic sculptural representation of phallus which is treated as the symbol of Shiva, and are enjoined to carry it in their body. This symbol, though associated immediately with human sexuality and therefore with the eros – sexual passion and procreation, signifies, according to the believers, the presence of Shiva, the primordial spirit.[26] According to Venugopal, a researcher on Lingayat religion, the *Linga* (known also as *Shivlinga*) turns out to be a potent symbol, which, embodies simultaneously the earthy dimension of impurity but at the same time, the purity of the pure spirit of Shiva. "This purity was predicated on the esoteric belief that the Linga, symbolising Shiva, the Cosmic Spirit, was always

[24] Michael Northcott, ed. *Urban Theology – A Reader* (London: Cassell, 1998), p. 5.

[25] C. N. Venugopal, "FACTOR OF ANTI-POLLUTION IN THE IDEOLOGY OF LINGAYAT MOVEMENT." *Sociological Bulletin*, Vol. 26, No. 2 (September 1977), p. 228; https://www.jstor.org/stable/23618919.

[26] Ibid., 228.

pure;"[27] and, "all those who wore the Linga on the body became everlastingly pure."[28] From the perspective of the theology of incarnation, Shiva's purity can be said to be identified through an embodiment in apparent impurity. It effectively mediates a transformation in the heart of the believers from a state of impurity to purity, and overcome the divide between them. As Venugopal surmises, "[I]ndeed one can say that Lingayatism rejected ritual pollutions because it predicated itself on the Purity of *Linga*."[29]

The Lingayats' teachings centre round the following precepts:

> (a) worship of Linga (representation of Phallus) as the symbol of Shiva, the Primordial Spirit; (b) rejection of Vedic sacrificial rites; (c) rejection of ritual pollutions; (d) emphasis on eradication through spiritual exercises (such as meditation) the three inner pollutions; 3 (e) belief in and practice of *astavarana* and *Panchachara* rites which embody the substance of *Lingayat* theology known as *Shakti* vis his *tad wai taf* and (/) insistence on the sanctity of work and equal opportunities for all in society.[30]

As we can see, at the heart of these precepts, we find the religious engagements of the Lingayats to overcome the ritual observance of purity and pollution. The godhead is presented as religiously pure in and through his supposed impurity; ritual pollutions are outrightly rejected; spiritual attempts are made to eradicate the 'inner pollutions' which could lie at the heart of an individual or a social group; and, an insistence is made to believe in the sanctity of work and equal opportunity for all.

Lingayat religion, therefore, can be an effective conversational partner in the public spaces for Indian Christianity to confront the obstacle of religiously and culturally indoctrinated and maintained aspects of purity and pollution. And this can go a long way in solving the problems of discriminatory segregations occurring in our living spaces, including the cities.

---

[27] Ibid., 230.

[28] Ibid., 230.

[29] Ibid., 228.

[30] Ibid., 228.

14

Ayya Vazhi's Emancipatory Potentials

The historical context of Ayya Vazhi (hereafter AV) was the early nineteenth century South Travancore (part of the erstwhile princely state of Travancore in the southern tip of the peninsular India). The society of the time was rigidly organised upon the hierarchical caste system, a system fervently safeguarded by the erstwhile political powers.[1] Travancore princely state, known to outside world as a 'Hindu State Par Excellence', had the ideology of *varnashrama dharma* (ethics based on religiously sanctioned distinction between the four *varnas*, the prototype of castes) deeply embedded into the cultural terrain, and the practice of it was observed meticulously and ruthlessly in the social realm. Accordingly, those at the social apex were the clans of Brahmins (internally divided as Nambudhri Brahmin, Tulu Brahmin, Tamil Brahmin, etc), and, the second in the ritual rank were the Nayars and Vellalars, who though considered as Shurdras as per the *varnashrama dharma*, were next in prominence here. The Nayars, numerically the highest in Travancore, were the most powerful people socially and politically. The kings, in all probability, had hailed from this group of people. Vellalars preponderated in Nancil Nadu, the bastion of paddy cultivation in South Travancore. It was these two categories of people who in point of fact 'owned', supervised and cultivated most of the lands as *de facto* Jenmies.[2] From among these people came the feudal lords who held the labouring class of people under subordination.

---

[1] Travancore then was ruled by the heirs of Marthanda Varma, a valiant king who had established the kingdom by amalgamating a number of independent political units, through usury, manipulation and violent suppression. But, by the beginning of nineteenth century, his monarchy had been so attenuated that the British could establish their hold over this kingdom through their manipulative tactics.

[2] Jenmie was a designation that stood for those who had the right of ownership of land as their birth right and not as something derived from any external agency. The Brahmins alone,

All other categories of people of South Travancore were treated as untouchable and polluting by the high castes and the ruling establishment. These 'polluting' people were victims to severe social ostracisation, political oppression and economic exploitation by the dominant. The oppressive measures imposed on them were so inhuman that Vivekananda, witnessing the social barbarity, remarked that 'it was a land of lunatics'. These subaltern masses of the society of South Travancore were primarily Shanars, Pallar, Sambavar, Pulayar and Parayar.

The Shanar, a people who populated thickly in South Travancore, were a Tamil race existing dinstinctively as a Tamil-speaking people in this Malayalam-speaking kingdom. They, apart from being agricultural labourers, followed a profession of toddy tapping and, on account of it, were considered a polluting caste. They had been further condemned as *untouchable, unapproachable,* and *unseeable.* They were not to read and write. They were violently prevented from using a number of public utilities such as roads, wells, streets, umbrellas, etc., etc. Their women were refused the use of upper cloth to cover their bosom. They had to maintain a distance of 12 feet while conversing with Nayars and 36 feet with Brahmin. Their labour was severely exploited in the name of a system of corvee labour called as *uliyam.* And, a head tax was imposed exclusively on these people. Besides these, a number of unmeaning taxes, like the tax for sporting a moustache, growing long hair, wearing jewels, etc. were imposed on these people.

However, as it was the case with the whole of India, Travancore too witnessed to an emancipatory identity formation of the subaltern people during nineteenth century, due to the advent of modernity. They began to assert themselves in various forms and fields. The introduction of the agents of modernity,[3] along with the supportive role played by the missionaries of Protestant Christianity, had contributed substantially to the emergence of emancipatory ideation and praxis among the subaltern people.

In this context of assertion, the Shanars could be singled out as a subaltern group that was definitively in a course of assertion for social emancipation and empowerment. The struggle for the right to use upper clothes for their women, even as their kindred were fighting for their right to temple entry in the neighbouring Tirunelveli region, was a telling instance of their disposition

---

and that too, indisputably, the Nambudhri Brahmin alone, were considered as Jenmies. But then, in the course of time, since the *varnashrama dharma* ideology had prevented the Brahmins from involving in the 'polluting' activity of cultivation, the care of land came into the hands of the Nayars and Vellalars, the ones next in the social order.

[3] By agents of modernity, I mean here the western education, the industrialisation, and the bureaucratisation along with the attendant rationalisation of social, political and economic spheres.

for undertaking emancipatory projects. A section of this people had joined the Protestant Christianity as part of realisation of their emancipatory aspiration.

It was against this background, a religious phenomenon called *Ayya Vazhi* arose among the *Shanar* people. This phenomenon owes its origin and early development to a person called Vaikuntasamy whose activities drew a large number of people who, in turn, by their actions and participation, progressively constituted this religious phenomenon in history.[4] Let us take a brief look at the life and activities of Vaikuntasamy.

1. Life and Activities of Vaikuntasamy

Vaikuntasamy was born as Muthukutti in the year 1809 at Sastankovil, a hamlet located in Agastisvaram taluk of the south Travancore. He was second child to Ponnumuthan and Veilal who belonged to the social group of the Shanars. Parents gave him a name as Mutisudum Perumal, the surname of which had been an exclusive privilege of the high castes, and, on that count, it had been objected to by the high castes. Sensing trouble, parents seemed to have changed the name to Muthukutti, a prosaic name commonly used by the people of the lower strata.

As a youth, Muthukutti earned his living as a palmyra climber and an agricultural labourer. At the age of seventeen, he married Paradevadai from the nearby village called Puviyur, and led a family life.

In his twenty-second year, he was struck by a severe illness that inflicted acute pain and suffering for a year. This disease was a cause of depression and desperation for Muthukutti and for his family. One day, his mother seems to have told that she had received an instruction in her dreams to bring her ailing son to the temple at Tiruchendur, in the year 1833 during the annual festival. As per her request, he was brought to Tiruchendur in a cradle, carried by his kith and kin.

In Tiruchendur, an important event, to the effect of a 'personal transformation' had taken place in the life of Muthukutti. R. Ponnu, who had studied this phenomenon, narrates the event as: "Muthukutti took a holy bath at the sea ... and the tides took him away and he was not to be seen. On the third day he appeared again claiming to have been born anew as Vaikuntasamy, an avatar of Vishnu... He then announced this to the people and involved himself in public service."[5] Today the followers of *AV* take this to be the central event of their faith whereby Muthukutti was born anew as the son of Vishnu.

After this event, Vaikuntasamy announced to the people that he had been instructed to undertake a *tavam*, a method of rigorous penance and meditation,

---

[4] We come to know about this phenomenon primarily from two sources. One, the religious books: *Akilathirattu* and *Arul Nool*; the other, the reports of the London Missionary Society.

[5] R. Ponnu, *The Life and Leadership of Vaikuntasamy* [Tamil], (Delhi: Karthik Publication, 1983), 43.

for the purpose of ushering in the age of *Dharma*, rule of righteousness, by incinerating the *kaliyugam*, the age of evil. He told the people that God no more needed 'offerings and bribes', that they needed not to pay the exploitive taxes to the rulers, that they should learn to live with dignity, and that they should wait for the dawning of the age of righteousness. After making such titular pronouncements, he proceeded and reached back his native place.

In his native place, the present Samithoppu, he undertook to perform the proclaimed penance which extended for six years. During this time, he seems to have performed healings with simple earth and water. Gradually, he became known to the surrounding areas and people congregated around him. In these congregations, Vaikuntasamy seems to have performed as a shaman[6] whose religious instructions and ritual actions had psychologically emboldened and socially kindled the emancipatory aspirations of the people.

1.1. Vaikuntasamy as a Shaman

With the authority of a shaman, he ventured out to dispel the fears of the people on 'evil spirits' and occult practices like witchcraft, sorcery, black-magic, etc. Shamanism seems to have worked as an effective pedagogic tool to impart the message of fearlessness. For example, once he seems to have told the congregation that, since he had come as 'the invincible avatar', his foes - the devils, demons, and evil spirits were to be incinerated. He, then, caused some of those in the congregation to get 'possessed' of the evil spirits. The 'possessed' ones came and danced in front of the crowd. He then ordered these evil spirits to make an oath, in front of the people, to surrender their powers and get burned up in flames. When he had finished his orders, those dancing under the duress of 'possession' got exhausted and fell flat on the ground. When the people witnessed to all these, their minds were greatly relieved of the fear of evil spirits!

1.2. Vaikuntasamy Pandaram

The fame of Vainkuntasamy had begun to spread in the regions of Travancore and Tirunelveli, and he had been gradually recognised as a religious person with extraordinary powers. In the religious parlance of the time, he seems to have been addressed as a Pandaram, a homo religiosus hailing from and serving the people of the lower strata. *Akilathirattu* (hereafter as *AT*), the religious book of *AV*, addresses him as Narayana Pandaram (Narayana – another name

[6] The term 'shaman' stands for a person who has mastery over the faculty of 'getting divinised', or 'getting into trance' (or, in traditional western terms, 'getting possessed') and instrumentalises it consciously. *The Encyclopaedia of Religion* notes that a shaman is a "person, either a Spirit medium or not", who "is regarded as controlling spirits, exercising his mastery over them in socially recognised ways" - Mircea Eliade, "Shamanism: An Overview", in *The Encyclopaedia of Religion,* vol. 13, pp. 202-208.

for Vishnu). Samuel Zechariah, a London missionary pastor, characterised him, in one of his books, as Muthukutti Pandaram.[7]

People flocked to him to listen to his instructions, "to be cured by him of different diseases,"[8] to witness, worship and serve a religious person undertaking penance. He encouraged the people to come together, irrespective of caste differences, around a well to take a ritual bath. He exhorted the people to dine together in his presence.

During these occasions, he gave out certain teachings that had emancipatory vibrations in the society. "Uplift of the lowly is *Dharma*" was a central refrain in his teachings (தாழக்கிடப்பாரைத் தற்காப்பதுவே தர்மம்). "When you live with self-respect, the evil would destroy itself" was another important line of teaching (மானமாக வாழ்ந்தால் மாளும் கலி தன்னாலே). "Live without fear" was yet another base-line teaching. He openly addressed the king as the wicked representation of evil and indicted him for exploiting the labour of the masses (உய்கொண்ட சான்றோர் உடம்புருகுந் தேட்டையெல்லாம், நாய்கொண்ட நீசன் நோகப் பறித்தனனே). He instructed the people not to pay taxes to the rulers (இறக்கும் இறைகள் இல்லையென்று சொல்லிடு நீ, வேண்டாமிறைகள் வேண்டாமென்று சொல்லிடு நீ ... அவனவன் தேடுமுதல் அவனவன் வைத்தாண்டிடுங்கோ, எவனெவனுக்கும் பதறி இனி அலைய வேண்டாமே).

1.3. Ordeals

Against the background of the growing popularity of Vaikuntasamy, and the convergence of people around him, a complaint seems to have been preferred against him to the ruler. *AT* speaks of this in the following words:

> ... from among the Shanars who pay levies and perform corvee services to us, a person claims that he has been born as incarnation of Vishnu, and that, on that account, he is going to rule the earth by destroying the wicked enemies. He has collected people of various castes into one place and has made them bathe and drink from the same well. It looks the Shanars are going to have a great future.[9]

---

[7] Cf. Rev. Samuel Zechariah, *The London Missionary Society in South Travancore Part I*, 1903, p. 200.

[8] *LMS Report for the year 1838*, p. 71.

[9] "நமக்கு இறையிறுத்து நாடூழியங்கள் செய்யும்
குமுக்காஇனம் பெருத்த கூண்ட சாணாரினத்தில்
மெய்கொண்ட பூமியெல்லாம் வேறொருவர் ஆளாமல்
நான்தான் முடிசூடி நாடுகட்டி ஆள்வேனென
தான்தானுரை பகர்ந்து சாதிபலதும் வருத்தி
ஒரு தலத்திலூட்டு வித்தானுற்ற தீரானதையும்
அருகிருக்குஞ் சாணாருக்கு அதிகவிதி தோணுதுகாண்
ஆகாத்த பொல்லாரை அழித்துப் போடுவேனென்றும்
சாகாவரங்கள் சாணாருக்கீவேனென்றும்
சொல்லியிருக்கிறான் சுவாமி வைகுண்டமென்று *AT.*, p. 267.

The king seems to have ignored the complaint initially, exclaiming whether it was possible for a low caste man to 'become an incarnation of Vishnu.'[10] But, given the reality of an already weakened monarchy due to the dominance of the British colonial power, the king could not remain unperturbed at this seeming challenge. He proceeded to take action on Vaikuntasamy.[11] He sent his soldiers and arrested and imprisoned him in an open jail at Tirvandrum, the headquarters of the Travancore kingdom.

During the imprisonment, an interesting episode, which led to his release, seemed to have taken place. On a particular day, in the presence of ministers, administrators, and different sections of the army, Vaikuntasamy was thrown into a tiger's cage. The tiger, contrary to the expectation of the onlookers, did not immediately jump onto its prey. The soldiers, being vexed at the strange behaviour of the animal, tried to provoke it. One of the soldiers used a spear to prod the animal to action. It so happened that the tiger caught hold of the spear, and, there ensued a tug of war between the tiger and the solider, and when the latter did not expect, the tiger left it abruptly. The sharp point of the released spear seems to have hit fatally a priest who was standing among the spectators.

The news of the death of a priest had unnerved the king and shocked the officials as per whose tradition and belief, killing of a priest was to fetch the divine wrath. Fearing of it, the king thought of freeing Vaikuntasamy from the prison. He seems to have ordered him to sign a condition that he would restrict his activities only to his own caste people, and that he would neither collect people of other castes around him nor instruct them. When the piece of document containing the condition was handed over to Vaikuntasamy, he seemed to have torn it into pieces and thrown it away. However he was released from the prison.

Having been released after three and three quarters of a month, Vaikuntasamy was carried back to his native place by his jubilant devotees. He came back to native village and set out to complete the remaining two years' penance as per the original plan. Once again, people gathered around him in great numbers.[12] He inspired a group of his devotees to undertake a religious

---

[10] Cf. *AT*., p. 268. "போத்தி நம்பூரி பிராமண சூத்திரகுலத்தில் பிறக்காமலித்த பிறத்தீண்டாச் சாண்குலத்தில் பிறக்க வருவாரோ பெரிய நாராயணரும்?"

[11] There is an information from oral tradition that the king took action against Vaikuntasamy at the behest of the British power to which the LMS missionaries had petitioned in this regard, because the growth of such a religious phenomenon was a hindrance to their missionary enterprise. I did not find any data on this in *AT* or LMS reports. However, that there was a Government interference to arrest the spread of this phenomenon of *AV* is attested to in the LMS Report of 1838 which reads as: "The Government, however, interfered, and the excitement quickly died away." - *LMS Report for the year 1838*, p. 71.

[12] Cf. *LMS Reports for the years 1843, 1847, 1858, and 1864*.

exercise called *Tuvaiyal Tavasu* – penance of cleaning. He initiated a lot of festivities around him. There were ceremonial processions held amidst singing, incantations and shouts of joy by the followers. Several rites and rituals were instituted during these occasions. All these gregarious ritual activities appeared to dispel the gloom and fear that surrounded the lives of the ordinary masses.

1.4. Later Part of Vaikuntasamy's Life

During the later part of his life, Vaikuntasamy was invited by his 'devotees' to their homes and entreated in a grand manner. By way of soliciting his blessings, his 'devotees' carried him to different places. He breathed his last in the year 1851 at the age of 42. Subsequent to his death, his body was interned in a tomb and, around that, a religious structure was raised later on. His devotees continue to visit this site until this day, and perform the rituals as they used to do when Vaikuntasamy was bodily present.

2. Emancipatory Proposition in a Religious Idiom

The life and activities of Vaikuntasamy, the ritual practices of the religious phenomenon and the mythography that evolved around this phenomenon together made an emancipatory proposition in the then existing context. Let us interpretatively look at one or two ritual practices and mythographical episodes.

2.1. Tuvaiyal Tavasu

Tuvayal Tavasu, literally meaning 'washing penance', an act of ritual washing of one's physique and clothes along with practice of self-abnegation and self-restraint, was a significant religious event that took place in the life of *AV*. By the late thirties of nineteenth century, when the phenomenon of *AV* had come to exist with certain 'excitement', a group of people, comprising of different age groups and genders, undertook to perform this unique exercise as directed by Vaikuntasamy. The LMS Report for the year 1838 has the following to say about this event:

> About 70 families of this sect, having subsequently established a community of goods, removed under the guidance of a man of some influence to a part of the seashore in Tinnevelly, where they erected huts, performed frequent ablutions, and often assembled to hear the dreams and visions of their leader and to witness the miracles he was said to perform.[13]

Having sold out their properties at half of their value by way of renouncing, the participants of this exercise seemed to have gone and camped at a place near the eastern seashore, called presently as Vahaipati, situated at about four KM to the north of Cape Comorin. They lived together and performed the

[13] *LMS Report for the year 1838*, p. 71.

following actions in a manner of a ritual: They took bath and washed their clothes in the seawater thrice everyday and cooked vegetarian meal with raw rice and green-grams, and ate it only once a day. They drank only the salty water and abstained from fish. Apart from washing, cooking, and eating, the remaining hours were spent on spiritual exercises.

There seems to have been some opposition to this practice. There is a verse in *AT* which says, "the wicked violently dispersed"[14] those that participated in this event. R. Ponnu notes that the high caste people caused troubles and tried to disperse the participants. But the participants seem to have withstood and continued the exercise.

As per the account of *AT*, the people performed this exercise for about six months. Once it was over, the participants went back to their native places. They were received with respect and reverence, and, addressed honourably as *Tuvaiyal Pandarams.*[15] The participants' external appearance seemed to have undergone a change to become brighter. *AT* says that the surrounding people who witnessed them exclaimed as follows:

> The dresses of the Nambudhri and other Brahmins have lost their shine, whereas that of the Shanars shine like the sun ... See what a change has come about for Shanars! The people who awaited avidly the arrival of fish and ate it even half cooked in a greedy manner, and chewed tobacco incessantly, have transformed themselves so much!

The LMS Report for the year 1892 puts it as: "It is true that their [the devotees of Vaikunda Swamy] bodies and their houses are more cleanly [sic] than those of the rest."[16]

This event, which is a cluster of ritual actions, seems to have served to enhance the image of the social persona of the adherents of *AV* to anchor it on a profound sense of self-worth. First of all, the very claim of these subaltern people to undertake a penance, that too with an added rigour in its execution, and its 'successful completion' were to contest the traditional claim that the high caste people alone were suitable for such spiritual exercises.

Secondly, the ritual actions of bathing and washing of their cloths thrice a day, apart from "establishing the importance of cleanliness"[17] to the adherents, seem to have served to project a 'dignified' image of their physique to the external society. Mary Douglas, in her anthropological study of human body vis-à-vis social control, opined that 'the physical body was a microcosm of

---

[14] Cf. *AT.*, p. 3.

[15] It means 'religious personalities who participated in this exercise of penance'.

[16] Quoted in M.S.S. Pandian, "Meanings of 'Colonialism' and 'Nationalism': An Essay on Vaikunda Swamy Cult", *Studies in History*, vol. VIII, 2 July Dec. 1992, p. 180.

[17] *Ibid.*, p. 180.

society.'[18] Drawing upon this inspiration, it may be said that the adherents of *AV*, by enhancing the social *representation* of their bodies, were actually negotiating for a respectable place in the social space of the time.

The new representation of their bodies was also to subvert one of the exploitative characteristics of the caste society. It seems to have challenged the ritual hierarchy of purity and pollution in an attempt at questioning the subordination of the subaltern people. As in the words of Partha Chaterjee, a prominent subaltern writer, "the essence of caste ... requires that the labouring bodies of the impure castes be reproduced in order that they can be subordinated to the need to maintain the bodies of the pure castes in their state of purity."[19] Against this oppressive dictate of the caste order, *AV* was attempting to redefine the representation of the subaltern physique in a manner of overthrowing the hegemonic stranglehold. And this attempt to "define a claim of proprietorship over one's own body, to negate the daily submission of one's body and its labour to the demands made by the dominant dharma"[20] was to subvert the oppressive caste order in a deeper manner. As in the words of Saurabe Dube, "the creation of a transformed body and a new 'self'" was "the transformation of an oppressive world held in place by the dominant symbolic order."[21]

2.2. Wearing of Headgear during Worship

One of the significant ritual actions that distinguished the *AV* male worshipper from others was 'wearing a headgear' during worship. Vaikuntasamy seems to have enjoined upon his male followers to tie a headgear when they came to worship their God.[22] Accordingly, the male followers seem to have tied a headgear during worship. In the course of time, it became a ritual action to be performed before the people entered the temple called *Pathi* to worship. The male devotees usually removed their upper garment and tied the headgear and entered the Pathi for worship. To this day it is meticulously followed.

This ritual practice of wearing a headgear during worship was, and is, something unique to *AV*, while the reversal is true of other temple worships. The significance of it comes to light when situated against the context of its emergence. In the nineteenth century Travancore society, the subaltern people had to live under severe restrictions imposed on the use of dress. They had to go without a cloth to cover the upper part of their body. In fact, the restriction

---

[18] Brian Morris, *Anthropological Studies of Religion - An Introductory Text* (Cambridge: Cambridge University Press, 1987), p. 229.

[19] Partha Chaterjee, "Caste and Subaltern Consciousness", *Subaltern Studies VI* (Delhi: Oxford University Press, 1994 [1989]), p. 203.

[20] *Ibid.* p. 204.

[21] Saurabh Dube, "Myths, Symbols, and Community: Satnampanth of Chattisgarh", *Subaltern Studies VII* (Delhi: Oxford University Press, 1996), p. 146.

[22] Cf. M. S. S. Pandian, "Meanings of 'Colonialism' and 'Nationalism'", p. 180.

was such that the people looked almost naked except a minimum of cloth to cover their loins. Imposing such a restriction onto the subaltern people, and maintaining it through ruthless violence was the order of the day.

Such a dress code was maintained because, among other things, it had come to be an arena of symbolic representation of the social power too. One of the tangible ways in which the dominant classes had been holding the subaltern people in submission was by imposition of such stringent codes on dressing. "Being bare above the waist was a symbolic caste code which affirmed the powerlessness of the subordinate castes in front of the upper castes in Travancore."[23] Therefore, when the subordinate classes began to assert themselves socially, in the wake of empowerment through education and other measures, the dispute of power came to be contested in the arena of dressing too. It is revealing in this regard that historically, in the nineteenth century Travancore, only serious contenders of social power came to be involved in the upper-cloth controversy. Consider the riots that took place between the Nayars, the traditional power wielders, on the one hand, and the Shanars, those on the process of assertion, on the other. Thus, it was a time when this cultural element of dressing had come to be one of the sites for contestation of social power.

It was against this background, Vaikuntasamy instructed his people to wear headgear when they came for worship. With this instruction, he sought to empower the subaltern masses in his own unique way. He, first of all, quite characteristically shifted the location of contestation of power from the general cultural to a specifically religious site. By bringing it directly under the purview of religion, he overtly 'disguised' the proponent, i.e. himself, from being a target of attack by the dominant, as it would have happened to a cultural reformer. Simultaneously, by choosing an effective tool of indoctrination i.e., ritualising an idea, he covertly challenged those that imposed such a degrading dress code.

With his unique method, Vaikuntasamy imparted certain empowering messages of self-dignity and courage. The Shanars had a custom called *urumalkattu* by which a boy, when attaining the age of manhood, was to wear a headgear, symbolising a crown. This ceremonial action seems to have given him certain self-worth, dignity, and responsibility.[24] Gradually this custom seems to have died down under the restrictions of the oppressive society. Having this fading custom at the background Vaikuntasamy introduced the ritual action of tying a headgear during worship. In order to appreciate the social impact of this ritual action better, it would do well to quote the words of Mr. Ponnukrishnan of Ambalapati who explained it graphically as follows: "Vaikuntasamy emboldened the people saying, 'tie your cloth not in your loins but on your head, let me see who is there to challenge it.'" Thus, it was an open

[23] M. S. S. Pandian, "Meanings of 'Colonialism' and 'Nationalism'", p. 169.

[24] Cf. R. Ponnu, *The Life and Leadership*, p. 64.

instruction to the followers of *AV* to rise up to the position of social dignity, and, simultaneously an implicit challenge to the oppressors.

Apart from these overtones of a challenging message, this ritual action also seems to have had a potency to instil inner strength, responsibility, and a sense of self-respect to the people. Mr Sankarapandi, one of my interviewees, said, "when one ties a headgear, he gets a certain strength and devotion." Wearing a headgear and standing in front of his God emboldened him psychologically to take on the oppressive social system. It may be contrasted with the practice of the subaltern people being compelled to untie the headgear at the sight of his master.

An Alternative Mythography

From the study of the phenomenon of *AV*, we come to know that a 'religious vision', formulated in a mythical language, had evolved along with ritual and other components of this religious phenomenon. How did this religious vision interact sociologically is an interesting dimension to come to know of. Let us take a brief look at it:

Myths have their unique dynamics and features. Apart from having the potentiality to "appeal to emotions and mobilize the psychic energies locked up in the collective unconsciousness,"[25] they can be statements of history of a social collectivity too. As noted by Saurabh Dube, myths "can be a form of ordering of historical consciousness and can embody specific cultural conceptions of the past."[26] They are, as noted by Vattamattam, metamorphoses of historical experiences of a community, sunk down into collective unconscious.[27]

A reading of the mythography of *AV* makes explicit the fact that the essence of this vision is an account of history, a religious history - a past, a present, and a future - constructed by weaving together of empirical facts as well as mythical accounts. It has appropriated myths from existing traditions and has repositioned or remodelled them in a new context to bring forth its own unique history, a history purported to contribute to the emergence of an emancipatory identity to its followers. Here lies the originality or specific contribution of the vision of *AV*, the subaltern religion.

This vision seems to unfold around three axiomatic typologies, namely *Shantor, Kaliyukam,* and *Tarmayukam*. It traverses through a past, a present, and a future in a teleological manner. It would do well to analyse and see how these basic concepts have been woven together to give a symbolic vision which is at once religious and social.

---

[25] S. Kappen, *Hindutva and Indian Religious Traditions* (Changanachery: Manusham, 2000), p. 56.

[26] Saurabh Dube, *The Untouchable Pasts*, p. 14.

[27] Cf. S. Vattamattam, "Introduction", in S. Kappen, *Hindutva and Indian Religious Traditions*, p. 13.

2.2.1. Shantor – The Subjects

Shantor is a name attributed to the people who are the subject of the religious vision of *AV*. It is both a religious and a social category in terms of its connotation. Today, most of the theologians of *AV* emphasise more on the religious dimension of this category than the social. They give it an inclusive character and universal reach to mean anyone who is noble, as the literal meaning of this *Shantor* word would have it, and anyone who believes in the vision of *AV*. However, the concept, as it occurs in *AT*, is much more specific, with a considerable importance attached to the social dimension of it, without, however, ruling out a space for universal connotation. In its specific and social reference, it represented the social group of the Shanars.

2.2.2. Inventing a Tradition

The first step of *AV* in making a people as subject of an emancipatory project seems to be empowering this people with a tradition, with a glorious past. It was an act of *inventing* a tradition that entailed a construction of a resourceful and dignified past. This implied an innovative use of materials, myths, symbols, folktales, etc., available in the cultural repertoire of the given society.

This process of *inventing traditions* contributes to constructing identities and cultural boundaries. In the words of Dimitra Gefou-Madianou, "this very process of invention is the creative process through which cultures and cultural boundaries are constantly negotiated."[28] Drawing upon the past of the society, *AV* invented its tradition and this very process became one of its methods for constructing an emancipatory identity for its subjects.

An episode regarding the divine birth of the *Shantor*, mentioned in *AT*, is a good example for drawing upon a prevalent folktale to provide a respectable parentage to the people. The folktale of *Ettu Kanikaiyar* (seven virgins), a known mythical story among the people, is woven into AV tradition to give a divine parentage to the people. Let me quote the episode as it is narrated in *AT*:

> The seven virgins, being faithful devotees of Vishnu, served regularly at his feet, with a 'lump' of water they could miraculously gather in their hands from the mythical river called the Ganges of Nectar where they bathed daily. One day, accosting these women, Vishnu requested them to serve him instead of Shiva, the other monotheist God, for a day. The women refused the request with certain haughtiness, saying they would serve only Vishnu, the all-powerful god. Having been refused, Vishnu wanted to teach them a lesson, and, at the same time, intended fulfilling the divine plan of bringing forth his children through them. He, then, took seven

[28] Dimitra Gefou-Madianou, "Cultural Polyphony and Identity Formation: Negotiating Tradition in Attica", *American Ethnologist*, 1999 26(2), pp. 412-439.

> 'seeds' from the seven worlds above, and, when the women got out of the water after their bath, made severe cold winds to blow. When the women were shivering due to the cold wind, Vishnu appearing there in the form of fire, made the women to embrace him, which they did instantly. During this embrace, Vishnu placed the seven 'seeds' inside the womb of the women, and they got conceived and delivered seven boys instantly. Realising that they had delayed their service to Shiva, the women left the babies in the river in a fist of fear and rushed to gather water. But, alas, they could no more gather the water in the shape of a ball. It was then they realised that they had been deceived. No more could they serve the feet of Shiva, nor did they have the bliss of rearing the babies. They then, undertook a rigorous penance and awaited, as it was promised to them, the manifestation of Vishnu as Vaikuntasamy.[29]

The social impact of this incorporated tale was enormous for the *Shantor*, as it comes out in the words of an interviewee:

> Respectable parentage is very important for a dignified social life. In Puranic stories, certain characters were degraded by making reference to their disrepute parentage. The Shantor people suffered silently under the yoke of oppression, and carried out the oppressive uliyam service without protest, thinking that they were born to do so since they were made to believe that they had emanated from the feet of *Brahman*. But Vaikuntasamy made them realise that they had had a divine birth, having been conceived in the womb of the seven celestial mothers with Vishnu as their father. This new realisation inculcated a sense of dignity to these people ... Our people, considering themselves to be unworthy, used to withdraw from the presence of Brahmins valuing them to be possessing divine attributes. But Vaikuntasamy, by making our people the children of Vishnu made them raise their heads in dignity ... Being considered as parent-less children the Shanar people had been socially ill-treated. But, Vaikuntasamy, by making known the seven virgins in public as their mothers, presented them to be a duly mothered children.[30]

Another episode called *feeding the children with the celestial nectar*, found in *AV* tradition, is a good example of how it sought to imaginatively critique the upholders of the exploitative socio-political system. A Brahmin priest and his wife are shown to have been implicated and punished for their selfish act of

[29] Cf. *AT.*, pp. 61-67.

[30] Interview with Mr. M. D. Periavan at his residence at Agastiswaram.

consuming the nectar that was meant for others as well. The punishment was that the priest and his wife were made to take birth on earth as palmyra trees to yield the nectar as juice. For the priestly class, who considered the profession of climbing the palmyra tree as polluting, it was a severe punishment indeed! This looks to be a veiled attack on the priestly class of the time, as selfish appropriators of the resources of livelihood that were to be available for all. Let us read the episode as it is narrated in *AT*:

> Shiva and Vishnu, wanting to feed the children with celestial nectar, commanded the celestial attendants to bring the same. When they went to bring the nectar, they found it emptied by a priest and his wife who 'dressing themselves as per the rules of the scriptures', had been drinking the whole measure of nectar to their full. By this, they had increased the fat in their own body, depriving others of their share. When the celestial attendants reported this matter to Shiva and Vishnu, the latter rebuked the priest and his wife and made them grow as palmyra trees on earth to feed his children perpetually by giving back the celestial nectar in the form of palm-juice.[31]

It is revealing to see how *AV*, utilising the symbols and traditions available with the religious universe of the dominant, is fashioning a tale of its own to critique the latter. The *celestial nectar* is a symbol borrowed from the tradition of the dominant, while the intention of the gods to feed the Shanar children with it, and, in the eventuality of the nectar having been consumed totally by the priest and his wife, making the latter to grow as palmyra trees on earth to yield the nectar in the form of saccharine sap are innovations born out of native imagination. This weaving of the borrowed with the native traditions, and fashioning of a tale to tell a message is one of the good examples of the creative imagination born out of the modernity-tradition interface of the subaltern agency operative in the *AV* tradition.

The narrative, then, proceeds to make the Shanar to be the privileged owners of the palmyra tree, which is made to yield the celestial nectar as its juice. The Shanar children are fed with this nectar. It is to be remembered that the profession associated with tapping the juice of palmyra tree, popularly known as 'toddy-tapping', was one of the factors that contributed to ostracising this people as a polluting people. In an act of emancipating the profession from its 'demeaning' marker, the tradition of AV makes the tree as a giver of the celestial nectar, and those who follow this profession, as agents of bringing to earth this valuable nectar in the form of juice. Thus, the tale privileges the Shanar over against the context of their being ostracised. The tale is a good example of how *AV* was conducting symbolic discourses having their impact on the social relations of the time.

[31] Cf. *AT*., pp. 69-71.

With these and similar episodes, AV was inventing a tradition for its people. By symbolically providing a people with a respectable parentage, a dignified name, etc., *AV* sought to invent a tradition, a past, for the Shanar, even while constructing a new identity for them.

2.2.3. Subverting the Present Kaliyugam

AV characterised the present age as *Kaliyugam*, an age dominated by the evil called *kalimayai.* The concepts of *kaliyugam* and *kalimayai* (the illusory evil) are age-old symbols, operative especially among the *sanskritic* Hindu tradition. It is a point to note here that the discourse on *kalimayai* was a predominant theme expatiated in art forms, especially in performing art forms, during the nineteenth century.[32] Sumit Sarkar, one of the leading historians from India, notes how the advent of modernity, along with the arrival of the colonial rule, and its impact of upsetting the caste hierarchy were read as effects of *kalimayai* by the upholders of the hierarchical caste system.[33] He observes that, "the evils of Kaliyuha had been associated always with the reversal of proper caste and gender hierarchy, with insubordinate ... Shudras lording it over upper-caste men."[34] He continues to observe that "for high – Hindu religion and philosophy, Kaliyuha normally is the most degenerate of times, when Shudras (low-castes) dominate over high-castes..."[35]

But what makes it unique for *AV* is the way this symbolic concept had been appropriated and infused with an alternate conception based on the historical experience of the people of *AV*. It turned out to be a condensed symbol that embodied the experience of the oppression of the people. *AT* elaborates this experience of oppression by enumerating the different types of exploitative measures - the social, the political and the economic – that the Shanar were submitted to.[36]

---

[32] Cf. Sumit Sarkar, *Writing Social History*, New Delhi: Oxford University Press, 1999 (1997), p. 206.

[33] Ibid., p. 191.

[34] Sumit Sarkar, Ibid., p. 191.

[35] Ibid., p. 188.

[36] உய்கொண்ட சான்றோர் உடம்புருகுந் தேட்டையெல்லாம்
நொய்கொண்ட நீசன் நோகப்பறித்தானே,
இப்படியே சான்றோர் இவர் தேடுந் தேட்டையெல்லாம்
அப்படியேனீசன் அவன்பறித்துத் தின்றாலும்,
ஞாயமுள்ள சான்றோர் நாமமது கேட்டதுண்டால்
நீயகுலத்தோர் விரட்டி நெடுந்தூரம் கொண்டடிப்பார் *AT.*, pp. 117-118.

ஒப்பமுள்ள சான்றோரை ஊழியங்கள் கொண்டடிப்பான்,
குளம் வெட்டச்சொல்லி கூலி கொடுக்காமல்
களம் பெரிய சான்றோரைக் கைக்குட்டை போட்டடிப்பான்,
சான்றோர்கள் தன்பனையில்த் தான்முளைத்த ஓலையெல்லாம்
வீணாக நீசன் வெட்டித் தாவென்றடிப்பான்,

For *AV*, caste oppression was considered to be the major evil that informed the symbol of *kalimayai*. While the high castes treated the violation of caste rules as characteristic of *kalimayai*, *AV*, in a reversal of roles, treated the legitimation and upkeep of the caste rules as characteristic of *kalimayai*.

Characterisation of the king of Travancore as *kalineesan* (wicked king) was an important feature in the mythography of *AV*. Apart from its political implications, it contributed to subversion of a religio-cultural order in which the king had a pivotal role. C.J. Fuller draws our attention to the fact that in the erstwhile princely states of India, "either the king is himself a form or incarnation of the tutelary state deity, normally a form of Vishnu, Shiva, or the gods …enshrined in the capital's principal temple, or he is the regent or prime minister (dewan) of the state deity."[37] The kings had almost become part of the pantheon of deities that engaged the religious imagination of the people. Koji Kawashima, in a study, shares the view that "political legitimacy grounded in religion was clearly the great difference between the princely states and British India."[38] The kings, thus, apart from being political agents, served as ritual figures too.

In the 'Hindu State' of Travancore, the princes who ruled the state claimed and, very sagaciously, forged too, a quasi-divine status, even as the people, in general, extolled them to the same. The words of Lt. Col. Sentleger, who was heading the operation to contain the rebellion initiated by the prime minister Velu Thampy against the British in 1809, that the people, "look up to the Rajah with a degree of respect, bordering on devotion,"[39] is an evidence to

---

வெட்டிக் கொடுத்தாலும் வெற்றியுள்ள சான்றோரை
கட்டிச் சுமவெனவே கைக்குட்டை போட்டடித்து,
சுமந்து போனாலுந் தொகையெண்ணமுங் கேட்டு,
பவந்து மொழிப் பேசிப் பணமும் மிகக்கேட்டடிப்பான் *AT*., p. 118.

கரியிறை பாட்டவிறை கண்டபாட்ட இறையும்,
தரிசிறை காணாத தறைபாட்ட இறையும்
ஆமிசங்களில்லாத அன்நீத வம்பிறையும்
நேமித்து வைத்த நிலையுள்ள சான்றோரை
அடித்துக் கைகெட்டி ஆண்பெண் வரைக்குமிட்டு,
இடித்தடைத்துப் பட்டினிகள் இரவு பகல் போட்டு,
பெண்ணானுடைய பெருமை மிகக்குலைத்து,
மண்ணாண்ட சான்றோரை வரம்பளித்து மாநீசன
சான்றோரைக் கண்ணில் தான்காண ஒட்டாமல்
வீணாட்டஞ் செய்து விரட்டியடித்து மிக
பம்பழித்துச் சான்றோரை பலசாதியின் கீழாய்
தும்பழித்து வேலை துாறுபடக் கொண்டனனே *AT*., pp. 118-119.

[37] C. J. Fuller, *The Champor Flame,* p. 107.

[38] Koji Kawashima, *Missionaries and a Hindu State Travancore 1858-1936* (Chennai: Oxford University Press, 1998), p. 6.

[39] As cited in Ibid., p. 5.

this point. The political leadership of the country found legitimacy among the people, to a large extent, on the basis of its putative divine character.

Over against this background, *AV*'s characterisation of the king as *kalineesan* obviously challenged the operationalisation of the above-mentioned concept of the divine kingship. It was a way of contesting the political leadership and the political system of the time. It is a point to note that the British, who supported the princely state of Travancore, were presented by *AV* in the same vein as *Venneesan*, meaning, 'the white wicked'. It means that *AV* challenged the king and his associates too. Added to it, the very identification of the present age as *kaliyugam* was a manner of disputing and challenging the established order of society. Incidentally, as we have noted earlier, the state of Travancore was projected to be a model of *Dharmarajyam* (kingdom of righteousness) exactly the opposite of what *AV* had characterised it to be. Thus, *AV*, through its symbolic religious vision, had sought to subvert the oppressive social and political institutions.

2.2.4. Dharmayugam - Projection of an Emancipatory Utopia

Utopia, a futuristic vision, plays a pivotal role in any emancipatory project, especially in that of the subaltern people. It is on a futuristic utopia that the present is grounded. It is an articulation of a future alternative to the present. As observed by a social scientist, "the articulation of social alternatives is the greatest service, which the utopian can perform for those of his fellows who are prisoners of the prevailing ideology and lack the imagination to escape even in spirit."[40] Situations of social distress, political oppression, and hegemonic dominance constrict the potential of emancipatory imagination of the masses. But, paradoxically enough, it is these situations that serve as fertile soil for emergence of "salvation beliefs"[41] and produce 'visionaries' or 'prophets' who bring forth proposals of emancipatory utopia.

AV, having emerged in a context of distress, proposes an emancipatory utopia under the banner of *Dharmayugam*. The core of the proposal was that Vaikuntasamy had come to establish and rule over a *Dharmayugam* in the place of the *kaliyugam*. Since the concept of *Dharma* comes as the lynchpin around which the grand concept of *Dharmayugam* revolves, an understanding of the latter needs to start with that of the former.

The concept of *Dharma*, proposed by *AV* as the catalyst[42] of ushering in *Dharmayugam*, is to be understood against the functioning of the concept in the then context. This concept, considered an archetypal one in the Indian ethos, was a weapon in the hands of the dominant to legitimate and maintain the

---

[40] Barbara Goodwin, *Social Science and Utopia – Nineteenth Century Models of Social Harmony* (New Jersey: Humanities Press, 1978), p. 204.

[41] Cf. M.Weber, "The Sociology of Religion", p. 27.

[42] Cf. *AT.*, 244.

ascriptive caste order. As noted by Micheal Mahar, "the 'old' dharma, rooted in Hindu religious thought, provides ideological support for the caste system and the Untouchable's inferior position within that system."[43] And, it was to this concept the dominant took recourse to for resolving the antagonism generated in the system. Ranajit Guha observed this fact as, "it was to dharma that the indigenous elite turned in order to justify and explain the initiatives by which they hoped to make their subordinates relate to them as non-antagonistically as possible."[44]

As noted above, Travancore kingdom at that time was being addressed by the elite as *dharmarajyam*, 'the land of charity'. This was to be so on account of the fact that the kingdom attached top priority to charity - of food, shelter, and wealth, to the Brahmins. Several ceremonies had been instituted to enlighten the public on this virtue of charity to Brahmins.

Against this background, *AV* came out with a proclamation that '*Dharma* was to uplift the lowly' and 'to do charity on food and on other means of subsistence to the lowly'. The scene of the lowly dining at the centres of *AV* could only be contrasted with the Brahmins being fed in the free inns of the palaces and temples. While the latter was a state-sponsored *Dharma*, the former supported by the lowly. By so doing, *AV* was, even as offering a new and alternate vision of *Dharma*, subverting the hierarchical caste order too.

What emerges in the analysis of some of the salient episodes from the mythography of *AV* is its concern for constructing an emancipatory identity to its people. By 'inventing a tradition' it had sought to empower a people with a dignified and glorious past, by subverting the present oppressive order it had sought to contest the authority of the socio-political institutions that kept the people under subordination. And, by providing an emancipatory utopia, *AV* sought to invest the people with an imagination of the emancipated future.

---

[43] J. Michael Mahar, "Agents of Dharma in a North Indian Village", in J. Michael Mahar (ed.), *The Untouchables in Contemporary India* (New Delhi: Rawat Publicantions 1998), p. 17.

[44] Ranajit Guha, "Dominance without Hegemony and its Historiography", *Subaltern Studies VI*, p. 244.

15

Tamil Buddhist Strivings for Freedom Exploring the Religious Initiatives of Pandit C. Iyothee Thasar

1. Not to be a Stranger in One's Own House

"Why did God make me an outcast and a stranger in mine own house? The shades of the prison-house closed round about us all: wall strait and stubborn to the whitest, but relentlessly narrow, tall, and unscalable to sons of night who must plod darkly on in resignation, or beat unavailing palms against the stone, or steadily, half hopelessly, watch the streak of blue above"[1] – wrote W. E. B. Du Bois in his *The Souls of the Black Folk*, conveying the agony in having to live a stranger's life in his own land of birth. Having to live as an "outcaste" victim of systemic caste prejudices in his own land of birth – South India, was the predicament Pandit C. Iyothee Thasar (1845-1914), a scholar of Tamil literature and a native medical practitioner had to contend with. The Pandit[2] did not remain resigned within the narrow walls of the 'prison-house'; the subaltern agency in him found expression in emancipatory initiatives he undertook to have a free and dignified life not merely for himself but for his people, who were treated as "outcaste" communities in their own land of birth. One among his well-known initiatives was to organise the *Sakya Buddhist Society* to spearhead the Tamil Buddhist religious movement in the northern part of the Tamil region, establishing units in other parts of India and abroad as well. A body of writings on this movement and the activities of the

[1] W. E. B. Du Bois, *The Souls of the Black*, ed. with introduction and notes by Brent Hayes Edwards (Oxford: Oxford University Press, 2007), 8.

[2] In the body-text, I use the phrase 'the Pandit', instead of his second name, following the convention to be found among the Tamil writers on the subject.

Pandit has recently come into existence in Tamil and English.[3] My study here is an attempt to explore the religious hermeneutical practice of the Pandit to overcome caste prejudices. I begin by giving a very brief account of his profile and that of Tamil Buddhism, and then go on to present a few interpretative instances from the Pandit, and conclude with a discussion on the relevance of the method he followed for his emancipatory project.

2. Pandit Iyothee Thasar (1845-1914) and Tamil Buddhism

Pandit Iyothee Thasar was born on May 20, 1845, to Mr. Kandasamy in Coimbatore[4] in the north-west region of the present-day Tamil Nadu. "He grew up in the Nilgiris and later settled in Madras."[5] He was given the name Kaathavaraayan, but later he changed it to Iyothee Thasar, incorporating the name of his teacher whom he greatly revered. The Pandit "was a native physician of repute in Siddha medicine."[6]

Even as his fame as a physician was becoming known, he became known also for his knowledge of the classical Tamil literature. He studied the Tamil classics and interpreted them for the contemporary context. His interest in Tamil literature, probably, was a 'patrimony' from his grandfather, who had been a Tamil scholar. However, a deep knowledge of Tamil classics and an exegetical interest in reclaiming the original meaning of Tamil words made him a unique Tamil scholar, to be addressed as a *Pandit* (meaning "the learned"). Combined with this exegetical interest was his conviction that the deeper semantics of Tamil embodied the beliefs and practices of Buddhism, which for him was once the religion of the Tamil people. From his younger days, he grew indignant towards the caste practices which oppressed the subaltern people. He intuitively perceived the deep nexus between caste and religion, and endeavoured to overcome the caste prejudices through a hermeneutical approach to religion.

As early as 1870, he organized the then 'lower' castes of the Nilgiris into *Advaidananda Sabha* (Association for Advaitic Bliss) an association for

---

[3] G. Aloysius has done yeoman service to compile the writings of the Pandit under the title *Iyothee Thasar Sinthanaikal I, II, III* [*The Thoughts of Iyothee Thasar*] in three volumes, and to study the emancipatory aspects of this movement. G. Aloysius, *Religion as Emancipatory Identity – A Bhuddhist Movement among Tamils under Colonialism* (Mumbai: New Age International Publishers, 1998); Gajendran Ayyathurai, "Foundations of Anti-caste Consciousness: Pandit Iyothee Thass, Tamil Buddhism, and the Marginalized in South India." Ph.D. Dissertation submitted to Columbia University, 2011; Dickens Leonard M. "Caste-less Community: Iyothee Thass (1845-1914) and Tamil Buddhism." Ph.D. Dissertation submitted to University of Hyderabad, 2017.

[4] Aloysius, *Religion*, 50.

[5] Ibid., 50.

[6] Ibid., 50.

living out the *advaitic* philosophical vision[7] to overcome the discriminatory caste divisions. However, his inner yearning for a dignified social living kept leading him to search for more effective transformative religions. After reading a booklet by a Buddhist bhikku in 1887, he was drawn to Buddhism.[8] After consulting Col. H. S. Olcott of the Theosophical Society of Madras, a known personality sympathetic to the concerns of the oppressed people, he journeyed to Ceylon in the year 1898 and "obtained the Panchashila[9] at the hands of the venerable Sri Sumangala Mahanayaka, the High Priest, Principal of the Vidyodaya College, Colombo."[10]

After coming back, he founded the *Sakya Buddhist Society* at Royapettah, Madras. History of Tamil Buddhism, as Aloysius observes,[11] is the history of the origin and development of the *Sakya Buddhist Society* which grew into a popular phenomenon during the early twentieth century. The Pandit was actively involved in establishing units of this Society among the Tamils, including those living in South Africa and Burma. These units were established "to explain the ancestral histories and Buddhist *thanmam*[12] to the casteless Dravidians[13] and through stability in virtue and religious discipline to help them towards progress."[14] As part of this process, members were recruited into the society with the rite of the *pancha silam*; Buddhist temples were built; rituals instituted; and other public activities were organized. An important activity among them was to organize lectures by known scholars of the time on the social condition of Tamil people. As Aloysius observes: "The Sakya Buddhist Society started its activities in 1898 with religious meetings on Sundays, semi-public lectures on socio-religious issues by learned men of all

---

[7] Advaita, as well known, is a major strand of Indian philosophy, emerging from the Upanishads and continuously being renewed by contextual interpretations by sages and gurus. Sankaracharya was perhaps the greatest figure in Indian philosophy to interpret the vision of *advaita* as ontology of 'non-dualist oneness'.

[8] Though appreciative of some aspects of Christianity, he opposed its 'proselytising' tendencies.

[9] A Buddhist rite of initiation.

[10] Aloysius, *Religion,* 50.

[11] Ibid., 50.

[12] *Thanmam* is a Tamil rendering of the Buddhist doctrine of '*Dhammam*' (anglicised form of the original word in Pali language). Dhammam was a Buddhist parallel or even a counter to Dharma, one of the central moral teachings of the Indian religio-philosophical corpus consisting of the Vedas, Upanishads, *Dharmasutras, Dharmasastras, Bhagavad Gita,* and *Puranas.*

[13] Dravidians are a conglomerate of racially unified but culturally differentiated people inhabiting the southern part of the Indian peninsula; and, they are generally differentiated from the Aryans, who inhabited / inhabit the northern parts.

[14] Aloysius, *Religion,* 56.

faiths and confessions and 'conversions' to Buddhism that is, taking of *pancha silam* and enrolling as members, though in small numbers, yet continuously."[15]

Once chosen as the religio-philosophical path for historical emancipation as well as for the ultimate liberation - *nirvana*,[16] the Pandit embarked upon the hermeneutical task of constructing the Tamil Buddhism, with the help of Tamil literary sources in an amazingly imaginative way. Beginning with the fundamental claim that not merely the Tamil country, but the whole of India was once Buddhist, he argued that the Vedas, Upanishads and other classical Indian systems too were originally Buddhist, and that the "fake Brahmins" had overlaid these classical systems with their own philosophies for their "self-aggrandisement"; he claimed that Buddhism was the *Ativedam*, i.e., the original Veda, and prescribed it for the members of the newly founded *Sakya Buddhist Society*. The Pandit involved himself in a life-time hermeneutical task of deconstructing the existing *puranic* myths and even the popular religious practices in order to disclose their original Buddhist content and character; and, went about constructing and spreading the *Ativedam* until the last breath of his life. His enthusiasm to lay a "substantial" foundation for Tamil Buddhism remained high all through his life. Thus he created a narrative site to contest the hegemony of the prejudice of caste and construct an emancipatory identity (both individual and collective) for the subaltern people, especially for the Dalit Parayar[17] community in the Tamil speaking regions.

The Pandit published a pamphlet in Tamil entitled, "Buddha: The Light without Distinction of Day and Night."[18] In this, he enunciated the lineaments of Tamil Buddhism, giving an account of Buddha's life, an account of the past glory of Tamils as per their classical ethical traditions, an explanation of the present degeneration of the status of Tamils due to the oppression by Brahmins, and the goal of redeeming the past glory.[19]

An important contribution he made both to Tamil and Tamil Buddhism was the launching of a weekly news magazine in 1907, which was originally known as *Oru Paisa Tamilan* (One Paisa Tamil Person) but changed to *Tamilan* (Tamil Person) within a year. Through his articles published in this magazine, he propounded Tamil Buddhism by retrieving the original Buddhist semantics embedded in Tamil and reconstructing an emancipatory identity to the Tamil Parayars. The magazine was run until the demise of the Pandit in the year 1914. As Aloysius observes: "For the Pandit, this was the most fruitful phase

[15] Ibid., 58.

[16] *Nirvana*, as per the Buddhist vision, is the ultimate 'liberation' or release from the cycles of rebirth.

[17] Parayar is one of the Dalit communities spread out through the southern part of India, especially in the Tamil speaking region.

[18] Ibid., 57.

[19] Ibid., 57.

of his entire life with several hundred pages of highly original, interpretative research and writing on Tamil history, culture and religion to his credit."[20]

He understood his work as a discovery of Buddhism, which for him, was, as mentioned above, the *adivedam*, i.e., the original Vedas of Tamils. In the year 1912, he published a work titled *Adivedam*,[21] which gave an account of the life and message of Lord Buddha interpreted from the perspective of emancipation of the subaltern people. This was being serialised in the *Tamilan* under the title "The Light of Ancient Tamils—Adivedam."[22] As Aloysius observes, the connection "between Buddhism and social emancipation was to be present perennially and pervasively in all the aspects of the growth of the movement"[23] of Tamil Buddhism.

Thus we see that the Pandit was actively involved in gaining freedom from the prejudicial system of caste. The Pandit's life and activities make an inspiring text for us to learn many lessons from. In this context, the present chapter explores the specific hermeneutical approach of the Pandit in relating religion to the project of social freedom to the subaltern people in case of the Parayars. It seeks to highlight the dynamics with which the Pandit integrated Tamil Buddhism into his emancipatory efforts.

3. Religion-in-Society Perspective and Beyond

Aloysius, as mentioned above, has explored the Pandit's Tamil Buddhism systematically. He has done it from the "religion-in-society" perspective, which certainly is very insightful. He situates the Pandit's initiative within the shift that occurred in religion, during the Post-French revolution modern era, from "transcendental-experiential to ethical-instrumental, individual-salvational to collective-liberational and from passive submission to and acceptance of the 'religiously given' to the active appropriation and construction of religious symbols and world views..."[24]

Though this religion-in-society perspective, with its constructivist underpinnings, sheds much light on the religious subjectivity or agency as propelled by aspirations for social emancipation, I argue that a religious perspective *per se* is needed to understand the depth of the religious agency of the subalterns. A religion-in-society perspective could face the danger of religion turning out to be an object of social engineering with the support of an ideology, thereby losing the very *religiousness*. I am aware that Aloysius is not pursuing a sociologically reductionist approach. He says, "Tamil Buddhism ... was a genuine religious movement of the subaltern... While critiquing

[20] Ibid., 65.

[21] Ibid., 75.

[22] Ibid.

[23] Ibid., 54.

[24] Ibid., 1-2.

ruthlessly the dominant definition of the Transcendent, the movement itself was positing a new form of humane and historically rooted notion of the supernatural as an alternative."[25] However, when he makes a claim in another place that "Just as organisation and symbolisation, the beliefs and ideologies too, of the Tamil Buddhists were a *subjective construction* (italics mine) of the subalternised communities...,"[26] the constructivism shows itself. Perhaps, the religion of the oppressed makes a *sui generis* opening, and that needs to be explored on its own, even while valuing the complementarity of sociological or anthropological insights.

Pandit's engagement with religion in the context of his aspiration for emancipation of the oppressed, was spontaneous, positive, and open-ended, i.e., he did not seek to *instrumentalize* religion and was open to the transcendental potentials of religion. While the ethical concern was pervasive in his religious quest, he pursued also transcendental religious ends like the 'eternal beyond death'. Explaining a difference between his Tamil Buddhism and a then existing Maha Bodhi Buddhism, the Pandit explained: "We believe that through Right Conduct and life of Right Path one should overcome sorrow, death and ego; but they (Maha Bodhi Buddhists) believe that there is no rebirth, or the eternal and nothing beyond death. The latter, negative formulations lead to the equations of human life to that of cattle and to the life of ethical abandon, which can lead neither the individual to deliverances from sorrow nor the society to harmony and love."[27] Thus, it can be seen that though the Pandit's religious initiatives fall within the general Buddhist religio-philosophical framework, and they cannot be reduced to humanist non-transcendental*ism*.

The general objective of the *Sakya Buddhist Society* that he founded after his conversion to Buddhism was stated, as mentioned above, as: "...to explain ... Bhuddhist *thanmam* ... through stability in virtue and religious discipline..."[28] "Through stability in virtue and religious discipline" are words that point to certain independent positions for ethics and religion, and they indicate his realization of the role of religion for nurturing emancipatory aspirations among subalterns. Certainly, ethics, the forte of virtue, is for him the yardstick to measure the presence of religion, but it is also the *vice versa*. He experiences both as associative realities, without one subsumed under the other. We find this happening in the way he approached both of them dialogically. Religion leads to ethics, while ethics leads to religion. It is a mutuality, enriching one another. We find this interplay of religion and ethics in the dynamics of his Tamil Buddhist strivings.

---

[25] Ibid., 145.

[26] Ibid., 129.

[27] Thasar cited in Aloysius, *Religion,* 145-46.

[28] As cited in G. Aloysius, *Religion,* 56.

4. Dynamics of Deconstruction and Reconstruction

The religious pursuit of the Pandit went with a sense of enquiry and wisdom. He would instruct his readers, or followers, to "inquire" into everything – beliefs, practices, etc., until one got answers satisfactory to enquiry, experience and sight. He treats "experience and reason"[29] as two epistemological criteria for the truthfulness of claims – religious or otherwise. He said: "Buddha *thanmam*[30] even if handed down by your great grandfather or grandfather, question it in your own enquiry and experience. If you realize its truth that it would lead to the welfare of your descendents, co-villagers and co-countrymen, then believe in it; but if found worthless in your enquiry and experience, leave it behind; that is why Buddha *thanmam* is named as the true *thanmam* (*meyyaram*)"[31] - an enquiring religion.

The Pandit's spirit of enquiry shined forth in "deconstructing" some of the age-old *puranic* role-models, that of Harichandra being the salient one. Needless to say the height of normativity this character had obtained in the Indian "cultural imaginary"[32] to signify honesty and truthfulness. Mahatma Gandhi, according to his autobiography, seems to have learned his lesson of truthfulness by listening to the story of Harichandra.[33] The Pandit was quite forthright in deconstructing this 'myth' of the truthfulness of Harichandra. He published an article with the title, "The Story of Harichandra's Truthfulness and the Details of how He Became a Liar."[34] He found this role-model characterised by umpteen number of lies, dis-loyalty to people, anti-women stances, and cowardice even to the extent of not being able to protect his wife. The Pandit was concerned about the concepts of 'truthfulness' and 'lie' that were being discussed in this *puranic* tale. He was agitated at the fact that Harihchandra was extolled as a truthful king because he, through trial and tribulations, kept his word to the Brahmins, but, on the other hand, disgracefully denied the request of two women from the lowly community for protection. This dissonance in

---

[29] Aloysius, *Religion,* 131.

[30] *Thanmam,* a Tamil word equivalent to *dhammam* in Pali language used by Buddhist texts; and it is a Buddhist adaptation of the word *dharma,* enunciated in Sanskritic texts from the Vedas.

[31] As cited in Aloysius, *Religion*, 131. *Meyyaram* in Tamil means 'true morality'.

[32] 'Cultural imaginary' is a phrase used by Graham Ward to stand for the corpus of symbols, narratives, art, artifacts, and beliefs a particular cultural world produces and sustains. It is a parallel to the concept of 'social imaginary' proposed by Charles Taylor.

[33] M. K. Gandhi, *An Autobiography or The Story of My Experiment with Truth* [trans. from the original in Gujarathi by Mahadev Desai in 1940 (Ahmedabad: Navajivan Publishing House), https://www.mkgandhi.org/ebks/An-Autobiography.pdf.

[34] Iyodhee Thasar, "The Story of Harichandra's Truthfulness and the Details of how He Became a Liar," in G. Aloysius, ed. *Iyotheethasar Sinthanaigal II* (Palayamkottai: Folklore Resources and Research Centre, 1999), 92.

the characterization makes Harihchandra a liar, and problematizes the very neutrality of the concepts of truth and lie.[35] He accuses the proponents of the story of lacking in discernment of truth and lie, and of propagating such lies in order to manipulate and cheat the gullible.

Even while deconstructing 'such myths', the Pandit constructs an alternate mythography of Tamil Buddhism. He gives an infancy narrative of Buddha, wherein he suggests a miraculous conception as well as birth to Buddha: "the mother of the child had a dream that a star came down and entered her womb;"[36] "when the child was born, a light emerged all over the world; a music emerged from heavens; the lame walked; love became boundless to bring peace and comfort; cattle and birds found their food; etc."[37] According to him, Buddha was born much before the advent of the Aryans into this subcontinent;[38] and the original Vedas were composed by the Buddha.[39] He claimed that the whole subcontinent was filled with Buddhism, and that the original Vedas and Upanishads were originally Buddhist texts.[40]

Pandit's writings come under the genre of mythical narratives, where analogy takes the upper hand to be effective in its dynamics. While he propounds a specific mythography within this grand genre that has been in existence for millennia together, what makes his mythography different from the traditional ones is the vision and concern to embody subaltern empowerment in the narratives. He intuitively draws upon the power of language to effect changes.

5. Pandit's Linguistic Approach to Religion

In both deconstruction and reconstruction, the Pandit followed a uniquely linguistic approach, aided by his amazing skill to alliteratively search for the semantics of a given linguistic code, and by his grammatically informed wide knowledge of the classical Tamil literary corpus. It was laudable that he could trace out meanings from such classics as *Manimekalai, Sudamani, Pinkalai Nikandu, Veerasoliam, Seevakasinthamani, Tirikural, Silapathikaram, Gnanavetti, Moodurai, Korkaivendan*, and many more. It was not only the

---

[35] The Pandit contends that "it looks as if there are 'Brahmin truth and lies' on the one hand, and 'Paraiyar truth and lies' on the other hand" (பறைப்பொய்ப் பாடப்பாரப்பொய், பறை மெய் பாடப்பார மெய் இருக்கின்றாப்போல் தோன்றுகிறது – 95).

[36] Iyothee Thasar, "Buddha – A Light that is Neither Night nor Day" in G. Aloysius, ed. *Iyotheethasar Sinthanaigal II* (Palayamkottai: Folklore Resources and Research Centre, 1999), 13.

[37] Iyothee Thasar, "Buddha – A Light that is…", 12.

[38] Iyothee Thasar, *Buddharathu Ativedam [Buddha's Ancient Veda]* (Chennai: Tamilkudi Arasu Pathipakam, 2010, originally published in 1912), 14.

[39] Iyothee Thasar, "Veda Vakkiyankalin Vivaram" [The Truth about Vedas] in G. Aloysius, ed. *Iyotheethasar Sinthanaigal II* (Palayamkottai: Folklore Resources and Research Centre, 1999), 79.

[40] Iyothee Thasar, "Veda Vakkiyankalin Vivaram", 80-82.

knowledge of the literary sources that gave the uniqueness to his linguistic approach, but also a deep confidence in approaching reality through language. Whether it was the religious or the social domain, he believed in the power of the language to work out transformations in them. Perhaps, it was this core confidence which spontaneously oriented him towards a religious solution to social problems, rather than social remedies on their own. He worked with the presupposition that knowing the 'genuine knowledge of the real and original meaning of the linguistic codes' (words or phrases) would result in ethical behaviour and religious observances resulting in justice, peace and harmony to the wider society, and to the oppressed in particular. This linguistic confidence of the Pandit and the dynamics of his approach can be appreciated much in the light of the now linguistic turn philosophy has taken; but I do not enter into this discussion here. I would like to descriptively analyse a few of the religious themes the Pandit had handled, in his attempt to construct the emancipatory religion.

5.1. Pandit's Debate on Kadavul (God)

It is generally being observed that classical Buddhism held a philosophically atheist position of 'no self', and 'no God'. The Pandit, on the other hand, "time and again rejected the allegation that Buddhist were atheists."[41] He took care to explain his position by expatiating upon the central linguistic code "God", *Kadavul* in Tamil. The original meaning of *Kadavul* for him was unconditional 'Goodness', implying a demand for 'doing good' and a life of intense orientation to this ultimate goodness. Those who know God would show it by their practice of justice, morality, and truthfulness, whose meanings emerge from out of a life-context, where they are used for right truth, right vision, right observance, right feeling, right charity, etc. Buddhists do accept God, *Kadavul*, in this existential sense. The Pandit, therefore, wondered how people could accuse Buddhists of not accepting/knowing God, *Kadavul*.[42]

His understanding of God, however, was not to be equated with the understandings of other theistic systems. He would not accept a Creator God, for example.[43] He found the claim on Creator God not emerging from experience and sight, which for him constitute the light of wisdom. The latter, according to him, would correspond to our experience and sight, and those which did not correspond to them were from "darkness", which would, in turn, lend itself for manipulation by priestcraft.

---

[41] Thasar, "Kadavul" [God], in G. Aloysius, ed. *Iyotheethasar Sinthanaigal II* (Palayamkottai: Folklore Resources and Research Centre, 1999 originally published in 1907), 26.

[42] Thasar, "Kadavul", 27; Thasar, "Kadavulilaiyo, Kadavulilaiyo" [Is there no God, Is there no God?" in G. Aloysius, ed. *Iyotheethasar Sinthanaigal II* (Palayamkottai: Folklore Resources and Research Centre, 1999 originally published in 1911), 168.

[43] Thasar, "Kadavulilaiyo, Kadavulilaiyo?", 168.

"Whoever seeks one's own benefit through religion will perish" is one of the assertions that keeps recurring in the writings of the Pandit. To drive home the point that the word *Kadavul*, God, was being used by various people for their own benefits, he narrated a story of a king and his minister: "the minister is aggrieved that the people do not mind him, and care only for their king; so he devises a plot and tells the king that the people are not respecting the king anymore; the king seeks his counsel to find remedy for this, and he advises him to announce to the people that they should come everyday to the palace and pay obeisance to their king, failing which they should pay a fine to the treasury. Thus, the minister got a revenue to his treasury."[44] This was to say that everyone seeks one's own benefit; especially through religion and faith. He finds the 'fake Brahmins' to be such self-seekers. While the original *anthanar* (Brahmins) were the Buddhists according to Thasar, others who came later with the name Brahmins began to misuse the Vedas, Upanishads and other religious resources for their own benefits, oppressing the real Brahmins, the *anthanar* – who practised the ideal of renunciation.

5.2. Associating Folk Deities with Buddhist Thanmam

The Pandit approached the folk deities astutely. He set aside some of them as "superstitious" when they did not contribute to an emancipatory practice. He denounced those who "bribed" these deities by sacrificing cattle and poultry to them. On the other hand, he redeemed through a linguistic excavation those folk deities that had transformative potential and assigned a due place in the Buddhist sacred canopy. It is amazing to read how he exegetically "identifies" Buddhist origins to several female deities of south India. For example, through his typical linguistic alliterative method, the Pandit begins with the first name of a deity known as *Pitari*, which consists of *Pita+ari*, wherein *Pita* stands for *tripitaka*, the Buddhist scripture and '*ari*' means 'to know'; not merely cognitive knowing, but announcing or proclaiming the *tripitaka* gives the name *Pitakari* to this deity, according to the Pandit.[45] This female deity was related by him with almost all the female deities known in the south, including *Avvai, Saraswathi, Ambikai, Kannakai,* and *Mariaththa*. Wherever these deities are celebrated, according to the Pandit, it is the Buddhist *thanman* that is celebrated and observed.

[44] Iyothee Thasar, "Kadavul", in G. Aloysius, ed. *Iyotheethasar Sinthanaigal II* (Palayamkottai: Folklore Resources and Research Centre, 1999 originally written in 1907), 27-28.

[45] Thasar, "Adi Mathathil Ammanai Sinthikkum Vivarum" [An Account of Meditating on Amman (a female deity) during the Month of Adi (a Tamil Month), in G. Aloysius, ed. *Iyotheethasar Sinthanaigal II* (Palayamkottai: Folklore Resources and Research Centre, 1999 originally published in 1907), 31.

5.3. Challenge to Christians

Proceeding with his linguistic exegesis, the Pandit dissects and interprets the word 'Christian' so as to evoke an ethical response. He understands a Christian to be someone who dwells within Christ, who, in turn, dwells in him. Dwelling in Christ means dwelling steadfastly within the observance of the ethical teachings of Christ, which is nothing but "loving God, and loving one another as oneself."[46] After proposing this ethical orientation to being a Christian, the Pandit challenges the so-called Christians whether they were really Christians, in the sense of dwelling in Christ. He finds a contradiction in them when they claim to be Christians, but address themselves as "Joseph Chettiyar, David Mudaliar, Savariappa Naidu and so on." He poses a sharp question: "how to understand the legitimacy of those who call others as 'pagans', even while they themselves keep the Christian names but observe the pagan castes?" Can those who enter into Christianity, but yet observe caste be identified as 'real' Christians? After posing such sharp questions, he gives a very pertinent piece of advice to the Christian priests based on a familiar theme from the Bible: "Those who humble themselves will be exalted, and those who exalt themselves will be humbled"; accordingly, he says, "when Christians consider themselves as high castes on earth, their status will be lowered in heaven, and so they need to be careful." He ends the section saying, "if there is one real Christian among thousand nominal Christians, the world will shudder, but, on the other hand, if there is not even one real Christian among ten thousand nominal Christians, the world will curse. Priests are the causes for both."[47]

5.4. Pandit's Linguistic Confidence

The Pandit criticised the so-called religions, and went in pursuit of a "real" religion that could bring freedom to the oppressed people. God, the central category of religion, was for him that virtuous code with which human beings could pursue their emancipation and freedom. The linguistic confidence of the Pandit needs more exploration, understanding and appreciation. Being a literary scholar in Tamil, he developed a confidence that by tracing the original meanings of the words, one could construct a history, an ethics, a religion, a programme for a movement, etc. He deconstructed the existing hegemonic myths and puranic tales, and reconstructed Taṃil Buddhism with the use of this method. In the process, he integrated the modern spirit of enquiry, religious pursuit of high virtues, and so on. He needs to be understood on his own terms, and his approach to religion needs to be understood on its own. Was the Pandit running against the boundaries to express his subaltern self?

---

[46] Thasar, "Kiristhavan Kiristhu Avan – Avan Kiristhu" [Christ as Christian, Christian as Christ], in G. Aloysius, ed. *Iyotheethasar Sinthanaigal II* (Palayamkottai: Folklore Resources and Research Centre, 1999 originally published in 1908), 99-100.

[47] Thasar, " Kiristhavan Kiristhu Avan – Avan Kiristhu", 101.

6. An Aura of Religiosity to the Colonial Rule

The Pandit's life had a creatively challenging background, which saw many forms of assertion from the subaltern people.[48] Obviously the most prominent factor present in the context was the inchoate Indian variant of modernity, emerging from the convergence of western colonial modernity, the traditions of dominant classes along with their efforts to reap the benefits of colonial modernity, and the emancipatory initiatives of the subaltern classes.

I wonder whether even post-colonialism has adequately articulated / described the vitality of this Indian modernity. Right from the time Edward Said threw the first stone upon *Orientalism*, the whole fund of literatures – religious, anthropological, philosophical, and sociological on the Orient, produced by both the colonisers and the natives, have been suspected of treating the Orient as passive, non-creative, civilizationally backward, retrogressive, and so on. The major intent of post-colonialism was to rectify the mistaken valuation of the Orient. However, even the latter seems to have become incapable of sufficiently appreciating the context-specific formations of modernity, because of their universal or continental frameworks of coloniality and post-coloniality.

It is a case in point that the Pandit greatly appreciated the role played by the British 'colonisers'. He went to the extent of adopting a religious observance to pay respect to the British rule. Every member of the Tamil Buddhist Society was enjoined to observe certain religious observances regularly, and one among them was paying obeisance to the British, because theirs was a reign characterised by justice, law, and compassion. He wrote: "The second act of veneration is to the British Raj which rules us. Why should we venerate them is because of their ethics of justice and the wellbeing they bestow upon us, and because of the freedom that they ensure us from fears of robbers, molesters, wicked persons, wild animals, and terminal diseases."[49]

The height of reverence he had accorded to the British cannot be understood within a post-colonial paradigm, and it certainly needs a contextual subaltern approach. The Dalit critique has a more situated and nuanced approach to colonialism, rather than a one-sided rejection; it has to negotiate between multiple layers of coloniality in their actual contexts of existence; for them, the empire is not just a linear power emerging from the western colonial

---

[48] As historians point out, several socio-religious movements emerged during this era. See for example, Stephen Fuchs, *Rebellious Prophets – A Study of Messianic Movements in Indian Religions* (Bombay: Asia Publishing House, 1965); Fuchs, *Godmen on the Warpath – A Study of Messianic Movements in India* (New Delhi: Munshiram Manoharlal Publishers Pvt Ltd., 1992); Kenneth W. Jones, *Socio-Religious Reform Movements in India* (Cambridge: Cambridge University Press, 1994).

[49] Thasar, "Buddharkalin Arikuri" [Characteristic traits of Buddhists] in G. Aloysius, ed. *Iyotheethasar Sinthanaigal II* (Palayamkottai: Folklore Resources and Research Centre, 1999 originally published in 1912), 431.

powers, but also the traditional, dominant hegemonies which cripple their lives in actual contexts of life.

Discussion

The Pandit, as can be seen from above, has gone about his emancipatory project with certain specific methodology. What is unique to the modern socio-cultural history of the subaltern people of India is that their emancipatory aspirations express themselves in religious idioms in terms of rituals and sacred mythographies. The umpteen number of socio-religious movements which emerged at the intersection of western modernity and Indian traditions bear witness to this specificity. Even well known modern Indian intellectuals and political leaders engaged themselves interpretatively with religions to pursue their social emancipatory goals. In a later period, Dr. B. R. Ambedkar's embrace of Buddhism in the year 1956 is a case in point.

Ambedkar's involvement in or encounter with religion has been, for a very long time, an important theme of interest in Ambedkar studies.[50] Several researchers have explored and continue to explore this dimension and have come out with interesting insights. Not a few scholars present Ambedkar's turn to religion as rational, secular, scientific, purely morality-based, and non-transcendental philosophical turn without any reference to God. Johannes Beltz, for example, writes that, "Ambedkar held Buddhism to be a social philosophy based on morality and science ... purified from all superstition, rituals, and theology, without any belief in God or worship in God, without prayers or sacrifices – Buddhism was nothing but morality... Ambedkar's most important innovation was in his viewing of Buddhism as totally secularist and anti-traditional."[51] In a similar vein, Valerian Rodrigues, in his introduction to the edited volume on the *Essential Writings of Ambedkar* notes that:

> Ambedkar acknowledged the power of religion and upheld its need, but there is no place in his religion for God and the transcendent. He subscribed to a secular religion, moving away from established religions geared towards the sacred vis-a-vis the profane... He felt that since human beings are part of this world, the primary role of religion is to safeguard the moral domain. Religion deploys sentiments, feelings and culture to secure the moral domain and make it universal.[52]

[50] Cf. Surendra Jondhale and Joahnnes Beltz, eds. *Reconstructing the World – B. R. Ambedkar and Buddhism in India* (New Delhi: OUP), 2004.

[51] Johannes Beltz, "Introduction" in Surendra Jondhale and Joahnnes Beltz, eds. *Reconstructing the World – B. R. Ambedkar and Buddhism in India* (New Delhi: OUP), 2004, 7-8.

[52] Valerian Rodriques, ed. *Essential Writings of B. R. Ambedkar* (New Delhi: Oxford University Press, 2002), 19.

These and similar views on Ambedkar's approach to religion have been prevalent for quite some time now. They are predominantly sociological, some anthropological, and a few even of religious studies, but more from the perspective of the history of religion, including the comparative religious approach.

However, there are new approaches being adopted today in an open-ended and explorative manner so as to understand the reality of Ambedkar's encounter with religion as best as possible. Debjani Ganguly's attempt is a good example. She contends that Ambedkar's religious experience, including his conversion, is "more often than not beyond the pale of sociological analysis,"[53] and she adds that "[I]n order to truly understand the significance of religious conversion from the point of view of the convert's life-world, one would have to engage with the phenomenology of faith and transcendence and their very singular manifestation in the individual lives of the converts."[54] Ganguly's view, along with several others who explore Ambedkar's religion from a post-secular perspective, opens a new perspective to Ambedkar's encounter with religion. I use the term 'encounter' to signify the orientation that occurred in Ambedkar towards religion. The term could point to the fact that religion engaged the mind of this modern individual who took on the dominant religious tradition in terms of a through-going critique, endeavoured to open a new 'religious horizon' through the Buddhist tradition, desired the social freedom of a people in terms of a religious imagination and practice, and finally ended with an act of religious conversion. All these, and many more dimensions, can constitute the phenomenology of Ambedkar's religion.

Similarly, the religious involvement of the Pandit too needs to be approached in an open-minded way, taking religion to be a *sui generis* experience that goes into the emancipatory assertion of subaltern people in the Indian context. Such involvement is uniquely pertinent in the context of the hegemony of caste, which reproduces itself with the aid of fossilized religious forms like myths, symbols, and narratives, i.e., religious forms reified to maintain the structures of power. The Pandit seeks after and encounters Buddhism in a new way and expresses his experience through the idiom of Tamil Buddhism. It is a way of reimagining the past of the subaltern people through a religious mythography, reclaiming dignity and power to the subalterns here and now and aiming at a new anti-caste community of freedom. It is a way of opening the horizons of history to the hitherto excluded.

As part of his religious encounter, the Pandit undertakes to 'deconstruct' the reigning oppressive mythical codes and figures in Tamil. He deconstructs, as seen above, the most popular mythical figure Harichandra, the symbol of

[53] Debjani Ganjuli, *Caste, Colonialism and Counter-Modernity – Notes on a Postcolonial Hermeneutics of Caste* (London: Routledge, 2005), 156.

[54] Ibid.

honesty and truthfulness, to reveal the lack of fairness and responsibility which constitute this mythical personality. He contends that such mythical figures are upheld by Brahminic mythography to deceive and hold the gullible under subjection.

The Pandit's linguistic exegesis is yet another method to obtain the 'true' meaning of words, which, according to him, reveals the Buddhist meanings. Here 'true' reflects the ethical standard of egalitarianism from the perspective of the subalterns, rather than the being in correspondence with an external objective reality. The way he does an exegesis of the word 'Christian', as mentioned above (p. 8), is a typical example. By tracing the root of the word to 'Christ', he interprets that a Christian is someone who 'becomes a Christ'; To become Christ means, for him, becoming a person who loves everyone without discrimination. On this hermeneutical axis, he denounces those 'Christians' who still carry their caste suffixes after their names. Thus, we see the Pandit critiquing the Tamil Christians for becoming victims of the caste order of discrimination; however, he promotes the cultivation of true Christian personalities too. Thus, we see an egalitarian gestalt emerging from the Pandit's endeavour of constituting the Tamil Buddhism.

Conclusion

Tamil Buddhism, initiated and developed through the *Sakya Buddhist Society* by the efforts of Pandit Iyothee Thasar, is a specific example of the way a hermeneutical approach to religion may meaningfully be integrated in efforts to overcome prejudices such as the caste related ones that are deeply entrenched in the Indian Society. The Pandit undertook to deconstruct the reigning myths or narratives to expose the oppressive intents invested in them by the 'fake Brahmins'. At the same time, he endeavoured to constitute Tamil Buddhism by constructing an alternate corpus of myths which were emancipatory in nature. In his endeavour he employed a hermeneutical approach, whereby he exegetically explored some salient religious terms in Tamil to argue that the deeper meanings they contained were not merely Buddhist in nature but also were emancipatory in content. Such hermeneutical exercises themselves, the Pandit believed, were methodologies for freedom from deep-seated prejudices. It is revealing to see that Ambedkar, a latter-day modern reformer, too took recourse to religion in a hermeneutical vein to overcome caste-prejudices during his time. One may do well to study these instances of religions in an open-minded way, treating religions as *sui generis* realities.

Bibliography

Adrados, Francisco R. "Indian and Greek Philosophy." *Annals of the Bhandarkar Oriental Research Institute*, Vol. 58/59, 1977-78, 1-8.

Ahmad, Aijaz. "The Making of India" *Social Scientist*, vol. 33, nos. 11-12, Nov-Dec, 2005.

Alles, D. Gregory, ed. *Religious Studies – A Global View*. London: Routledge, 2008.

Aloysius, G. *Religion as Emancipatory Identity – A Buddhist Movement among the Tamils under Colonialism*. Mumbai: New Age International Publishers, 1998.

_______ (ed). *The Thoughts of Iyothee Thasar I (Religion and Literature)*. Palayamkottai: FRRC, 1999.

Anderson, Walter K and Shridhar D. Damle. *The RSS – A View to the Inside*. New Delhi: Penguin Random House India, 2018.

Amaladoss, Anand. ed. *Indian Christian Thinkers*. Vol. 2, Chennai: Sathya Nilayam, 2006.

Amaladoss, M., John T. K., and Gispert-Sauch G. eds. *Theologizing in India*. Bangalore: TPI, 1981.

Amaladoss, Michael. *Blessed are the Peacemakers – Theological Reflections*. Chennai: The New Leader Publications, 2012.

_______. *Making Harmony – Living in a Pluralist World*. Chennai: IDCR, 2003.

_______. *Peace on Earth*. Mumbai: St. Paul's, 2003.

_______. *Beyond Inculturation – Can the Many be One*. New Delhi: Vidyajoti & ISPCK, 1998.

_______. *Life in Freedom – Liberation Theologies from Asia*. Anand: Gujarat Sahitya Prakash, 1997.

Alam, Javeed. "Public Sphere and Democratic Governance in Contemporary India." In *Multiculturalism, Liberalism and Democracy*, edited by Rajeev

Bhargava, Amiya Kumar Bagchi and R. Sudharshan, 323-347. New Delhi: Oxford University Press, 1999.

Arockiadoss, Peter. *Equal and Free*. Dindigul: Vaigarai Publications, 2010.

Audard, Catherine. "French Republicanism and 'Thick' Multiculturalism." In *Multiculturalism, Liberalism and Democracy,* edited by Rajeev Bhargava, Amiya Kumar Bagchi and R. Sudharshan, 116-137. New Delhi: Oxford University Press, 1999.

Ayyathurai, Gajendran. "Foundations of Anti-caste Consciousness: Pandit Iyothee Thasar, Tamil Buddhism, and the Marginalized in South India." Ph.D. Dissertation submitted to Columbia Universit, 2011.

Banchoff, Thomas. "Jesuit Higher Education and the Global Common Good." In *The Jesuits and Globalization – Historical Legacies and Contemporary Challenges,* eds. Thomas Banchoff and Jose Casanova, 239-260. Washington, DC: Georgetown University Press.

_______ ed. *Religious Pluralism, Globalization, and World Politics.* Oxford: Oxford University Press, 2008.

_______ *Democracy and the New Religious Pluralism*. OUP, 2007.

Banerjee-Guha, Swapna. "Neoliberalising the 'Urban': New Geographies of Power and Injustice in Indian Cities." Economic and Political Weekly , May 30 - Jun. 5, 2009, Vol. 44, No. 22 (May 30 - Jun. 5, 2009), pp. 95-107; https://www.jstor.org/stable/40279062.

Barret, Richard. "The Survival of Reason: Reflections on 'Fides et Ratio'" New Blackfriars, Vol. 81, No. 955, Special Issue: Fides et Ratio (September 2000), pp. 360-376, 24-12-2019 06:48 UTC.

Bauman, Chad M. *Christian Identity and Dalit Religion in Hindu India, 1868-1947*. Grand Rapids, Michigan: William B Erdmans Publishing Company, 2008.

_______ *Pentecostals, Proselytization, and Anti-Christian Violence in Contemporary India*. New York: Oxford University Press, 2015.

Berger, Peter, ed. *The Desecularization of the World: Resurgent Religion and World Politics*. Washington, DC: Ethics and Public Policy Center, 1999.

Berger, Peter L and Richard John Neuhaus. *To Empower People – From State to Civil Society*. USA: American Enterprise Institute, 1977.

Bergunder, Michael. *The South Indian Pentecostal Movement in the Twentieth Century*. UK: William B. Eerdmans Publishing Company, 2008.

Beverley, Eric Lewis. "Colonial Urbanism and South Asian cities." *Social History*, November 2011, Vol. 36, No. 4 (November 2011), pp. 482-497; https://www.jstor.org/stable/2307265.

Bhagwan, Manu and Anne Feldhaus. *Speaking Truth to Power – Gender, Power and the Subaltern Question in India*. New Delhi: OUP,

Bhargava, Rajeev. *The Promise of India's Secular Democracy*. OUP, 2010.

_______ (ed). *Secularism and its Critics*. New Delhi: OUP, 1998.

Bordoni, Linda "Pope urges Sri Lankan leaders to initiate dialogue for common good" Pope urges Sri Lankan leaders to initiate dialogue for common good - Vatican News accessed on 25 Sept. 2022.

Brown, Judith M. and Robert Eric Frykenberg, eds. *Christians, Cultural Interactions, and India's Religious Traditions*. Grand Rapids, UK: William B. Eerdmans Publishing Company, 2002.

Boyd, Robin. *An Introduction to Indian Christian Theology*. New Delhi: ISPCK, 1969.

Bunnell, Tim, Goh, Daniel P. S., Lai, Chee-Kien and Pow, C. P. "Introduction: Global Urban Frontiers? Asian Cities in Theory, Practice and Imagination," *Urban Studies*, Vol. 49, No. 13, Special Issue: Global Urban Frontiers? Asian Cities in Theory, Practice and Imagination (OCTOBER 2012), pp. 2785-2793: https://www.jstor.org/stable/10.2307/26144113.

Cali, Dennis D. "John Paul II's Papal Encyclicals as Dialectic", in *The Rhetoric of Pope John Paul II*, eds. Joseph R. Blaney and Joseph P. Zompetti. 233 – 256. Lanham: Lexinton Books, 2009.

Casanova, Jose. *Public Religions in the Modern World*. Chicago: Chicago University Press, 1994.

Cavanaugh, William T. *The Myth of Religious Violence – Secular Ideology and the Roots of Modern Conflict*. Oxford: Oxford University Press, 2009.

Chandhoke, Neera. *Beyond Secularism: The Rights of Religious Minorities*. New Delhi: OUP, 1999.

Chathanatt, John, SJ. *Unto the Margins – Pope Francis and His Challenges*. Bangalore: Claretian Publications, 2013.

_______ "Pope Francis and India – Mutual Enrichment and Challenges." In *Pope Francis as a Global Actor: Where Politics and Theology Meet*, eds. ALYNNA J. LYON, CHRISTINE A. GUSTAFSON, AND PAUL CHRISTOPHER MANUEL, 245-266. Palgrave Mcmillan, 2018.

Chatterjee, Nandini. *The Making of Indian Secularism – Empire, Law and Christianity 1830 – 1960*. UK: Palgrave Macmillan, 2011.

Chhibber, Pradeep K. and Sandeep Shastri. *Religious Practice and Democracy in India*. Delhi: Cambridge University Press, 2014.

Copley, Antony. *Religions in Conflict – Ideology, Cultural Contact and Conversion in Late-Colonial India*. Delhi: Oxford University Press, 1997.

Coulter, Michael L. "Serving the Person through the Political Community Reflections on Compendium Chapter 8," *Catholic Social Thought American Reflections on the Compendium*, eds. D. Paul Sullins and Anthony J. Blasi. UK: Lexington Books, 2009.

Cowan, Robert Bruce. "Friedrich Schlegel's Indictment of Indian Philosophy in "Uber die Sprache und die Weisheit der Indier." *The German Quarterly*, Vol. 81, No. 3 (Summer, 2008), 322-338.

Dalmia, Vasudha. *Religious Interactions in Mughal India*. New Delhi: OUP, 2014.

Datta, Dhirendra Mohan. "The Contribution of Modern Indian Philosophy to World Philosophy." *The Philosophical Review*, Vol. 57, No. 6 (Nov. 1948), 550-572.

Das, Veena et al. *Tradition, Pluralism and identity*. SAGE, 1999.

Desai, A. R. "National Integration and Religion," *Sociological Bulletin*, Vol. 12, No. 1 (March 1963), pp. 53-65, Accessed: 04-10-2019 05:55 UTC.

De Vries, Hent and Lawrence E. Sullivan, ed. *Political Theologies – Public Religions in a Post-secular World* (abridged edition). New Delhi: Orient Longman, 2007.

Desphande, Satish. *Contemporary India – A Sociological View*. New Delhi: VIKING, 2003.

Desrochers, John. *The Social Teaching of the Church in India*. Bangalore: NBCLC/CSA, 2006.

Douglass, R. Bruce and David Hollenbach, eds. *Catholicism and Liberalism – Contribution to American Public Philosophy*. Cambridge: Cambridge University Press, 1994.

Dreze, Jean. "Dr Ambedkar and the Future of Indian Democracy." In *The Radical in Ambedkar – Critical Reflections,* edited by Suraj Yengde and Anand Teltumbde, 170-180. Gurgaon: Penguin Random House India, 2018.

Dube, Saurabh. *After Conversion – Cultural Histories of Modern India*. New Delhi: YODA Press, 2010.

Echeverria, Eduardo, J. "Once Again, John Paul II's Fides et Ratio", Philosophia Reformata, Vol. 69, No. 1 (2004), pp. 38-52

Embree, Ainslie T. "A South Asian Dilemma: The Role of Religion in the Public Sphere." The Brown Journal of World Affairs , Summer/Fall 1997, Vol. 4, No. 2 (Summer/Fall 1997), pp. 137-149; https://www.jstor.org/stable/24590023.

Etzioni, Amitai. *From Empire to Community – A New Approach to International Relations.* New York: Palgrave Macmillan, 2004.

Everett, William Johnson. *Religion, Federalism and the Struggle for Public Life – Cases from Germany, India and America*. Oxford: Oxford University Press, 1997.

Faggioli, Massimo. 2021. *The Liminal Papacy of Pope Francis – Moving toward Global Catholicity*. Bangalore: Theological Publications in India.

Farias, Kranti, K. *The Christian Impact in South Kanara*. Mumbai: Church History Association of India, 1999.

Fernando, Leonard and G. Gispert-Sauch. *Two Thousand Years of Faith – Christianity in India*. New Delhi: Penguin India, 2004.

Fitzgibbon, Éamonn. "Together on the Way - Pope Francis and Synodality." The Furrow, Vol. 68, No. 10 (October 2017), pp. 532-539; https://www.jstor.org/stable/44738620.

Ford, David F, et.al. *Fields of Faith – Theology and Religious Studies for the Twenty-first Century*. Cambridge: Cambridge University Press, 2005.

Freeman, Curtis W. *Undomesticated Dissent – Democracy and the Public Virtue of Religious Nonconformity*. Texas: Baylor University Press, 2017.

Ganjuli, Debjani. *Caste, Colonialism and Counter-Modernity – Notes on a Postcolonial Hermeneutics of Caste*. London: Routledge, 2005.

Ganeri, Jonardon. "Intellectual India: Reason, Identity, Dissent." *New Literary History*. Vol. 40, No. 2, Spring 2009, 247-263.

Geetha, V. and Rajan, Nalini. *Religious Faith, Ideology, Citizenship*. London: Routledge, 2011.

Giri, Ananta Kumar. *The Modern Prince and The Modern Sage – Transforming Power and Freedom*. New Delhi: SAGE, 2009.

Goel, Sita Ram. *History of Hindu-Christian Encounters*. New Delhi: Voice of India, 1989.

Gonsalves, Francis SJ, et.al. *Towards Renewing Church and World – Revisiting Vatican Council II through the Eyes of Pope Francis*. New Delhi: ISPCK, 2020.

Gottschalk, Peter. 2001. *Beyond Hindu and Muslim – Multiple Identity in Narratives from Village India*. OUP.

Graham, Elaine. "What Makes a Good City? - Reflections on Urban Life and Faith." *International Journal of Public Theology*, 2 (2008), 7–26.

Hargarden, Kevin. A Pope on a Neoliberal Island." Studies: An Irish Quarterly Review , Vol. 108, No. 430, Goodbye to All That? Ireland after the Pope (Summer 2019), pp. 172-184; https://www.jstor.org/stable/10.35939/studiesirishrev.108.430.0172.

Hollenbach, David, SJ. *The Common Good and the Christian Ethics*. UK: Cambridge University Press, 2004.

Harris-White, Barbara. *India's Market Society – Three Essays in Political Economy*. New Delhi: Three Essays Collectives, 2005.

Hedlund, Roger E. *Quest for Identity - India's Churches of Indigenous Origin: The 'Little Tradition' in Indian Christianity*. New Delhi: ISPCK, 2000.

Helm, Paul, ed. *Faith and Reason*. Oxford: Oxford University Press, 1999.

Hvithamar, Annika, et.al. *Holy Nations and Global Identities – Civil Religions, Nationalism and Globalisation*. Leiden: BRILL, 2009.

International Theological Commission, *Synodality in the Life and Mission of the Church*. Synodality in the life and mission of the Church (2 March 2018) (vatican.va) https://www.vatican.va/roman_curia/congregations/cfaith/cti_documents/rc_cti_20180302_sinodalita_en.html.

International Journal of Public Theology. "Editorial: Special Issue - Public Theology and the City" *International Journal of Public Theology*, 2 (2008) 1–6.

Iseult Honohan, *Civic Republicanism* (UK: Routledge), 2002.

Jaffrelot, Christophe and Narender Kumar, eds. *Dr Ambedkar and Democracy*. New Delhi: Indian Institute of Dalit Studies and Oxford University Press, 2018.

Jaoul, Nicolas. "The Politics of Navayana Buddhism – Reinterpreting Ambedkar's Turn to Religion." In *The Radical in Ambedkar – Critical Reflections,* ed. Suraj Yengde and Anand Teltumbde, 281-292. Gurgaon: Penguin Random House India, 2018.

Jeanrond, Werner G & Aasulv Lande, eds. *The Concept of God in Global Dialogue*. Orbis Books, 2005.

Jenkins, Richard. *Social Identity*. New York: Routledge, 2008 (third edition).

Jondhale, Surendra and Joahnnes Beltz, eds. *Reconstructing the World – B. R. Ambedkar and Buddhism in India*. New Delhi: OUP, 2004.

Joseph, John E. *Language and Identity – National, Ethnic and Religious*. New York: Palgrave Macmillan, 2004.

Juergensmeyer, Mark. *Global Rebellion: Religious Challenge to the Secular State*. California: University of California Press, 2008.

________. *Terror in the Mind of God: The Global Rise of Religious Violence*. Berkeley: University of California Press, 2003.

________. *The New Cold War? Religious Nationalism Confronts the Secular State*. Berkeley: University of California Press, 1994.

________ ed. *Religion in Global Civil Society*. Oxford: Oxford University Press, 2005.

Kakar, Sudhir and Kathrina Kakar. *The Indians – Portrait of a People*. New Delhi: VIKING, 2007.

Kanjamala, Augustine. *The Future of Christian Mission in India – Toward a New Paradigm for the Third Millenium*. Bengaluru: Theological Publications in India, 2016.

Kakar, Sudhir and Kathrina Kakar. *The Indians – Portrait of a People*. New Delhi: VIKING, 2007.

Kennedy, Mark R. and Ricardo Calleja. "How Pope Francis is Shaping the Environment of Business." The Journal of Corporate Citizenship, No. 64, Theme Issue: The United Nations Global Compact and the Encyclical Laudato Si (December 2016), pp. 79-97; https://www.jstor.org/stable/10.2307/90003793.

Keys, Mary M. *Aquinas, Aristotle and the Promise of the Common Good.* New York: Cambridge University Press, 2006.

Kim, Sebastian C. H. *In Search of Identity – Debates on Religious Conversion in India.* New Delhi: Oxford University Press, 2003.

Kinvall, Catarina. *Globalization and Religious Nationalism in India – The search for Ontological Security.* USA: Routledge, 2006.

Kundu, Amitabh. "Making Indian Cities Slum-Free: Vision and Operationalisation." *Economic and Political Weekly,* APRIL 27, 2013, Vol. 48, No. 17 (APRIL 27, 2013), pp. 15-18; https://www.jstor.org/stable/23527179.

Kuttianimattathil, Jose. *Practice and Theology of Interreligious Dialogue.* Bangalore: Christu Jyothi Publications, 1995.

Laborde, Cecile. *Liberalism's Religion.* Cambridge: Harvard University Press, 2017.

Lal, Vinay, ed. *Political Hinduism – The Religious Imagination in Public Spheres.* New Delhi: OUP, 2009.

Larson, Gerald James (ed). *Religion and Personal Law in Secular India: A Call to Judgement.* Delhi: Social Secular Press, 2001.

Leonard, Dickens, M. *Caste-less Community: Iyothee Thasar (1845-1914) and Tamil Buddhism.* Ph.D. Dissertation submitted to University of Hyderabad, 2017.

Lewis, V. Bradley. "Catholic Social Teaching on the Common Good," in *Catholic Social Teaching – A Volume of Scholarly Essays,* eds. Gerard V. Bradely and E. Christian Brugger, 247-280. Cambridge: Cambridge University Press, 2019.

Loomba, Ania. *Colonialism / Post-colonialism.* 2nd ed. New York: Routledge, 2005.

Mahadevan, Kanchana. "Rethinking Power – Aesthetics, Dialogue, Hegemony." In *The Modern Prince and The Modern Sage – Transforming Power and Freedom,* ed. Ananta Kumar Giri, 98-136. New Delhi: SAGE, 2009.

Maitra, S. K. "Reason in Hindu Philosophy: Classical and Contemporary." *Philosophy East and West.* Vol. 11, No. 3 (Oct., 1961), 125-142.

Maliekal, Jose. *Standstill Utopias? Dalits Encountering Christianity.* New Delhi: ISPCK, 2017.

Mangalwadi, Vishal. *Missionary Conspiracy – Letters to a Postmodern Hindu.* Mussoorie, UP: Nivedit Good Books Distributors Pvt., Ltd. 1996.

Maritain, Jacque. *The Person and the Common Good.* Notre Dame: University of Notre Dame Press, 1972 (1946).

Melakandathil, Pius, Joy L. K. Pachuau and Tanika Sarkar, eds. *Christianity in Indian History – Issues of Culture, Power and Knowledge.* New Delhi: Primus Books, 2016.

Menon, Dilip. *Blindness of Insight – Why Communalism in India is about Caste?.* Navayana, 2004.

Menon, Krishna A. G. "Imaging the Indian City." *Economic and Political Weekly*, Nov. 15-21, 1997, Vol. 32, No. 46 (Nov. 15-21, 1997), pp. 2932-2936; https://www.jstor.org/stable/4406063.

Mohan, Dinesh. "Moving around in Indian Cities." *Economic and Political Weekly*, NOVEMBER 30, 2013, Vol. 48, No. 48 (NOVEMBER 30, 2013), pp. 40-48; https://www.jstor.org/stable/23528921.

Mukherji, Nirmalangshu. "Academic Philosophy in India." Economic and Political Weekly, Vol. 37, No. 10 (Mar. 9-15, 2002), pp. 931-936, Stable URL: https://www.jstor.org/stable/4411839, Accessed: 28-12-2019 03:50 UTC.

Narayanan, Vasudha. "The History of the Academic Study of Religion in Universities, Centres, and Institutes in India." *Numen*, vol. 62, No. 1, Special Issue – *De-Orienting Religious Studies: Four Genealogies of the Study of Religion in Modern Asia*, 2015, pp. 7-39.

Narai, Iqbal. "Cultural Pluralism, National Integration and Democracy in India," *Asian Survey*, Vol. 16, No. 10 (Oct., 1976), pp. 903-917, Accessed: 04-10-2019 05:54 UTC.

Nehru, Jewaharlal. *The Discovery of India.*

Nijman, Jan. "India in the Urban Revolution." *Indian Anthropologist*, July - December 2012, Vol. 42, No. 2 (July - December 2012), pp. 1-17; https://www.jstor.org/stable/41922303.

Northcott, Michael, ed. *Urban Theology – A Reader.* London: Cassell, 1998.

O'Brien, David J. and Thomas A. Shannon, eds. *Catholic Social Thought – Encyclicals and Documents from Pope Leo XIII to Pope Francis.* Maryknoll: Orbis, 3rd edition, 2016.

Oddie, Geoffrey A. *Hindu and Christian in South-East India.* London: Routledge, 2017.

Olivera, Jelson Roberto de, Clovis Ultramari. "The Eutopian City: The Challenge of Urban Conviviality in the *Laudato Si'* and *Fratelli Tuttii* Encyclicals." 154-173. *International Journal of Public Theology.* Volume 16, No. 2, 2022.

Oommen, T. K. And Hunter P. Mabry. *The Christian Clergy in India – Volume 1 – Social Structures and Social Roles*. New Delhi: SAGE, 2000.

Pandikattu, Kuruvilla, SJ, ed. *Pope Francis – His Impact on and Relevance for the Church and Society – Commemorating Five Years of His Papacy*. Pune: Jnana-Deepa Vidyapeeth & Christian World Imprints, 2018.

Pandithar, Iyotheethasar. *Buddha's Ativedam*. Chennai: Tamilkudi Arasu Pathipagam, 2010.

_______. *Iyotheethasarin Aaivukal 1 & 2*. Tamilkudi Arasu Pathipagam, 2010.

Panikkar, Raimon. *The Fullness of Man – A Christophany*. New York: Orbis & New Delhi: ISPCK, 2006.

_______. *The Intra-Religious Dialogue*. Bangalore: TPI, 1978.

Pajin, Dushan. "The Legitimacy of the Term 'Philosophy' in an Asian Context: The Beginnings of Indian Philosophy." *Journal of Indian Philosophy*, vol. 15, No. 4, 1987, 349-362.

Patil, R. R. and James Dabhi, eds. *Dalit Christians in India*. New Delhi: MANAK Publications Pvt. Ltd., 2010.

Patrick, Gnana . "Pope Francis, Culture of Encounter, the Common Good, and Dharma: Public Theological Conversations Today," *Theological Studies*, Vol. 84(2), 2023, 212-228. DOI 10.1177/00405639231171730.

Paranjape, Makarand R. *Cultural Politics in Modern India – Postcolonial Prospects, Colourful Cosmopolitanism, Global Proximities*. London: Routledge, 2016.

Phan, Peter C. "Pope Francis' Encyclical *Laudato Si'* in Dialogue with Asian Religions." In *Towards Renewing Church and World – Revisiting Vatican Council II through the Eyes of Pope Francis*, eds. Francis Gonsalves SJ, Arjen Tete SJ and Dinesh Braganza SJ, 377-397. New Delhi: ISPCK, 2020.

Pinchard, Alexis. "Does the Concept of theoria fit the beginning of Indian Thought?" in *Universe and Inner Self in Early Indian and Early Greek Thought,* ed. Richard Seaford, 118 – 133. Edinburg: Edinburg University Press, 2016.

Pushparajan, A. 2018 *The Mahatma and Christian Mission Today – Revisiting Pope Francis' Evangeli Gaudium in the Light of Gandhian Insights*. Bangalore: Asian Trading Corporation.

Rajagopal, Arvind. *The Indian Public Sphere – Readings in Media History*. New Delhi: Oxford University Press, 2009.

Rodriques, Valerian ed. *Essential Writings of B. R. Ambedkar*. New Delhi: Oxford University Press, 2002.

Saksena, S. K. "Authority in Indian Philosophy", Philosophy East and West, Vol. 1, No. 3 (Oct., 1951), pp. 38-49, https://www.jstor.org/stable/1397171, Accessed: 26-12-2019 07:30 UTC.

Sarkar, Tanika. "Hindutva's Hinduism." In *Public Hinduisms*, eds. John Zavos, et. al. 264-282. New Delhi: SAGE Publications India Pvt. Ltd. 2012.

Sidhwani, Pranav. "Spatial Inequalities in Big Indian Cities." Economic and Political Weekly, Vol. 50, No. 22 (MAY 30, 2015), pp. 55-62; https://www.jstor.org/stable/24482493.

Spinner-Halev, Jeff. "Hinduism, Christianity, and Liberal Religious Toleration," *Political Theory*, Vol. 33, No. 1 (Feb., 2005), pp. 28-57.

Pope Benedict XVI, *Deus Caritas Est*. Rome: Holy See.

Pope Francis. *Life after the Pandemic*. Citta del Vaticano: Libreria Editrice Vaticana, 2020.

Pope John Paul II, *Compendium of the Social Doctrine of the Church*. Rome: Holy See.

Pope John Paul II, *Centesimus Annus*, https://www.vatican.va/content/john-paul-ii/en/encyclicals/documents/hf_jp-ii_enc_01051991_centesimus-annus.html.

Pius XI, *Divini Redemptoris*. https://www.vatican.va/content/pius-xi/en/encyclicals/documents/hf_p-xi_enc_19370319_divini-redemptoris.html.

Puthanangady, Paul ed. *Popular Devotions*. Bangalore: National Biblical Catechetical and Liturgical Centre, 1986.

Rafael Luciani. "Pope Francis and the Theology of the People", in Justin Beaumont, ed. *The Routledge Handbook of Postsecularity*. New York: Routledge, 2019.

Rafael, Luciani. 2020. "Francis and the Pastoral Geopolitics of Peoples and Their Cultures: A Structural Option for the Poor." *Theological Studies* 2020, Vol. 81(1) 181–202 © Theological Studies, Inc. 2020 Article reuse guidelines: sagepub.com/journals-permissions DOI: 10.1177/0040563920906135 journals.sagepub.com/home/tsj.

Rayan, Samuel. *Doing Theology – Indian Christian Reflections on Theologizing in India Today* [Collected Writings of Samuel Rayan, SJ], vol. II, edited by Kurien Kunnumpuram, SJ. New Delhi: ISPCK, 2013.

________. *Nature, Woman and the Church – Indian Christian Reflections on Ecology, Feminism and Ecclesiology* [Collected Writings of Samuel Rayan, SJ], vol. I, edited by Kurien Kunnumpuram, SJ. New Delhi: ISPCK, 2013.

________. *In Spirit and Truth – Indian Christian Reflections on Spirituality and Worship* [Selected Writings of Samuel Rayan, SJ, vol. II, edited by Kurien Kunnumpuram, SJ. Mumbai: St. Paul's, 2012.

________. *Jesus – The Relevance of His Person and Message for our Times* [Selected Writings of Samuel Rayan, SJ, vol. I, edited by Kurien Kunnumpuram, SJ. Mumbai: St. Paul's, 2011.

Rao, Anupama. "Ambedkar's Dalit and The Problem of Caste Subalternity." In *The Radical in Ambedkar – Critical Reflections,* edited by Suraj Yengde and Anand Teltumbde, 340-358. Gurgaon: Penguin Random House India, 2018.

Roberts, Nathaniel. *To Be Cared for – The Power of Conversion and Foreignness of Belonging in an Indian Slum*. New Delhi: Nayayana, 2016.

Robinson, Rowena. *Christians of India*. New Delhi: SAGE, 2003.

Robinson, Rowena and Sathianathan Clarke, eds. *Religious Conversion in India – Modes, Motivations, and Meanings*. New Delhi: Oxford University Press, 2003.

Robinson, Rowena and Joseph Marianus Kujur, eds. *Margins of Faith – Dalit and Tribal Christianity in India*. New Delhi: SAGE, 2010.

Robinson, Rowena, ed. *Minority Studies*. New Delhi: Oxford University Press, 2012.

Rowlands, Anna Roper. 2021. *Towards a Politics of Communion – Catholic Social Teaching in Dark Times*. T&T Clark, 2021.

Sadananda , Daniel Ratnakara and Solomon Paul J., eds. 2021. *Rethinking Ecclesia: Being and Becoming Christ Communities towards a Borderless Church*. New Delhi and Chennai: CSI Synod Communications.

Sahay, Keshari N. *Christianity and Culture Change in India*. New Delhi: Inter-India Publications, 1986.

Sahoo, Sarbeswar. *Pentecostalism and Politics of Conversion in India*. UK: Cambridge University Press, 2018.

Sandel. Michael. *Liberalism and the Limits of Justice*. Cambridge: Cambridge University Press, 1998.

Sanna, Gouthama. *C. Iyotheethasa Pandithar*. New Delhi: Sakithya Academy, 2005.

Sen, Amartya. *The Argumentative Indian – Writings on Indian Culture, History and Identity*. London: Penguin Books, 2005.

Sharma, Arvind. *Methodology in Religious Studies – The Interface with Women's Studies*. New York: State University of New York Press, 2002.

Sikka, Sonia. "Teaching Religion and Philosophy in India." *India International Centre Quarterly, Vol. 40,* No. ¾, 2013, 131-148.

Sniegocki, John. *Catholic Social Teaching and Economic Globalization – The Quest for Alternatives* . Wisconsin: Marquette University, 2009.

Soares-Prabhu, George. *Theology of Liberation: An Indian Biblical Perspective* [Collected Writings of George M. Soares-Prabhu], vol. 1, edited by Francis X. D'Sa, Pune: JDV, 2000.

________. *Biblical Spirituality of Liberative Action* [Collected Writings of George M. Soares-Prabhu], vol. 1, edited by Scaria Kuthiralkkattel, Pune: JDV, 2000.

________. *Biblical Theology for India* [Collected Writings of George M. Soares-Prabhu], vol. 2, edited by Scaria Kuthirelkattel, Pune: JDV, 1999.

________. *Biblical Themes for a Contextual Theology Today* [Collected Writings of George M. Soares-Prabhu, vol. 1, edited by Isaac Padinjarekuttu, Pune: JDV, 1999.

Stiltner, Brian. *Religion and Common Good – Catholic Contributions to Building Community in a Liberal Society*. Lanham: Rowan & Littlefield Publishers, Inc., 1999.

Stout, Jeffrey. *Democracy and Traditions* (Princeton: Princeton University Press, 2004.

Swarup, Ram. *Hindu View of Christianity and Islam*. New Delhi: Voice of India, 1992.

Tach, Laura M. "Diversity, Inequality, and Microsegregation: Dynamics of Inclusion and Exclusion in a Racially and Economically Diverse Community." *Cityscape*, Vol. 16, No. 3, American Neighborhoods: Inclusion and Exclusion (2014), pp. 13-46; https://www.jstor.org/stable/10.2307/26326904.

Teixeira, Alfredo, Alex Villas Boas and Jefferson Zeferino. "Public Theology in the Context of the Religious Dualization Phenomneon in Multiple Modernities," *International Journal of Public Theology*. Volume 16, No. 2, 217-237, 2022.

Thankavelu, K. *Forerunner of Tamil Nationalism – Iyotheethasap Pandithar*. Chennai: Tamilkudi Arasu Pathipagam, 2010.

Thapar, Romila. *The Public Intellectual in India*. New Delhi: ALEPH Book Company, 2015.

Thayil, Thomas. *The Latin Christians of Kerala*. Bangalore: Kristu Jyoti Publications, 2003.

Varshney, Ashuthosh. *Ethnic Conflict and Civic Life in India – Hindus and Muslims*

Venugopal, C. N. "Factor of Anti-Pollution in the Ideology of Lingayat Movement." Sociological Bulletin, Vol. 26, No. 2 (September 1977), pp. 227-241; https://www.jstor.org/stable/23618919.

Verma, Vidhu. "Conceptualising Social Exclusion: New Rhetoric or Transformative Politics?" Economic and Political Weekly, December 10, 2011, Vol. 46, No. 50 (December 10, 2011), pp. 89-97; http://www.jstor.com/stable/41319488.

Vivekananda, Swami. *My India – The India Eternal*. Calcutta: The Ramakrishna Mission Institute of Culture, 1993.

Vithayathil, Tina, et.al. "Only 'Good People', Please: Residential Segregation in Urbanising India." India International Centre Quarterly, Winter 2016–Spring 2017, Vol. 43, No. 3/4, The Contemporary Urban Conundrum (Winter 2016–Spring 2017), pp. 45-54; : https://www.jstor.org/stable/26317313.

Wilfred, Felix. *Christians for a Better India.* New Delhi: ISPCK, 2015.

________. *Theology to Go Public.* New Delhi: ISPCK, 2013.

________. *Asian Public Theology – Critical Concerns for Challenging Times.* New Delhi: ISPCK, 2010.

________. *Margins – Site of Asian Theologies.* New Delhi: ISPCK, 2008.

________. *The Sling of Utopia – Struggles for a Different Society.* New Delhi: 2005.

________. *Asian Dreams and Christian Hope – At the Dawn of the Millenium.* New Delhi: ISPCK, 2003.

________. *On the Banks of Ganges – Doing Contextual Theology.* New Delhi: ISPCK, 2002.

________. *From the Dusty Soil – Contextual Interpretation of Christianity.* Chennai: Department of Christian Studies, 1995.

________. *Beyond Settled Foundations – The Journey of Indian Theology.* Chennai: Department of Christian Studies, University of Madras, 1993.

________. *Sunset in the East? – Asian Challenges and Christian Involvement.* Chennai: Chair in Christian Studies, 1991.

________. "New Impetus for Integral Ecology: Theological Significance of *Laudato Si.*" In *Theology for an Inclusive World*, au. Felix Wilfred, 151-173. New Delhi: ISPCK, 2019.

Zachariah, K. C. *The Syrian Christians of Kerala – Demographic and Socio-Economic Transition in the Twentieth Century.* New Delhi: Orient Longman, 2006.